W9-CXR-866

40 km

PENDLETON

EASTERN OREGON

SOUTHERN OREGON

Idaho

Oregon

Nevada

Kennewick
Mabton
Prosser
Walla Walla
Touchet
Columbia R.
Umatilla
Hermiston
Milton-Freewater
Athena
Weston
Flora
Promise
Maxville
Arlington
Cecil
Echo
Pendleton
Minam
Wallowa
Zumwalt
Imnaha
Wasco
Rock Creek
Glex
Ione
Lexington
Pilot Rock
Eagle Cap
Train Rides
Elgin
Lostine
Joseph
Enterprise
Moro
Clem
Heppner
Nye
Kamela
Summerville
Island City
Cove
Wallowa Mts
Wallowa Lake
Kent
Condon
Ruggs
Hardman
Eastern Oregon
Fire Museum
Starkey
La Grande
Union
Telocaset
Homestead
Mayville
Lonerock
Ukiah
North Powder
Pondosa
Carson
Oxbow
Clarno
Fossil
Kinzua
N. Fork
John Day R.
Dale
Eastern Oregon
Museum
Haines
National Historic
Oregon Trail
Interpretive Center
Halfway
Spray
Ritter
Ah Hee
Diggings
Bourne
Richland
Cambridge
Painted Hills
Painted Cove
Nature Trail
Hamilton
Kimberly
Long
Fox
Granite
Baker City
Midvale
Thomas Condon
Paleontology Center
Mitchell
Dayville
Mount
Vernon
Kam Wah Chung
State Heritage Site
Bates
Salisbury
Hereford
Durkee
Bridgeport
Lime
Weiser
Rebecca
Ochoco
National Forest
Paulina
John Day
Table Rock
7815
Unity
Eldorado
Huntington
Brogan
Jamieson
Ontario
Payette
Fruitland
New
Plymouth
Suplee
Izee
Seneca
Silvies
Strawberry Mtn.
9038
Ironside
Malheur
National Forest
Willowcreek
Westfall
Vale
Nyssa
Parma
Brothers
Hampton
Ochoco
National Forest
Trout
Creek
Beulah Res.
Beulah
Drewsey
Harper
Adrian
Nampa
Deschutes
National Forest
Burns
Harney
Warm Springs
Res.
Buchanan
Juntura
Riverside
Dry Creek
Marsing
Homedale
Glass Buttes
6385
Riley
Lawen
Crane
Lake
Owyhee
Christmas
Valley
Wagontire
Malheur National
Wildlife Refuge
Narrows
Princeton
Crowley
Upper Cow
Lake
Aikali Lake
Silver
Lake
Harney
Lake
Malheur
Lake
Diamond Craters
Outstanding Natural
Area
Jordan Valley
Arock
Jordan Cr.
Antelope
Res.
Diamond
Steens
Mountain
Wilderness
Sheepshead
Mts
Rome
Owyhee R.
Hot Springs
Paisley
Lake
Abert
Abert Rim
Fremont
National
Forest
Valley Falls
Plush
Hart Mountain
National Antelope
Refuge
Warner Pk.
8017
Alvord
Desert
Andrews
Alvord
Lake
Basque
Cliffs
Fairylawn
Crump
Lake
Lakeview
Adel
Pueblo Mountains
Fields
Trout Creek Mts
Goose
Lake
New Pine
Creek

INSIGHT GUIDES

OREGON

PLAN & BOOK
YOUR TAILOR-MADE TRIP

BRAZIL

CHILE

ECUADOR

TAILOR-MADE TRIPS & UNIQUE EXPERIENCES CREATED BY LOCAL TRAVEL EXPERTS AT INSIGHTGUIDES.COM/HOLIDAYS

Insight Guides has been inspiring travellers with high-quality travel content for over 45 years. As well as our popular guidebooks, we now offer the opportunity to book tailor-made private trips completely personalised to your needs and interests. By connecting with one of our local experts, you will directly benefit from their expertise and local know-how, helping you create memories that will last a lifetime.

HOW INSIGHTGUIDES.COM/HOLIDAYS WORKS

STEP 1

Pick your dream destination and submit an enquiry, or modify an existing itinerary if you prefer.

STEP 2

Fill in a short form, sharing details of your travel plans and preferences with a local expert.

STEP 3

Your local expert will create your personalised itinerary, which you can amend until you are completely satisfied.

STEP 4

Book securely online. Pack your bags and enjoy your holiday! Your local expert will be available to answer questions during your trip.

BENEFITS OF PLANNING & BOOKING AT INSIGHTGUIDES.COM/HOLIDAYS

PLANNED BY LOCAL EXPERTS

The Insight Guides local experts are hand-picked, based on their experience in the travel industry and their impeccable standards of customer service.

SAVE TIME & MONEY

When a local expert plans your trip, you save time and money when you book, even during high season. You won't be charged for using a credit card either.

TAILOR-MADE TRIPS

Book with Insight Guides, and you will be in complete control of the planning process, from the initial selections to amending your final itinerary.

BOOK & TRAVEL STRESS-FREE

Enjoy stress-free travel when you use the Insight Guides secure online booking platform. All bookings come with a money-back guarantee.

WHAT OTHER TRAVELLERS THINK ABOUT TRIPS BOOKED AT INSIGHTGUIDES.COM/HOLIDAYS

Trip to Portugal

Every step of the planning process and the trip itself was effortless and exceptional. Our special interests, preferences and requests were accommodated resulting in a trip that exceeded our expectations.

Corinne, USA   ★★★★★

Trip to Vietnam

The organization was superb, the drivers professional, and accommodation quite comfortable. I was well taken care of! My thanks to your colleagues who helped make my trip to Vietnam such a great experience. My only regret is that I couldn't spend more time in the country.

Heather   ★★★★★

DON'T MISS OUT BOOK NOW AT
INSIGHTGUIDES.COM/HOLIDAYS

CONTENTS

LEGEND
φ Insight on
📷 Photo story

THE BEST OF OREGON: TOP ATTRACTIONS

△ **Crater Lake National Park.** The crown jewel of the state, this national park centers on a sapphire lake in a rugged volcanic caldera. It offers epic backcountry hiking, boat rides, and winter adventures. See page 164.

▽ **Portland.** Effortlessly hip and open-hearted, Oregon's urban hub is a melange of one-off shops, craft coffeehouses, food trucks, and arts spaces. Sprawling green areas such as Forest Park are crisscrossed with hiking trails. See page 101.

△ **Oregon Coast Highway.** US Route 101 spools out for the entire length of Oregon's stellar Pacific coastline, threading together quaint lighthouses, sand-fringed state parks, maritime forests, and wildlife-viewing spots. See page 136.

△ **Mount Hood.** An emblem of the state, the snow-plastered hulk of Mount Hood rises in northwestern Oregon and offers some of the state's premier ski resorts. It is a haven for hikers and bikers in summer. See page 193.

△ **Painted Hills.** Streaked with ocher, burnt red, and butter yellow, the Painted Hills contain fossils from 39 million years ago. They were formed over eons, as volcanic activity deposited layer upon layer of cooled ash. See page 179.

△ **Jacksonville.** Steeped in Old West history, Jacksonville sprouted when prospectors struck gold in the region in the 1850s. Now, the city's stuck-in-time Downtown remains intact thanks to its National Historic Landmark accolade. See page 154.

▷ **Oregon Dunes National Recreation Area.** Stark and otherworldly, this 31,500-acre (12,700-hectare) sweep of champagne-colored dunes is one of Oregon's great wonders. It is a popular place for ATV riding, hiking, and camping. See page 142.

◁ **Multnomah Falls.** This thundering cascade plunges 620ft (190 meters) over a craggy sheet of basalt. A short, paved trail leads to arched Benson Bridge, a 1914-built structure that affords astonishing views of the falls. See page 195.

▽ **Columbia Gorge Discovery Center & Museum.** One of the standout museums in the state, this educational beacon holds exhibits on Indigenous cultures, geology, and wildlife. A nature trail runs through the flora-filled grounds. See page 199.

△ **Willamette Valley wine country.** A temperate climate and fertile volcanic soils make this sheltered valley a top growing region. Pinot Noir and Chardonnay are signatures here., though creative winemakers experiment with a range of varietals. See page 124

THE BEST OF OREGON: EDITOR'S CHOICE

Yaquina Head Lighthouse.

ONLY IN OREGON

Covered bridges. There are more than 50 of these charming landmarks across Oregon. Many are in Lane County, where they are joined up on themed tours. See page 131.

Lighthouses. Typically perched on rugged headlands, historic beacons stud the stirring Pacific coastline. You can stay in the 19th-century keeper's cottage at Heceta Head Lighthouse. See page 148.

North American Bigfoot Center. Run by a local researcher, this offbeat museum in Boring is dedicated to sasquatch and includes artifacts such as footprint casts. See page 194.

Steller sea lions. These hulking (and invariably cute) marine mammals collect on rookeries and haul-outs along the Pacific coastline. See them at Sea Lion Caves near Florence. See page 141.

Timberline Lodge, Mount Hood. The 1936 ski lodge is a base camp for winter adventures. It also served as the exterior for the Overlook Hotel in Stanley Kubrick's *The Shining*. See page 202.

MUST-SEE MUSEUMS

Portland Art Museum. Oregon's signature art museum holds a fine store of Northwestern paintings, plus precious relics from the region's Indigenous cultures. See page 102.

Columbia Gorge Discovery Center & Museum. Learn about the mind-boggling geology of the mighty Columbia River Gorge, as well as Native American history and the Lewis and Clark Expedition. See page 199.

High Desert Museum. Exhibits at this center in Bend showcase basketry from Oregon's Plateau tribes and a replica of an 1800s Oregon Trail wagon. See page 170.

Kam Wah Chung State Heritage Site. A part of Eastern Oregon's Chinese heritage is preserved at this site, which once served as a general store, medical clinic, and private residence. See page 181.

Oregon Museum of Science and Industry (OMSI), Portland. Kids will love this interactive learning center, whose highlights include a working fossil preparation lab and a planetarium. See page 108.

Wildcat Creek Covered Bridge.

Portland Art Museum.

NATIVE AMERICAN HERITAGE

Native American Chief.

Indigenous songs and artifacts like beaded moccasins. See page 177. **Old Chief Joseph Gravesite.** Located near Joseph, this is the burial site of a Nez Perce leader who refused to cede his homeland to white settlers in the 1800s. See page 184. **Quintana Galleries, Portland.** Jewelry, masks, model totem poles, and contemporary paintings are included in this Indigenous-owned art collection (access is by appointment only). See page 105. **Chachalu Museum and Cultural Center.** This museum tells the story of the ancestral lands belonging to the Confederated Tribes of the Grand Ronde, including a devastating fire in 1856. See page 123.

Tamástslikt Cultural Institute. The history and culture of the Cayuse, Umatilla, and Walla Walla tribes is explored at this state-of-the-art museum at the Umatilla Reservation. See page 189. **The Museum at Warm Springs.** Celebrating the heritage of the Warm Springs, Wasco, and Paiute peoples, this cultural center includes audio recordings of

BEST BEACHES

Whaleshead Beach. A steep track leads down to this serene strand, named for a sea stack that resembles a breaching whale. See page 147. **Cannon Beach.** This iconic beach is dominated by mammoth monolith Haystack Rock, home to an abundance of birdlife including tufted puffins. See page 136. **Indian Beach.** Surfers flock to this windswept beach, part of Ecola State Park, whose

maritime forest trails offer spectacular vistas. See page 136. **Secret Beach.** A trail off the Samuel H. Boardman State Scenic Corridor uncovers this diminutive sandy crescent. You might have it all to yourself. See pages 69 and 147. **Nye Beach.** This sandy strip fronts buzzy Newport, with its family-friendly cafés, ice-cream parlors, and beachfront hotels and condos. See page 140.

Kayaking on the Coquille River.

OUTDOOR ADVENTURES

Snowshoeing at Crater Lake. From winter through to late spring, the volcanic wonderland is covered in several feet of snow, making the lake's sapphire waters pop. See page 157. **Paddling on the Coquille River.** Kayaking trips are popular on this tidal river, which features Indigenous fishing weirs as well as routes through a National Wildlife Refuge. See page 145. **Biking the Sandy Ridge Trail System.** Cyclists of varied abilities flock to this prized 27km (17

mile) -long trail network in the forested foothills of the Cascade Mountains. See page 202. **Hiking the Pacific Crest Trail (PCT).** The mother of all West Coast hiking routes, the PCT beats a 732km (455 mile) -long path across Oregon through awesome mountainscapes and old-growth forests. See page 163. **Skiing on Mount Hood.** An icon of Oregon, this Cascades peak has some of the state's best powder, with standout resorts like Timberline Lodge. See page 202.

Whaleshead Beach.

Fort Rock in Oregon's backcountry.

MOST SCENIC ROAD TRIPS

Pacific Coast Highway. A grand dame among Oregon's scenic roads, Highway 101 slinks down the Pacific seaboard linking up lighthouses, beaches, and marine-life viewing spots. See page 136.

Historic Columbia River Highway. Drink in views of the mighty Columbia River and its gaping basalt gorge and detour for scenic waterfall hikes. See page 195.

Journey Through Time Scenic Byway. Rugged river canyons, rich fossil beds, and ancient hills striped with color await on this route through Eastern Oregon. See page 180.

Mount Hood Scenic Byway. The pyramidal form of the Cascades peak is on fine display on this route sweeping from Hood River to Wood Village. See page 201.

Oregon Outback. Rugged stretches of Oregon's southern and central backcountry are revealed on this dramatic route featuring Fort Rock and Summer Lake. See page 163.

Hummingbirds flitter in Crater Lake National Park.

FINEST WILDLIFE VIEWING

Crater Lake National Park. Elusive black bear, coyote, and mountain lions roam this volcanic playground, while migratory warblers, hummingbirds, and raptors fill the skies. See page 160.

Shore Acres State Park. There are few more life-affirming moments than seeing a whale breach in the Pacific Ocean. This park's clifftop trails offer a front-row view. See page 143.

Dean Creek Elk Viewing Area. Up to 100 Roosevelt elk graze in this lush string of pastures off Highway 38. There is also a small outdoor exhibit. See page 89.

Rogue Wild and Scenic River. Oregon is blessed with 34 Wild and Scenic Rivers – black bear ramble along the banks of the Rogue, which is populated with otters and Chinook salmon. See page 152.

Malheur National Wildlife Refuge. A birdwatcher's dream, this protected swathe of the High Desert is a habitat for species including great white pelicans, night herons and Canada geese. See page 191.

The Columbia River Highway is a scenic drive.

TOP FESTIVALS AND EVENTS

Portland Rose Festival. A city tradition since 1907, this wholesome event includes colorful parades, fairground rides, and street food on the waterfront. See page 75.

Oregon Country Fair, Veneta. Oregon's creativity is unleashed at this summer event near Eugene – it includes folk concerts, quirky art displays, and circus acts. See page 211.

Oregon Shakespeare Festival (OSF), Ashland. Lovers of the Bard should head to Ashland for the OSF theater company's annual season, which includes productions of his great tragedies and comedies. See page 74.

Portland Pride. The LGBTQ+ community is celebrated with bright processions, parties, and live concerts and street food in Portland's waterfront park. See page 59.

Pendleton Whisky Music Fest. Big names such as Flo Rida and Macklemore have graced the stage at this major music event in Eastern Oregon. See page 188.

BIG-HITTING SMALL TOWNS

Jacksonville. This gold rush jewel in Southern Oregon is notable for its well-preserved Old West architecture and annual arts festival. See page 154.

Florence. The ornate Siuslaw River Bridge watches over this coastal beauty, on the doorstep of the Oregon Dunes National Recreation Area and Heceta Head Lighthouse. See page 141.

Baker City. A dose of Wild West history is on offer in this Eastern Oregon mining town, heralded for its craft drinks scene and access to rugged backcountry. See page 182.

Hood River. A solid arts heritage and the bounty of the Hood River Valley make this town a delight for creative types and discerning foodies. See page 197.

Cottage Grove. As quaint as they come, this Willamette Valley town is known for its charming covered bridges and biking trails. See page 130.

Baker City sculpture.

Portland Rose Festival.

MONEY-SAVING TIPS

National parks pass. Frequent visitors to US national parks should buy an "America the Beautiful" pass ($80), which covers entrance fees for the holder, a vehicle, plus any passengers, at over 2,000 federal recreation sites. www.nps.gov/findapark/passes.html.

CityPass. The Oregon GetOutPass provides admission to a range of state attractions, including the Tillamook Air Museum, the Oregon Jewish Museum and Oaks Park, plus a selection of walking and biking tours, restaurants and family-friendly attractions like bowling and laser tag. www.getoutpass.com/locations/oregon.

Free museums. Many museums offer free entry or deals at select times during the month – check out the First Thursday event in Portland's cool Pearl District. Always-free museums include the Oregon Rail Heritage Center in Portland and the Jordan Schnitzer Museum of Art in Eugene.

State parks. An annual pass to Oregon's state parks will likely save you money. It costs $30 (www.stateparks.oregon.gov) – otherwise, entry will generally set you back around $5–10 per day.

Rainbow over Crown Point and the Vista House in the Columbia River Gorge.

John Day Fossil Beds National Monument.

Rural Mitchell town in Oregon.

The mighty Cascade Range ripples 420km (260 miles) along the state.

A FREE SPIRIT

Artsy cities, volcanic marvels, and a coast chiseled by the Pacific Ocean – Oregon has ceaseless wonders, both natural and man-made.

Willamette Valley is behind a crop of fine wines.

Mother Nature has done spectacular things in Oregon. She carved out the volcanic mass of Mount Mazama, then blasted it to pieces, filling its belly with the sapphire-hued Crater Lake. She dropped curtains of water over great hunks of basalt, and threaded rivers through yawning canyons. Peaks pierce the skies, and caves knot together beneath the ground. The natural world is Oregon's main calling card, and its rich bounty unfolds right across the state. The powerful Pacific Ocean sculpts the shoreline, which reveals itself in a series of rocky headlands and driftwood-strewn beaches.

Inland, the Cascade Range is the state's backbone, thrusting 420km (260 miles) across its entire length – the main showstopper, Mount Hood nudges 11,240ft (3,436 meters) and is known for its stellar skiing. Farther east, Oregon's High Desert unfurls in vast, sagebrush-flecked sweeps.

History is buried in the rocks here, too. The John Day Fossil Beds are some of the richest on the planet, divulging secrets about ancient periods of climate change and curious creatures that walked the Earth in distant epochs. To explore here is to be reminded that mankind is a mere drop in the ocean.

Still, though, in the shadow of nature, humanity has also made its mark. Ancient rock art tells of Indigenous cultures who have been calling these lands home for millennia, while ghost towns – evidence of Oregon's 19th-century gold rush – are scattered about the state like bones.

Abandoned Blue Ridge Mine.

Oregon's vibrant cities are part of its appeal too. Renowned for its freewheeling spirit and unwavering creativity, Portland is the state's urban hub. Come to feast on world cuisine from food trucks, explore hip neighborhoods, and continue your outdoor pursuits in the city's renowned green spaces. Meanwhile, mountain towns such as Bend and Ashland, in Central and Southern Oregon respectively, are famed for their craft beer and cool arts scenes. And then there's the food. Fertile regions such as the Willamette and Hood River valleys grow a cornucopia of produce that is whipped into imaginative dishes by forward-thinking chefs – all perfect fuel for a mountain of adventures.

Blue-toned fossil beds.

A LAND OF ICE AND FIRE

Layered fossil beds, ancient volcanoes, and relic-packed museums reveal clues about Oregon's natural history.

Oregon's history is written into its rock. Over millions of years, the state's epic landscape has been shaped by tectonic plate shifts, ice-age floods, and volcanic eruptions, which have spawned mountains and carved gorges. It also has some of the richest fossil beds in the world, and continued excavations by paleontologists have turned up evidence of long-extinct flora and fauna.

Very few dinosaur fossils have been discovered in Oregon: the state was covered by an ocean when these prehistoric beasts existed on Earth. Still, a few have been found, including an intact ornithopod vertebra in Central Oregon.

Picture Gorge Basalts.

FERTILE FOSSIL BEDS

Oregon is a mecca for geology enthusiasts. The John Day Fossil Beds National Monument sprawls out in Eastern Oregon, comprising 14,000 acres (5,665 hectares) of layered, sedimentary rock spat out by volcanic eruptions. It paints a picture of Oregon that dates back some 44 million years, beginning with the Clarno Nut Beds. These rocky strata preserve relics from a time when Central Oregon was humid and swamp-like, with a semi-tropical climate. An impressive number of ancient nuts and seeds have been discovered here, offering clues about 175 distinct species, all of which are now extinct. Experts believe that crocodiles, tortoises, and ancestors of the modern-day catfish existed during this period.

Further sheets of rock reveal yet more secrets. The Bridge Creek Assemblage dates back around 33 million years and captures a period of climate change in Oregon's ancient history. During this time, the temperature dropped between 37°F (3°C) and 43°F (6°C) and Oregon's subtropical woodlands gave way to more temperate ones. The region was covered with tracts of hardwood forest, not too dissimilar from those in the modern-day Southeastern states – these early trees are distant relatives of today's alders, oaks, maples, and elms.

A VOLCANIC LEGACY

Over the millions of years that followed, the landscape was altered by intense periods of volcanic activity, which carpeted those ancient forests in ash and pumice. The creatures that roamed the Earth during this period seem almost to belong to the realm of the mythical: lumbering "bear-dogs" and ferocious feline creatures called nimravids thrived in Oregon's woodland. The climate continued to become cooler and drier too, and eventually grasslands began to emerge. Early horses and camels flourished in the developing savannahs.

But around 16 million years ago, eruptions released mighty flows of molten basalt that choked the grassy landscape. The Picture Gorge Basalts – striking columned rock formations at the southern entrance to the John Day Fossil

Crater Lake became a national park in 1902, with legislation signed by then president Theodore Roosevelt, whose passion for conservation was well known.

Mount Hood's Eliot Glacier, the largest in Oregon.

⊘ CURIOUS CRITTERS

Fossil discoveries across Oregon have unearthed secrets about various weird and wonderful species. Among them is the formidable-sounding saber-toothed salmon (*Oncorhynchus rastrosus*). It is thought that the mammoth species would have been 6–8ft (1.8–2.4 meters) long and would have existed in Oregon's waters until about 5 million years ago. In 2014, two skulls were discovered near the Central Oregon city of Madras. Experts studied the excavated fossils and found that the salmon's teeth may have protruded sideways from its jaw, like warthog tusks, rather than jutting downward like those of a saber-toothed tiger, as previously thought.

Beds National Monument's Sheep Rock Unit – are visual reminders of this volcanic activity. It wasn't until these basalt layers cooled that life began to return: mylagaulids, a kind of ancient rodent, are among the species that would have been found here.

COLUMBIA RIVER GORGE AND THE MISSOULA FLOODS

To the north, the Columbia River Gorge was similarly contoured by basalt flows. The region once existed as a flat plateau, though tectonic activity over eons had created a highly volcanic landscape. Then, around 17 million years ago, those ancient volcanoes exploded, unleashing powerful basalt flows that later cooled and hardened into robust layers of rock – thousands of feet thick in places.

Fast forward many epochs, and North America was gripped by the last Ice Age. During this period vast swathes of the continent were covered by a mighty glacier known as the Cordilleran ice sheet. As that glacier moved southward over time, a giant ice dam formed, blocking the Clark Fork River, and creating the mammoth Lake Missoula. It is thought that the ice dam could have been around 2,000ft (610 meters) high, and existed between 18,000 and 12,000 years ago.

Eventually, however, the dam burst, releasing 2,000 cubic kilometers (500 cubic miles) of rushing water that beat a path toward the Pacific Ocean. The dam reformed and burst repeatedly over several thousands of years and, each time, the fast-moving torrent chewed away at the basalt layers of the Columbia Plateau, eventually forming the Columbia River Gorge. The flood washed across Oregon's Willamette Valley too.

Those waters contained fertile silts and sediments from across the USA's Northwest, which seeped into the valley floor. The region still owes its fruitful plains to this ancient flooding event.

MOUNT MAZAMA

One of the most significant eruptions in Oregon's history, the impact of Mount Mazama's cataclysmic explosion was felt far beyond the boundaries of Crater Lake National Park, where the gaping caldera it left behind is protected. The ancient volcano, which once rose to around 12,000ft (3,000 meters), in fact began exploding around 420,000 years ago – during this time, the lava flows hardened into rocky crags, such as the 400,000-year-old Phantom Ship, which peeps out of Crater Lake. However, it was 7,700 years ago that a seismic eruption changed the face of the region forever. The enormous blast caused the entire upper part of the volcano to collapse, leaving a yawning caldera. Ash was deposited as far away as southwestern Canada, and the valleys that surrounded the peak were caked in up to 300ft (91 meters) of the stuff. The explosion created new vents too, and soon emerged additional formations such as Wizard Island, which still

pierces Crater Lake's impossibly blue waters. It is thought that Mount Mazama last erupted around 4,800 years ago.

Given Mount Mazama's volcanic record, experts believe that it will erupt again. However, due to the relatively low magma stores, it is not at all likely to be on the same scale as the event 7,700 years ago.

The extraordinary lava-sculpted landscape.

⊘ ON THIN ICE

The first glacier to be identified in Oregon was the Sandy Glacier on Mount Hood, in the early 1870s. This discovery was made toward the end of the region's Little Ice Age, a period of cooling that lasted from around 1300 to 1900. Since then, Oregon's glaciers have retreated at a concerningly rapid rate. Now, it is thought that there are around 463 glaciers across the state, existing in the Cascades and the eastern Wallowa Mountains. The most significant are Mount Hood's Eliot Glacier – the largest in the state – and Collier Glacier on North Sister (one of the Three Sisters in the Cascades Range).

Portrait of the 1804 Lewis and Clark Expedition by Frederic Remington.

DECISIVE DATES

10,000 BC
Indigenous peoples inhabit areas such as Central Oregon's Paisley Cave, where ancient human feces have since been found. Native Americans are known to have been living in the state since time immemorial.

1543
Spanish explorers may have got their first glimpse of the Oregon Coast.

1730s
Native Oregon tribes acquire horses from the Shoshone people, expanding trade routes and shifting traditional lifeways.

1778
Captain James Cook first sees the Oregon Coast, naming the headland Cape Foulweather due to the treacherous conditions.

1781
A deadly smallpox epidemic takes hold of Oregon's Indigenous communities as Euro-American settlers arrive in the region.

1792
Captain Robert Grey becomes the first non-Indigenous person to sail into the Columbia River and he names the waterway after his ship.

1804
The Lewis and Clark Expedition, which would explore the USA's western reaches and ultimately culminate in Oregon, begins.

1811
John Astor, head of the Pacific Fur Company, establishes a trading post at Astoria, representing Oregon's first European settlement.

1840s
The first wagons roll onto the Oregon Trail, a major east–west migrant route on which an estimated 300,000 to 500,000 people traveled.

1843
Oregon City is the first place west of the Rocky Mountains to be incorporated as a city.

1846
A very early portage railroad is constructed, connecting Oregon City and Canemah with horse-drawn trains over a wooden track.

1850
The Donation Land Claim Act is passed, granting white settlers 320 acres of 'free' land, encroaching on traditional Indigenous territories.

1850–1851
Prospectors discover gold along Josephine Creek in Southern Oregon.

1855
The Coast Reservation is established, one of many reservation sites used to forcibly relocate Indigenous communities from their traditional homelands.

1859
Oregon is admitted into the Union as the 33rd state.

1902
Crater Lake National Park is established in Oregon.

1905
Portland hosts the Lewis and Clark Centennial Exposition, garnering national attention for the wider Pacific Northwest region.

Internment camp for Japanese Americans in 1942.

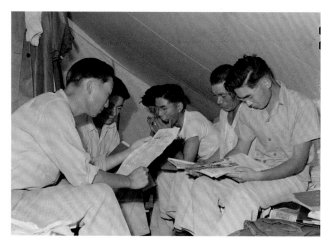

Antique map of Oregon.

1912
Women in Oregon win the right to vote, after multiple failed attempts at suffrage.

1916
Prohibition is enacted in Oregon, banning the manufacture or sale of liquor.

1922
The Oregon School Bill comes into force, closing private institutions and disproportionately affecting the Catholic community.

1929
The financial crash affects most of Oregon's major industries, including logging, fishing, and mining.

1933
The Tillamook Burn – a series of devastating wildfires affecting the state's coast northwest – begins.

1940
Portland International Airport (then called the Portland–Columbia Airport) is dedicated in October.

1941
The Japanese attack on Hawaii's Pearl Harbor sends shockwaves across the nation. The strike kills 2,403 people, including soldiers and civilians. Oregon's Japanese population suffers fierce discrimination as a result.

1942
Executive Order 9066 is signed by Franklin D. Roosevelt, authorizing the removal of those peoples deemed a "threat" to West Coast security to "relocation centers." This order greatly impacts Oregon's sizable Japanese population.

1954
Congress terminates the Klamath Indian Tribe, effectively relinquishing federal responsibility.

1964
Mega sportswear brand Nike is founded in Eugene.

1966
The soaring Astoria–Megler Bridge is completed.

1974
The John Day Fossil Beds National Monument is created by Congress.

1980s
Tribes including the Confederated Tribes of Grand Ronde; the Confederated Tribes of Coos, Lower Umpqua and Siuslaw; and the Klamath Tribes are restored.

2002
The Biscuit Fire becomes the largest recorded wildfire in Oregon history; it is sparked by lightning hitting the Rogue River–Siskiyou National Forest and went on to char almost a half a million acres.

2015
The use and possession of recreational marijuana is legalized in Oregon.

2020
The murder of George Floyd at the hands of police in Minneapolis sparks widespread protests across the states, including in Portland. Crackdowns by federal forces in Portland cause widespread controversy.

2022
Eugene hosts the World Athletics Championships at Hayward Field.

2022
The repeal of Roe v. Wade leads to a controversial abortion ban in at least 13 states, though it remains legal in Oregon.

2024
A total solar eclipse will cross North America, beginning in Oregon on the morning of October 14.

Astoria–Megler Bridge.

Chief Umapine, Cayuse.

FIRST PEOPLES

Before the encroachment of white settlers, diverse Indigenous tribes with distinct cultures lived on this land for thousands of years.

Before white settlers made their way west, Indigenous peoples had occupied this land for many millennia. In fact, archaeological finds suggest that human habitation in modern-day Oregon could date back more than 14,000 years.

Theories as to how humans came to be on the North American continent abound. Many people believe that America's earliest settlers came from Asia via the Bering Land Bridge, an ancient plain thought to have connected the two continents. That plain was revealed toward the end of the last Ice Age, when water became locked up in glaciers, causing sea levels to lower. Early peoples were likely following their food source – mostly large (and now extinct) mammals such as mammoths, mastodons, and steppe bison – across the bridge. Other experts refute this theory and believe instead that First Peoples arrived there by boat.

EARLY CIVILIZATION

First Peoples settled in various pockets of what is now Oregon. Many collected in the center of the state, around Fort Rock, and dozens of pairs of sandals made from twined sagebrush bark were discovered in Fort Rock Cave in 1938. Thought to be more than 9,000 years old, they are widely tipped as the oldest shoes in the world. Around an hour south, in Paisley, archaeologists also discovered coprolites, or fossilized feces, in 2008. The feces have been described as the oldest biological evidence of humans in North America and is thought to date back around 14,300 years. The excrement contains DNA and experts say that it confirms theories that the continent's earliest peoples came from Northeast Asia.

Evidence of early humans has also been discovered in The Dalles area along the Columbia

The Klamath, one of Oregon's Plateau tribes.

River. Here, archaeologists found fish and animal bones, and tools such as stone scrapers, thought to be around 10,000 years old. Ancient stone tools have been found along the Oregon Coast, too.

LIVING OFF THE LAND

Though unified by their reverence for Mother Earth and their binding relationship with the land, the First Peoples of Oregon settled in distinct groups, each with complex cultures and different languages – for thousands of years, there were as many as 60 tribes across what is now Oregon and they spoke in at least 18 different tongues.

First People's cultures are intrinsically linked to their homelands, and the state's incredibly varied terrain dictated the lifestyle and hunting practices of early tribes. For example, Native Americans such as the Coquille, whose land covered around a million acres of southwestern Oregon, fished at estuaries and in sheltered bays on the coast. They ate both shellfish and saltwater and freshwater species. These reliable, year-round food sources enabled the tribe to avoid the need to move around between seasons – they typically lived in permanent villages in homes made from cedar planks. Early Coquille people spoke a rich tapestry of languages, from Miluk around the lower Coquille River, to a variety of Athabaskan dialects to the south and east. Though many of these early languages have sadly died out, the modern Coquille Tribe is working to connect its members to their ancestral tongues. Thankfully, the artistry and craftsmanship of the Coquille peoples endures. They once carved tools from hardy volcanic blueschist rock and made basketry from spruce roots, and today a generation of tribal artisans is breathing new life into age-old traditions, creating intricate baskets and beadwork.

Away from the coast, there was more movement among the First Peoples of Oregon. Plateau tribes

Klamath chief overlooking Crater Lake National Park.

⊙ STORYTELLING TRADITIONS

Storytelling is a vital and precious part of Native American heritage. Oral histories, tales and stories have long been passed down through generations, helping Indigenous peoples of various tribes make sense of their origins, their ancestors, the natural world, and their place in it. Many of these stories relate to how the First Peoples of Oregon came to be, often featuring an all-powerful Creator who first planted humans on Earth.

Several groups, including the Molalla people of the Cascades – today, part of the Confederated Tribes of the Grand Ronde – tell stories of the Coyote who intended to "make the world." However, as the Coyote went about his quest, a Grizzly Bear challenged him to a fight. Thus, the pair of animals engaged in a contest swallowing hot rocks. Unfortunately, while Grizzly downed the hot stones, Coyote cunningly sneaked strawberries instead.

When Grizzly inevitably died, Coyote carved him up and scattered his remains, throwing his heart to what would become Molala Country, in order that its people should become good hunters.

Meanwhile, the Klamath people tell stories of the Creator Kamukamts, who canoed on a great lake and eventually ran into a Pocket Gopher who helped him on his quest to build the world.

generally shifted location with the seasons, moving to suitable areas for hunting and/or gathering, then setting up semi-permanent winter villages. This way of living applied to the various tribes of the Klamath Basin, who lived in the land east of the Cascades Range. In spring they fished in rivers, including the Sprague where the annual C'waam Ceremony is still commemorated – this ancient celebration is intended to welcome these endemic fish back to the waters as they swim upriver to spawn. They would also dig for root crops like wild onion and bitterroot. In summer, tribespeople would head into mountain areas to pick huckleberries, drying their bounty in forest clearings ready for the winter. As they traveled through the warmer months, the Klamath typically lived in tule-mat shelters made from bulrushes and reeds, which they gathered from rivers in dugout canoes. In winter they favored pit houses that were warm and had space for storage.

Some Native Americans were even identified by their food sources. For example, the Northern Paiute, who occupied the Great Basin area, were distinguished as Wadikishitika ("juniper deer eaters"), Agaitika ("elk eaters"), or Gidutikad ("groundhog eaters"), among other things.

A THRIVING TRADE

Long before the arrival of white settlers, trade was an extremely important part of life for the First Peoples of Oregon. The region's contrasting landscapes meant that different natural resources were readily available to different Native American groups, and instead of swapping goods for money, they operated on a barter system. They directly exchanged items of similar worth, from seashells and baskets to animal hides, foodstuff, and natural materials for weaponry.

The Cayuse, Walla Walla, and Umatilla tribes were extremely proficient traders, controlling a vast trade route that struck into the Great Basin and pushed north into Canada – the tribes mainly dealt in dried foods such as fish, plus roots and berries. There was also a great deal of trade along the Columbia River. The Chinooks would accumulate vast stores of dried salmon, while the Kalapuyans of the Willamette Valley traded plants such as camas, whose bulbs were used as sweeteners. (Later, in 1805, Nez Perce peoples would save travelers on the Lewis and Clark Expedition from starving by sharing their

camas bulbs.) Meanwhile, coastal tribes would gather shells and trade materials that could be fashioned into tools. Social stratification was sometimes decided by material wealth. For example, in the Coos, wealth was determined by a person's store of items such as dentalium shells or gray pine seeds. The wealthiest member of society became the chief of the village – though he was obliged to use his riches to benefit the entire community. The village members would reward the generosity by bestowing food and gifts upon the chief.

The Umatilla people of the Plateau region.

⊙ CONTROLLED BURNS

Fire was an integral part of the land management for First Peoples, and controlled burns were common. Typically, these burns would take place in late summer, after the harvest. The fires would "clean up" the forest, removing weeds, wiping out insects, and leaving behind fertile ash. Various root crops, trees and plants spawning nuts and berries would thrive after a burn and the thinned underbrush would create ideal habitats for elk and deer, which the Indigenous peoples hunted. This practice was rife in the Willamette, upper Umpqua, and Rogue Valleys – in parts of Oregon such as the Willamette Valley, "prescribed" or "cultural" burns still form part of Indigenous lifeways.

It is thought that as early as the 1640s, coastal tribespeople may have interacted with foreign ships making landfall on the Pacific Coast. The eventual arrival of Europeans and US citizens – which is often wrongly pinpointed as the beginnings of commerce in the region – ultimately disrupted trading routes and traditions that have existed for thousands of years.

EQUINE ENDEAVORS

Horses had reached the Columbia Plateau by the 1730s – the animals were passed up through Indigenous trade routes, beginning in early Spanish settlements in northern Mexico. The Cayuse are thought to have been the first Native Americans in Oregon to gain horses. It is said that the Cayuse came into contact with Shoshone people mounted on horses in the first part of the 18th century, and at first they thought they were riding elk. Once the Cayuse realized that these animals were new to their lands, they asked the Shoshone if they could trade something for the creatures. Initially, the Shoshone were reluctant – however, the determined Cayuse laid down all

Horses revolutionized life for the Cayuse and other tribes and transformed trading routes.

⊘ BOUNTY OF THE RIVER

Salmon has long been of great importance to the Native Americans of Oregon. Various waterways across the state, including the Columbia River, were once swollen with salmon that, after spending a great portion of their lives in the Pacific Ocean, would swim (sometimes thousands of miles) back to their birthplace to spawn their own young.

Hundreds of thousands of salmon were caught by First Peoples every year: they could be eaten right away, dried for winter, or even traded for other goods. Salmon species are considered a "First Food" and are included in the origin stories of some Indigenous tribes, with many believing the fish was a gift from the Creator. They were also celebrated in First Foods ceremonies, a tradition continued by many of the Plateau tribes today.

However, over the years, habitat degradation, invasive species, and overfishing has led to the gradual decline of Chinook salmon in certain parts of the state. This is true of the Coquille River watershed area, where the Coquille Indian Tribe and the Oregon Department of Fish and Wildlife have joined forces to try to bring the species back from the brink. The government are depending on Indigenous knowledge and practices to revive fish populations, including the management of a hatchery and the control of invasive bass.

their wares and the Shoshone finally consented, handing over a stallion and a mare. Eventually, the mare gave birth to a colt.

The acquisition revolutionized life for the Cayuse, and also the neighboring Umatilla and Walla Walla tribes, and transformed traditional trading routes. The horses allowed the Native Americans to travel great distances and to exchange previously inaccessible goods. The animals themselves were also exchanged for skins or other valuable items. The Cayuse became incredibly skilled equestrians. The horses also enhanced

and treaties were broken. The sovereignty of tribal peoples was routinely ignored, and Native Americans often ended up with a fragment of their promised land (which was already just a slither of their traditional ancestral homes).

Little to no regard was given to the distinct cultures and lifeways of Oregon's many Indigenous peoples: the reservation system lumped separate tribes onto single swathes of land, while attempts at assimilation included day and boarding schools for Indigenous children. Later, in the 20th century, the abrupt termination of the trea-

A Shoshone community living in traditional buffalo-hide teepees.

the people's abilities in war, and they used them to hunt deer and elk. As horse ownership spread, raids became more commonplace too.

Ultimately, the horses thrived in the hills and valleys of the Columbia Plateau and eventually the Cayuse began a program of selective breeding. The result was a distinctive breed known as the Cayuse pony or mustang, which was revered for its speed, endurance, and strength.

RESERVATIONS

The reservation system changed the lives of the Native Americans of Oregon immeasurably. Long journeys to newly prescribed lands (which were often much less bountiful when it came to natural resources) led to disease and death,

ties (which ended federal responsibility for tribes) led to widespread unemployment and poverty.

NATIVE AMERICANS TODAY

Today, there are nine federally recognized tribes in Oregon, many of which are coalitions between historically distinct groups with their own cultures and lifestyles. They are self-governing, sovereign nations and, for many, they fight an ongoing campaign to regain the rights to the ancestral lands ceded during the reservation system. Various organizations preserve precious Indigenous traditions: among them is Portland-based Wisdom of the Elders, which makes video recordings of tribal leaders to protect quickly fading aspects of culture, from oral legends to languages.

Meriwether Lewis of the iconic Lewis and Clark Expedition.

EUROPEAN AND US ENCROACHMENT

From early explorer ships to the Lewis and Clark Expedition, European and US citizens were curious about the Pacific Northwest.

It is thought that Spanish explorers would have first caught sight of the Oregon Coast back in 1543, on an expedition led by Juan Rodríguez Cabrillo. However, it would be another two centuries before foreigners would stake their claims in the region – when they did, their movements proved devastating for Oregon's long-standing Indigenous communities.

EARLY EXPEDITIONS AND THE BEGINNINGS OF THE FUR RUSH

Captain James Cook, a Yorkshire-born explorer, led three voyages across the Pacific Ocean between 1768 and 1779. During his journeys, he produced detailed maps of stretches of the Oregon Coast, naming natural phenomena such as Cape Foulweather and Cape Perpetua. He also described resources harbored by Native Americans, such as sea otter furs. Word of the furs piqued interest in the region and triggered the "fur rush" to the Pacific Northwest.

Rhode Island-born Robert Gray was among those who heard Cook's descriptions of the valuable otter pelts and he sailed out to the region in 1787. When it came to trade, Gray was aggressive in his approach – on several occasions, he killed Indigenous peoples who would not exchange their wares at a price that he saw fit. He sold the furs he had acquired in Macao and returned to the East Coast. Then, he embarked on a second voyage in 1790 and ultimately sailed into the Columbia River in 1792 (the first non-Indigenous person to do so), naming the waterway after his ship. On this second excursion, Gray destroyed entire Native American villages.

The fur trade boomed in the decades that followed. Though many Native Americans embraced it at first, the practice ultimately

Captain James Cook, 1728–79.

⊘ DOCTRINE OF DISCOVERY

The colonialism by Europeans and the United States was justified by the "Doctrine of Discovery," which was first issued by Pope Alexander VI way back in 1493. The doctrine granted Christian explorers absolute power to seize "New World" land that they had "discovered" and, in degrading the humanity and sovereignty of Indigenous peoples, was used to legitimize land grabs at their expense. This eventually morphed into a concept called "Manifest Destiny," which encapsulated the belief that the US was destined and duty-bound to expand westward. This vision idealized colonialism and hailed new territories as promised lands.

changed their way of life. Some tribes abandoned their subsistence lifestyle in favor of commerce systems created by the fur traders. Tools and weapons from the eastern US and Europe also flooded into the daily lives of Native Americans, leading to the demise of some Indigenous handicrafts. Diseases such as smallpox and measles decimated populations of Native Americans, who had no immunity to European-borne diseases. Epidemics swept through the region in the late 18th century, with deadly smallpox gripping Indigenous communities in 1781. Entering

Meriwether Lewis on his early expeditions.

⊙ PACIFIC FUR COMPANY

Several years after the conclusion of the Lewis and Clark Expedition, one of the most infamous American companies of the 19th century was founded. The American Fur Company was established by John Jacob Astor in New York state in 1808, and its subsidiary – the Pacific Fur Company – was set up in 1811. The company led to the first permanent American settlement in Oregon. Astor sent fur traders west to Oregon in 1811 and they built Fort Astoria at the mouth of the Columbia River. Astoria bloomed over the decades and today it is recognized as Oregon's oldest city. Despite this, the War of 1812 meant that the Pacific Fur Company did not take Oregon's Pacific Coast by storm as Astor had hoped.

the 19th century, malaria was also rife. It is estimated that, in regions including the Portland Basin and the Willamette Valley, between 80 and 90 percent of the Indigenous population was wiped out. This meant abandoned villages, overflowing cemeteries, and the erasure of culture as Native Americans began to be outnumbered by non-Indigenous settlers. The weakened numbers left them vulnerable to attack, too.

The first known African American to set foot in the Oregon region was sailor Markus Lopeus, who arrived in Tillamook Bay in 1788 with Captain Robert Gray. It is thought that Lopeus was killed in a clash with Indigenous peoples.

LEWIS AND CLARK EXPEDITION

The Lewis and Clark Expedition is one of the most talked-about journeys in American history. Meriwether Lewis – born in Virginia in 1774 – was tasked with exploring territories west of the Mississippi River by President Thomas Jefferson in 1804. The request followed the Louisiana Purchase, through which the USA acquired the vast Louisiana territory from France in 1803. Lewis enlisted former military man William Clark as the expedition's co-leader and the pair struck out from St Louis, Missouri, with the Corps of Discovery in 1804. The Corps numbered around 47, including many unmarried young men and an enslaved person named York.

The expedition would take two years and cover some 8,000 miles. On several occasions, the expeditioners were saved by the kindness of the Native Americans who they met along the way. The travelers encountered the Nez Perce people along the Lolo Trail, which beats a path through the Bitterroot Mountains. By this point in their journey, the Corps were bone-tired, with many of them also suffering from frostbite and dehydration. The Nez Perce gave the travelers food and water and allowed them to rest before they continued their journey.

As they pushed west, the explorers shared insights on the region with dignitaries waiting back home, and when they finally reached the Pacific Ocean in the winter of 1805, they established a camp in Oregon, near what is modern-day Astoria. They also established a trading post on the Columbia River and eventually built Fort Clatsop, where they spent a challenging winter.

The team began their return journey in 1806, ultimately splitting into two groups, one led by Clark, the other by Lewis. They returned to the city of St Louis in September 1806.

THE OREGON TRAIL

The Oregon Trail is one of the most notorious chapters in the state's history. Following the expeditions of early 19th-century explorers, and in the wake of a booming fur trade, a period of mass migration to America's West Coast occurred.

Between about 1840 and 1860, it is estimated that upward of 300,000 people made the harrowing overland journey toward the Willamette Valley and other parts of the West Coast. Travelers would need to cover some 2,000 miles of ground in rickety wagons, typically pulled by mules or oxen, and they would generally be on the road for around six months.

The expedition was an unforgiving one: travelers were at the mercy of Mother Nature as the trail coursed through America's stark and craggy terrains. The route hugged the Missouri and Platte rivers, striking through vast plains in Nebraska and Wyoming, then tracing the Snake River in Idaho. Upon entering Oregon Country, it traversed the forested Blue Mountains before following the mighty Columbia River to The Dalles region, where travelers would often continue part of their journey on water. (The creation of the Barlow Road in 1846 presented an overland option.) Travelers would cross rivers, weather storms, and brave mountain passes. They also faced diseases such as cholera.

There were sometimes clashes with Native Americans as the potential settlers continued westward, though many early interactions are thought to have been peaceful. It is estimated that at least 20,000 people died making their way along the trail, though that figure may of course be conservative.

The travelers typically operated in groups called "companies," camping together and sharing provisions. Written-up constitutions would determine leadership and divide duties among the group. And by the time they reached Oregon Country (or struck out toward destinations such as California or Utah), they were exhausted and often impoverished, having spent funds or lost possessions along the way.

Nevertheless, preserved diary entries from travelers nod to the abundance of Oregon's fertile lands, which the new arrivals farmed with vigor. Homesteads were cheap and easy to come by, and soon the new population swelled to 5,000. In 1848, Oregon became a named territory.

John Jacob Astor, founder of the Pacific Fur Company.

⊘ THE HOLMES FAMILY

Robin and Polly Holmes were enslaved by American politician Nathaniel Ford, who brought the couple and their three-year-old daughter west on the Oregon Trail in 1844. The group set out from Missouri, where slavery was still legal, and arrived in Oregon, where it was prohibited. However, upon arrival and in the following years, Ford denied the couple and their children (eventually numbering five) emancipation. In 1849, Robin managed to negotiate freedom for himself, Polly, and their infant son by agreeing to prospect for gold on Ford's behalf. Yet, Ford still refused to emancipate the other children. Eventually, a court battle ensued and in a landmark case, the judge ruled in Holmes' favor.

Gold was first struck in Oregon in the early 1850s, changing the face of the state forever.

A VIOLENT ERA

As non-Indigenous immigrants settled in the Oregon Territory, and established new industries and traditions, life was irrevocably altered for Native American communities.

The population in Oregon continued to explode after the region was granted territorial status – and this was helped along exponentially by the Donation Land Claim Law. Passed by Congress in 1850, the law endowed white male citizens and their wives with 320 acres (130 hectares). The only requirement was that they must make 'improvements' to the land over a four-year period. The law notably excluded Black people.

Naturally, the law and the resulting influx of further white settlers had a devastating impact on the region's existing Indigenous populations. Native Americans were driven from their homes as non-Indigenous citizens made claims on the land. It is estimated that by 1855 (when the law terminated) some 30,000 white immigrants had flooded into the territory.

RESERVATIONS AND TREATIES

As non-Indigenous settlers continued their claims on the Oregon Territory, so began the Reservation Era. This period of Oregon's checkered history saw Native Americans forcibly moved from their homelands in exchange for little or no monetary funds and directed to federally assigned and approved reservations. These reservations were typically on land with scant natural resources. Some treaties allowed Indigenous peoples to fish and hunt on their ancestral homelands; others did not.

As early as 1851, treaties were agreed with as many as nineteen tribes and bands in the territory. Spearheaded by Superintendent of Indian Affairs for the Oregon Territory Anson Dart, these treaties ceded some 6 million acres (2 million hectares) to the US, creating

China store in Portland between 1895 and 1910.

◎ ROGUE RIVER WAR

Tensions between the Indigenous tribes of the Rogue River and the non-Indigenous settlers who flooded in on the Oregon Trail, plus local miners, heightened during the 1850s. Native Americans were already wary of settlers after fur-trappers killed tribe members in 1834, but between 1855 and 1856, the Rogue River tribes, the US army, and volunteers clashed in a series of deadly armed conflicts – collectively known as the Rogue River War. There were fatalities on both sides: estimates put the number of war dead at between 235 and 267 Indigenous peoples, and around 50 non-Indigenous soldiers. Post-war, most of the surviving Native Americans were forcibly removed to reservations.

reservations for various tribes, including the Chinook people on the Columbia River. However, though the treaties were signed by Indigenous communities, they were never

---

Oregon was admitted to the Union in 1859, becoming America's 33rd state, just two years before the start of the American Civil War in 1861.

John Smith, Chief of the Grand Rondes.

ratified by Congress as the treaties failed to move the tribes east of the Cascades as the US powers-that-be had intended. Dart was forced to resign.

From 1853, Dart's successor, Joel Palmer, continued negotiations with Indigenous leaders and reignited efforts to move them east. Eventually, Palmer formed treaties with many of Oregon's western tribes, including the Chinook, Umpqua, and Kalapuya peoples. Seven treaties were ratified by Congress. Tribespeople were typically removed from their lands and placed into temporary reservations, as the permanent reservations set out in treaties were developed.

The Coast Reservation was one of the key sites that Native Americans in western Oregon were moved to. The reservation, which stretched out for around one million acres (400,000 hectares) on the western flank of the Coast Range, became home to 27 tribes that would once have lived independently from one another. Meanwhile, the forcible removal of Indigenous peoples to the Grand Ronde Reservation is described by the modern-day Confederated Tribes of Grand Ronde as Oregon's "Trail of Tears."

Indigenous peoples of various descent were marched from the temporary Table Rock reservation to the federally created Grand Ronde Reservation, which encompassed 60,000 acres (24,000 hectares) in the Coast Range. The journey lasted approximately 33 days and there was a sizable death toll.

⊘ RIVERS OF GOLD

Prospectors first struck gold in Oregon in the 1850s, in the Blue Mountains, and mines sprouted along the John Day, Grand Ronde, and Snake rivers. The earliest miners used placer methods, separating minerals from gravel and sand deposits; hydraulic and hard rock (or lode) operations came later. Many laborers were Chinese and often suffered discrimination. Chinese mining operations were often afforded less fertile lands than those run by white people, and tensions grew when reserves dwindled. One of the most tragic incidents occurred in 1887 when 34 Chinese miners laboring in Deep Creek, Hells Canyon, were tortured and then murdered by a gang from Wallowa County. Six men were

believed to have committed the crime – however, three of the indicted fled and the others were pardoned by the jury. The site, which became known as the Chinese Massacre Cove, now has a memorial to the victims.

Many of Oregon's towns have roots in mining. Jacksonville and Baker City began as mining camps before mushrooming into towns. These hastily established settlements, with saloons and hotels, were often dangerous, with loose systems of law and order. Post-1860s, mining began to decline. Nonetheless, it remains a key Oregon industry today and companies dig for lithium, gold, and other minerals. Mines litter the state, with clusters in the southwest and northeast.

OREGON AND THE CIVIL WAR

Oregon was a juvenile state in 1861, when Confederate forces fired shots on South Carolina's Fort Sumter, igniting the American Civil War. Before that, it is estimated that several hundred

In 1862, Oregon passed a law banning interracial marriage and also imposed a $5 annual tax on minorities, including Black and Chinese people.

Though there were political divides across the region, Oregon had voted in its majority for abolitionist and Democrat Abraham Lincoln, and the state raised two regiments in support of the Union war effort: the 1st Oregon Infantry and the 1st Oregon Cavalry. Among the notable Oregonians to be killed in the war was Edward Dickinson Baker, an acting senator who died in the Battle of Ball's Bluff.

Union forces gained victory over the Confederacy, and the war ended in April of 1865. When Oregon ratified the Fourteenth

Gold prospector armed with rifle and burro (donkey) carrying supplies.

African Americans had passed into the region on the Oregon Trail – some of them free, others enslaved by settlers. The Organic Laws of Oregon, which had been passed in 1843, prohibited slavery. But although slaveholders were forced to relinquish their human "property," Oregon's Black Exclusion Laws – the first of which was passed in 1844 – prevented free Black people from remaining in the state, lest they be punished with lashings.

In 1849, further laws stopped Black people from entering the state at all, while in 1857, they were prohibited from owning property, signing contracts, or voting. Thus, despite Oregon's outward ban on slavery, it was an incredibly inhospitable place for African Americans.

⊘ ASSIMILATION

Despite terms laid out in treaties, the US routinely rejected the sovereignty of Indigenous tribes. In Oregon, particularly throughout the late 19th century, various methods were implemented in attempts to assimilate Native Americans into US society. Day and boarding schools were established for Indigenous children, typically with the involvement of Christian missionaries. Sometimes, children were forcibly removed from their parents and taken to schools far away from their ancestral homes. These schools peddled Euro-American values: children were often punished for speaking in their Indigenous language, were prohibited from wearing traditional dress, and were forced to study the bible.

Amendment – which was passed in Congress in 1866 and promised all citizens "the equal protection of the laws" – the state's multiple exclusion laws were rendered obsolete. However, they were not axed from the state Constitution until 1926.

THE RAILROAD

Shortly after Oregon was admitted into the Union, railroads began to crisscross the state. The Oregon Steam Navigation Company installed tracks along the Columbia

Civil war reenactment near Salem.

River as early as 1862. Fast forward a decade and the Oregon and California Railroad joined Portland with Eugene – by 1887, it had found its way across the California border. The Northern Pacific Railroad was also completed in 1883.

The federal government poured substantial funds into railroad development in the region and granted companies such as the Oregon and California Railroad vast swathes of land. The impact of the railroad on Oregon was two-fold. On the one hand, the building of the network created jobs in the state, while the increased connectivity provided further opportunities for trade and more ready access to natural resources. Chinese laborers worked in

railroad construction in great numbers through the 1870s (when the mining industry was in a decline after its boom from the 1850s to mid-1860s). The railroad was also great news for Oregon's flourishing agricultural industry. As refrigerated rail cars joined up Oregon, regions such as Hood River Valley – still known for its many fruit farms – boomed.

EARLY LOGGING INDUSTRY

The development of the railroad spurred on another industry: logging. This one, however, was already established: Portland earned its "Stumptown" nickname way back in the mid-1800s, when forestland was rapidly cleared to make way for an exploding population. Immigrants had poured into the region during the Gold Rush, and they continued to do so as the railroad was constructed, so the need for timber increased exponentially. Oregon's lumber industry also supplied mining operations in California through the 1800s and, later in the century, extensive rail networks allowed the practice to mushroom in previously inaccessible parts of the state.

Logging was mostly concentrated in two principal regions: the Western Cascades, with their soaring Douglas firs and mountain hemlocks, and rugged Eastern Oregon, with its ponderosa pines. Hulking sawmills sprung up along Portland's waterfront and in coastal communities such as Coos Bay. By the end of the 19th century, it is estimated that as much as 100 million board feet of lumber was exported from the Lower Columbia River area every year.

DWINDLING RESERVATIONS

As industry fizzed across Oregon, it was, once again, often at the expense of the state's Indigenous peoples. The 1887 General Allotment Act, or Dawes Act, authorized President Grover Cleveland to carve up reservation land, and grant parcels of it to individuals for farming – this worked in direct contrast to tribal nations' traditional communal ownership of their ancestral homes.

It is estimated that this new law reduced tribal lands by around 90 million acres (36 million hectares) up until the 1930s, when it was finally revoked.

Actress Margaret Vale at the Woman Suffrage Procession in Washington D.C. on March 3, 1913.

MODERN OREGON

The 20th century was a period of flux in Oregon, with boom times and busts, and pressures and progress that would change the face of the state forever.

Throughout the 18th and 19th centuries, Oregon and the West were held up as the promised land – a utopian world of unfettered fortune and opportunity. Riverbeds were laced with gold; volcanic soil produced fat fruits; forests sacrificed endless timber. Thousands listened to the lore and by the turn of the century, westward expansion had changed Oregon immutably. The region's urban hub, Portland, was a city of more than 80,000 people.

In 1873 and 1893, periods of economic downturn had created uncertainty across the nation, including in Oregon. However, by the early 1900s, recovery was widespread. Mining operations were no longer at their mid-19th-century zenith but work on the railroad continued and Oregon's logging industry showed little sign of waning.

Portland on the cusp of the 20th century.

The New Age was the first Black-owned newspaper in Oregon – it was published by businessman Adolphus D. Griffin, beginning in 1896.

MIGRATION CONTINUES

In the late 1800s and early 1900s, waves of migration continued in Oregon. The African-American population swelled significantly, as many arrived to work as porters on the railroad. Immigrants from European countries such as Italy, Hungary, and Greece also arrived – by the turn of the century, it is estimated that 17 percent of the population had been born somewhere other than the United States. This diverse mix of migrants worked across Oregon's booming industries, from logging and mining to fishing and farming.

Growth across the state was helped along by the 1902 Reclamation Act – the law brought about various irrigation and hydropower projects across the fast-developing West. The city of Hermiston, a stone's throw from the Columbia River, grew out of the project and served as its headquarters.

The process of urbanization was also evident during the early 1900s. Portland's population continued to mushroom – helped along by the Lewis and Clark Centennial Exposition, held in 1905 – and so did that of other urban cores, such as Eugene, Ashland, Medford, and Salem. The number of people living in the modern-day capital tripled between 1900 and 1910.

SUFFRAGE

Women's suffrage organizations had formed as early as the 1870s in hubs such as Salem and Albany. Early figureheads of the movement included Abigail Scott Duniway, who was born in Illinois, but migrated west with her family on the Oregon Trail in the 1850s. Yet, while the first vote on women's suffrage might have taken place in 1884, those 'against' won with a 72 percent majority. The second vote occurred in 1900 and it was much closer this time: suffrage was voted down by just 52 percent and the tight margins further emboldened activists.

Oregon's suffrage movement gained momentum after the turn of the century and in 1905, the

Abigail Scott Duniway, a pioneer of women's suffrage.

⊘ LAND FRAUD SCANDALS

Portland's Pioneer Courthouse was the battleground for one of the early 20th century's most scandalous legal cases. The basis of the trials was the exploitation of homestead laws, which allowed for the sales of public lands to Oregon settlers. However, it was discovered that many fraudulent claims had been made (some under entirely fabricated names), with General Land Office officials accepting bribes to push them through. Later, these fraudulently acquired lands were sold on to lumber and farming operations for major profits. Among the almost 100 people convicted were Senator John H. Mitchell and US District Attorney John Hall.

> *The Indian Citizenship Act was passed in 1924, granting citizenship to Indigenous peoples, though they were still not afforded the right to vote.*

National American Woman Suffrage Association held its convention in Portland – well-known activists such as Susan B. Anthony attended the national event. Soon, grassroots suffrage groups were springing up across the state, but despite vigorous campaigns, the concept was struck down in the ballot box several more times (in 1906, 1908, and 1910).

By 1912, both Washington to the north and California to the south had granted women the right to vote. At this time in Oregon, there were around 70 groups, representing diverse populations, campaigning for suffrage across the state. Votes were cast in a final ballot in 1912 and supporters of suffrage finally won – 52 percent were in favor of women's right to vote. Early pioneer Abigail Scott Duniway was asked to write and sign the state's Equal Suffrage Proclamation.

WORLD WAR I AND THE DEPRESSION

Oregon's natural resources were mined during World War I (1914–1918), and the economy boomed. Its Sitka spruce trees were harvested for timber to build aircraft, and thousands of soldiers were sent into the state's maritime forests to accelerate operations. Meanwhile, large shipyards sprouted on the coast, in communities including Coos Bay and Astoria.

Yet, shortly after the boom came a bust. When the war ended and demand for wood (and wheat, another of Oregon's major exports) shrank, so too did the economy, and many of the state's workers found themselves unemployed. Nevertheless, so much industrial might had been built up during the wartime effort that Oregon bounced back in a timely manner. The lumber industry in particular gained pace again through the 1920s.

However, the financial crash of 1929 triggered another downturn, this time affecting every industry, from logging and fishing to mining. Employment across the state dropped by one-third. Mines and mills were left abandoned through the 1930s as operations ceased, and a number of Oregonians left in vain pursuit of work elsewhere.

DIVIDED ATTITUDES

The 1920s were a period of flux and contradictions in Oregon. Tensions grew between non-Indigenous settlers and Indigenous communities, and this decade saw the rise of hate groups such as the Ku Klux Klan. However, in apparent opposition to this, further rights were granted to Indigenous peoples, and the Black Exclusion Law written into Oregon's Constitution was finally repealed in 1926.

By the early 1920s, the Ku Klux Klan's national membership had surpassed two million people. The white supremacist group unleashed a campaign of hate against Oregon's Jewish, Catholic, and Black populations, beginning in 1921, when Ku Klux Klan recruiter Luther Powell arrived in Medford in Southern Oregon. In a series of meetings, Powell heard that white Oregonians were worried about crime and also, for the most part, abhorred Catholicism. He set up a Ku Klux Klan chapter in response.

The KKK injected cash into local churches and spread their messages (which hinged on a promise to end lawlessness, under the guise of national pride and patriotism) with parades and other public events. In 1922, the Oregon School Bill came into force, outlawing all private schools in the state, and thus closing Catholic institutions. It is thought that by 1923 Oregon had around 58,000 Klan members. Alongside Catholics, Oregon's Jewish, Black, and Asian populations were menaced and sometimes physically attacked. At this point in time, the Oregon Alien Land Law was also enacted: this prohibited Chinese and Japanese people from buying land in Oregon.

Eventually, opposition to the KKK grew, and most of Oregon's chapters had disbanded by the middle of the decade. In 1927, the Constitution was altered to remove voting restrictions for African and Chinese Americans.

WORLD WAR II

The United States entered World War II after the devastating attack on Hawaii's Pearl Harbor by Japanese forces in 1941. The surprise military strike killed 2,403 Americans (including 68 civilians) and destroyed a vast store of Navy ships. Following the

The Umatilla Army Depot opened in Hermiston in 1941.

⊘ JAPANESE INTERNMENT CENTERS

Japan's role in World War II exacerbated the discrimination that Japanese citizens in the US had already faced for decades. Civilians suffered threats and violence – most devastating of all, though, was Executive Order 9066, signed by wartime president Franklin D. Roosevelt in 1942. The order stipulated that all individuals who posed a threat to national security should be removed to "relocation centers." The ruling was then used to forcibly displace and incarcerate thousands of Japanese Americans along the West Coast.

First, individuals were required to report to temporary "assembly centers." At its peak, the Portland Assembly Center reached a population of more than 3,600 people. Next, they were transferred to the relocation centers. Most people from Portland were relocated to Minidoka, Idaho, while people from the Hood River area and southwest Oregon were moved to Tule Lake in California. The camps were essentially prisons, located in stark desert plains and ringed by barbed wire. Due to the poor construction of the centers, prisoners were exposed to the elements, while a lack of basic sanitation meant conditions were dire and disease was rife. Though the Japanese were eventually free to leave the camps by January 1945, most had lost land and livelihoods and only a portion of those from Oregon chose to return.

incident, the Pacific Northwest region was on high alert. Blackouts were ordered along the Oregon Coast and in western counties, as officials feared further strikes. The Beach Patrol, which was composed of some 24,000 men, was also formed – the organization kept watch over Oregon's coastline in anticipation of enemy ambush.

In June 1942 Fort Stevens, on the north coast of Oregon near Astoria, was attacked by Japanese submarines. Seventeen shells were fired but no damage occurred, and US troops did not return fire. A few months later, a Japanese pilot

Japanese citizens faced prejudice during World War II.

⊘ TILLAMOOK BURN

The Tillamook Burn – a series of devastating fires in Oregon's northwestern coastal region – wreaked economic havoc from the 1930s. The first fire started in 1933 and is thought to have been sparked by friction when a large log was dragged over another fallen tree. For almost two decades afterward, fires were reignited as the dead trees from previous blazes served as tinder. Over the entire period, it is thought that around 355,000 acres (143,663 hectares) were burned in the region. Important logging areas vital to Oregon's economy were ravaged and by the early 1950s, private landowners, unable to pay taxes, were forfeiting large plots to the state.

Improved infrastructure attracted tourists, too. Travelers were drawn in by such epic landscapes as Crater Lake National Park and scenic byways such as coastal Highway 101.

dropped bombs over the Siskiyou National Forest – the intent was to spark destructive woodland fires that would ultimately distract the US from the war effort. Luckily, the conditions were wet, so the resulting blaze was quickly brought under control and the destruction was much less than anticipated.

Sadly, though, in 1945 six people were killed by a Japanese balloon bomb near Bly in Southern Oregon. Local minister Archie Mitchell and his pregnant wife Elsie took five Sunday school children out to a picnic. Elsie ran up ahead with the children while her husband parked the car and gathered lunch – however, in that time, Elsie and the children happened across a balloon bomb, which exploded, killing them all. They became the only civilian fatalities during World War II on the continental United States.

For the most part, Oregon's economy boomed during the war. As was the case during World War I, there was a high demand for lumber, while shipyards in the Portland area built hundreds of emergency vessels. Near Troutdale, a large-scale aluminum plant churned out metals for aircraft. There were more women in the workforce than ever before, with a major female presence in Oregon's shipyards. Many African Americans moved west to work in this industry.

POSTWAR OREGON

The second half of the 1940s rang in the end of a dismal period of Depression and war and, for many Oregonians, the 20th century seemed to spread out Eden-like before them. Oregon's population continued to balloon, and the state's key industries were still booming. This was a period of technological advancement for the state and for the nation as a whole. Across the region, many farming processes became mechanized. Sophisticated irrigation systems and chemical fertilizers enhanced crop growth, while powerful tractors made tillage easier.

Mammoth logging trucks and modern chainsaws strengthened the lumber industry, and logging was bolstered by housing demands from the soaring post-war population. Major hydro-electric dams, including Bonneville Dam in the Columbia River Gorge, meant that power was not cripplingly expensive. Roads across the state were improved in line with a rise in car owner-ship, another boon for Oregon's key industries.

The trend toward urbanization, which was evident at the turn of the century, continued in post-war Oregon. Places such as Portland and Eugene gained sprawling suburbs, while rural communities began to shrink – particularly in places where smaller farms could not compete with larger, mechanized operations.

BURGEONING COUNTERCULTURE

Through the late 1960s and 1970s, the so-called "hippie movement" was in full swing across the nation, with many protests sparked by opposition to America's involvement in the Vietnam War. On the West Coast, San Francisco's Haight-Ashbury neighborhood is most readily associated with hippies but, unsurprisingly, Oregon had its own counterculture movement. Anti-war marches took place across Portland and protestors formed barricades at Portland State University (and were met with police violence). Meanwhile, Vortex I, a state-sponsored rock music festival that was specifically intended to distract youngsters who might disrupt American Legion's annual conven-tion in Portland, went down in history.

Throughout this period, many hippies descended on Oregon's rural areas and formed communities where alternative lifestyles flour-ished. These places typically upheld values of

pacifism and were concerned with green ways of living and artistic pursuits. One such place is Alpha Farm in Deadwood, a commune estab-lished in 1972. Self-described as "an extended family-style community," it still exists today.

BLAZING A GREEN TRAIL

Today, Oregon is often heralded as one of the greenest states in the union – a leader in the field of renewable energy and a fierce protec-tor of its wild spaces. The concept of the nat-ural world as something to be preserved and

Logging thrived due to post-war housing boom.

⊘ TERMINATION

Following the war, the concept of "termination" unleashed further assaults on the ancestral home-lands of Native American communities. Termination essentially threatened to reverse established rela-tionships with Indigenous tribes and the federal government, leaving previously negotiated territories under threat.

The policy was formally adopted in 1953, with the House Concurrent Resolution 108, which called for an end to federal responsibilities for Native Americans. The ultimate goal was assimilation. The Klamath Termination Act was passed in 1954 and many enrolled Klamath tribe members were given lump sums of

money for their reservation land – the alternative was to keep their shares in the land and participate in a trust scheme managed by the United States National Bank of Oregon.

That trust relationship was eventually terminated, too, and all remaining shareholders received payouts. Sadly, what followed for the Klamath people was mass unemployment and a lack of access to basic resources such as education.

Other tribes, including the Siletz, Coquille, Coos, and Grand Ronde, also yielded to termination in this decade. Federal recognition of Oregon's various tribes came later in the 1970s.

CIVIL RIGHTS MOVEMENT

In Oregon and beyond, African American communities have suffered discrimination for centuries – meanwhile, grassroots activism and widespread protests have demanded civil rights and justice.

Portland protests after the death of George Floyd at the hands of police in Minneapolis.

During and immediately after World War II, the African American population rose in Oregon, and specifically in Portland. This increase upset some white citizens, who became increasingly hostile toward their Black neighbors. African Americans were excluded from some labor unions and protests arose in communities that had seen particularly high levels of immigration. In Portland, police violence against African Americans spiked and grassroots civil rights efforts gained pace.

Due to the high levels of migration, appropriate housing was an issue. One supposed solution was the city of Vanport, a large temporary housing project that catered to workers on Portland's Kaiser Shipyards. A significant portion of the population here was African American – however, the Columbia River tragically flooded the settlement in 1948, killing 15 people and leaving some 18,500 people displaced, spelling further disaster for Portland's Black community.

Landmark events were too happening across the wider US: in 1954, Brown v. Board of Education of Topeka ruled that segregated schools were unconstitutional, while in Arkansas, the nation watched as Governor Orval Faubus used National Guard troops to bar the entry of nine Black students to a previously all-white school.

Back in Oregon, through the 1950s, political change was afoot. In 1951, Oregon repealed its law preventing interracial marriages. The Oregon Fair Housing Act was also passed in 1957, stipulating that landlords or agents could not discriminate "solely because of race, color, religion, or national origin." Oregon finally ratified the 15th Amendment in 1959 (some 15 years after it had been adopted by the US) – the Amendment states that "no government may prevent a citizen from voting based on that citizen's 'race, color, or previous condition of servitude'."

In 1964, the landmark Civil Rights Act was enacted by Congress: it outlawed unequal voting rights, segregated schools and workplaces, and all discrimination based on color, race, national origin, and gender. However, policy did not always reflect national or local attitudes, and the new legislation sparked backlash in some white communities.

In Portland, tensions came to a head in 1967, with what became known as the "Albina riot." The city's Black citizens came out to Irving Park to protest their treatment by police officers, and the two groups clashed.

Portland also made the headlines in 2020, following the death of George Floyd in Minneapolis at the hands of white police officer Derek Chauvin. Hundreds of people marched out on the city's streets to protest Floyd's death and to support the Black Lives Matter movement. Many demonstrations were peaceful, however some culminated in violent encounters between protestors and police. The decision of then-president Donald Trump to send in federal agents to confront demonstrators was also controversial. Chauvin lost his job and was sentenced to 22.5 years in prison for the murder of Floyd.

enjoyed through recreation came to the fore in the 1960s and 1970s. Tom McCall, who served as state governor of Oregon from 1967 to 1975, was vocal about environmental issues – and particularly the degradation of the Willamette Valley due to industrial use and waste. He was responsible for spearheading hundreds of environmental bills during his time in office. These included the 1967 Oregon Beach Bill, which prohibited private development on the state's spectacular shoreline. In the early 1970s, the Bottle Bill also mandated that certain beverage

into the economy. The sportswear brand has also helped pave the way for Eugene's excellent record in track and field sports – the World Athletics Championship was held here in 2022.

Technology company Intel is another firm with a major presence in Oregon – it is headquartered in Hillsboro, northwest of Portland, and employs more than 21,000 people in the state. In fact, modern-day Oregon's largest export industry is now electronic products.

It is the presence of these behemoth brands that has put Oregon on the world stage.

Hayward Field on the University of Oregon campus in Eugene hosted the World Athletics Championship in 2022.

containers be returnable, in efforts to control litter, while the Bicycle Bill required new highways to include facilities for cyclists and pedestrians. Portland's waterfront park is named after McCall.

MODERN URBAN HUBS

Now, more than four million people live in Oregon, and around half of these reside in the Portland metro area. Today, the city is defined by its patchwork of independent businesses, but footwear giant Nike has also greatly influenced the region, since its founding in Eugene in 1964. The modern-day headquarters are in Beaverton, a short jaunt west of Portland, employing thousands of Oregonians and injecting millions

⊘ WILDFIRES

Wildfires are a natural part of the lifecycle of Oregon's forest ecosystems, though experts warn that continued climate change will lengthen and exacerbate fire seasons. The wildfire season in 2020 was particularly destructive, ravaging around 1.1 million acres (400,000 hectares) and destroying around 4,000 homes. Labor Day weekend saw especially devastating blazes, displacing hundreds of Oregonians. Thankfully, the 2021 season was not as calamitous as the previous year, but still some 825,000 acres (335,000 hectares) were burned. The Bootleg Fire in the Klamath Lake area was the most significant blaze.

📷 GHOST TOWNS

While other industries prospered through World War II, the conflict sent many of Oregon's mining operations into decline. As once-booming settlements were abandoned, eerie ghost towns across the state were left to molder.

Oregon's mining industry boomed in the mid-1800s after gold was struck in Eastern and Southern Oregon, and as operations mushroomed, so too did Gold Rush settlements – typically, they sprouted with blacksmith shops, banks, hotels, and a saloon or two, plus maybe a bank, post office, church, or school. Some began with only a few prospectors and, if the area's gold deposits were rich enough, would grow to boomtowns accommodating several thousand residents.

However, when those rivers of gold dried up and miners moved on to pastures new, many Western towns were deserted. In 1942, as World War II raged on, President Roosevelt declared mining a non-essential activity. Thus, mines across the state temporarily halted their operations or ceased them for good. Over the decades that followed, other towns have been abandoned due to shuttered farming operations, rerouted railroads, or devastating fires.

Today, Oregon's ghost towns are haunting reminders of yesteryear: they range from the tired, scattered bones of old buildings left to decay by the roadside, to empty but well-preserved towns with reinforced structures and interpretive panels. Some of the most notable are Golden and Buncom, both located in Southern Oregon.

Fort Rock Ghost Town, or Fort Rock Valley Homestead Museum, in the high desert of Central Oregon.

Wooden granary in 1870-built Boyd, a thriving farming community turned deserted town in Wasco County.

Abandoned wooden house in Antelope, Wasco County.

Haunting reminders of mining towns and farming hubs.

Golden by name...

This aptly named settlement in Southern Oregon was built in the mid-1800s, when gold was discovered near Coyote Creek. Operations here began with small placer mines, though the Americans who established the settlement quickly abandoned it. When they moved on to milk richer deposits in Idaho, Chinese laborers worked the land for decades.

By the 1880s, hydraulic methods for mining had taken the industry by storm and American workers settled back in, displacing the Chinese. Golden grew rapidly during this period and by 1890, it was a fully-fledged town with around 100 residents.

However, Golden was built differently to most mining towns: instead of rowdy saloons and bordellos (brothels), the community centered on a pair of churches. The town eventually fell into decline in the 1920s, after gold deposits in the region were depleted. Since then, its buildings have been used in several Western movies and today they are protected as a State Heritage Site, welcoming a steady stream of curious tourists walking in the shadow of prospectors. Visitors can see a fascinating collection of abandoned buildings, including a haunting wooden church, a former school, and an old community store for local supplies.

Old West Prison Wagon, or a "tumbleweed wagon."

An abandoned BBQ restaurant in Kent, another casualty of the railroad industry.

Ghost town of Hardman, a bustling farming hub that went into decline in the 1920s thanks to a rerouted railroad.

Deadstock Coffee in Downtown Portland blends sneaker culture with excellent coffee.

A DIVERSE PEOPLE

The state is diverse when it comes to people, places, and politics – but a passion for the outdoors is something most Oregonians have in common.

Shaped by city dwellers and country folk, liberals and conservatives, Indigenous and newcomers, Oregon's cultural landscape is as varied as its terrain. But one uniting force is a kinship with nature, whether that is through the state's thriving logging and farming industries, or through its exhilarating outdoor adventures.

INDIGENOUS HERITAGE

That binding connection to the land began with Native Americans. Since time immemorial, a rich tapestry of Indigenous tribes has drawn upon the state's natural larder, fishing from its rivers, hunting elk in the Blue and Wallowa mountains, and gathering roots and berries from forests. Before the westward migration of US settlers, there were as many as 60 tribes speaking at least 18 languages in the region that is now Oregon. But as non-Indigenous colonizers encroached on Indigenous territories through the late 18th and early 19th centuries, the Native American population of Oregon was decimated and displaced. Epidemics of diseases such as smallpox and measles wiped out around 90 percent of the Native Americans here.

Now, Indigenous peoples account for around 1.8 percent of Oregon's total population (around 4.2 million people), according to the US Census Bureau. There are currently nine federally recognized tribes in the state, most of which are unions between historically distinct groups from similar regions. The tribes are: the Burns Paiute of Harney County; the Confederated Tribes of Coos, Lower Umpqua and Siuslaw Indians; the Confederated Tribes of Grand Ronde; the Confederated Tribes of Siletz; the Confederated Tribes of Umatilla Reservation; the Confederated Tribes of Warm Springs; Cow Creek Band of Umpqua Indians; the Coquille

Happy Canyon Princess at Portland Rose Festival.

Indian Tribe; and the Klamath Tribes. The tribes are recognized as sovereign nations with their own governments, law enforcement, and court systems, and they work to protect the interests of tribal members – that relates to issues including land management, healthcare, education, and housing. The tribes are dedicated to preserving their ancestral cultures and traditions, which were degraded over time as settlers moved in. Another concern is reclaiming homelands that were taken through a discriminatory 19th-century reservation system that forcibly relocated Native Americans.

OREGON DEMOGRAPHICS

Portland is often held up as a beacon of progress and inclusion, but the state of Oregon has not always been an easy place for minorities. In fact, systematic oppression through the centuries means that modern-day Oregon has an overwhelmingly white population. According to the US Census Bureau, 86.7 percent of Oregonians identify as white, followed by 13.4 percent Latino, 5.4 percent Asian American, 4 percent multiracial, 2.2 percent Black and 1.8 percent Native American. The Oregon Territory passed its first Black Exclusion Law in 1844, some 15 years before it was admitted into the Union. The law prohibited African Americans from making a

Southeast Portland's Jade District is one of its most diverse neighborhoods – Chinese, Vietnamese, and Japanese restaurants jostle for space with Asian grocery stores and karaoke bars.

permanent move to Oregon, threatening a punishment of lashings if they disobeyed. Further laws in 1849 and 1859 – the year that Oregon became a state – strengthened these rules and

Chinese and Japanese gardens are one of the ways that Portland celebrates Asian culture.

⊘ NORTHERN PAIUTE LANGUAGE

The Northern Paiute communities recognize the Great Basin region of the US as their ancestral homeland, and they include the Burns Paiute tribe, whose reservation extends across some 13,500 acres (5,500 hectares) in Eastern Oregon. This particular group has made significant efforts to protect their cultural heritage and identity. The Wadatika Yaduan Language Preservation Project was established to preserve the ancient tongue of this Indigenous group – thousands of Northern Paiute words and phrases were spoken by Native speakers, recorded, and saved to protect the vernacular from extinction.

prevented Black people from buying property or making contracts.

The laws were repealed in 1926, though racist language in the constitution was not altered until 2002. In more recent history, Black Portlanders were displaced from the Albina District during the building of Interstate 5 and – as is common in America's biggest cities – gentrification has pushed many African Americans to the city's fringes. In recent years, the city has attempted to make reparations for this by building subsidized apartments in the neighborhood and giving preference to formerly displaced peoples – a program that has garnered mixed reactions. Today, Portland's small Black community is among its most creative and entrepreneurial:

Black culture manifests in a variety of ways across Portland, from food carts selling soul and fusion food, to a hip-hop-themed winery and Downtown tasting room pioneered by Oregon's first black winemaker, Bertony Faustin.

Oregon's Asian populations have also been met with intolerance, discrimination, and violence over the years. Sizable numbers of Chinese people migrated to the state from the 1850s onward, usually coming to work as miners. For the most part, they were encouraged to make the move by US merchants who loaned the Chinese money for

numbered around 2,000 in 1950 (compared with more than 10,000 at the turn of the century).

Particularly after Chinese Exclusion Acts were passed, the Japanese labor market was heavily tapped. A busy Japantown emerged in Portland and the 1907–08 Gentlemen's Agreement allowed Japanese men to fly their wives to the States. In the 20th century, most of Oregon's Japanese community worked in agriculture. However, in 1923, the Alien Land Law was passed, prohibiting the Japanese (and Chinese) from owning their own farms.

Across rural Oregon, ranchers, farmers, and lumberjacks work the land as they have done for centuries.

their travels and promised them good work that would support their families back home and eventually allow them to return. The majority were young men and, in the decades that followed, they also took jobs in railroad construction, at canneries, and in agriculture. However, as the populations of Chinese increased, so too did white settlers' hostility toward them. Many faced individual counts of derision and violence, while raids on their neighborhoods were not uncommon. In 1882, the first federal Chinese Exclusion Act was passed, banning the entry of most Chinese people to the USA for ten years. Interracial marriage was prohibited, too. The exclusionary law was made permanent in 1902 and stood right up until 1943. As such, Chinese populations dwindled until they

⊘ THE OREGON COWBOY

The Oregon cowboy has not achieved legend status in quite the same way that its southwestern counterparts have, but these humble characters are an integral part of Oregon's culture, identity and economy. In fact, beef remains one of Oregon's key agricultural exports. Long-running events such as the Pendleton Round-Up – a popular and storied rodeo established back in 1910 – signal the importance of this heritage to Oregonians. The Round-Up event celebrates both traditional cowboy culture and Native American customs and takes place in the first full week of September each year.

The attack by Japanese forces on Pearl Harbor in 1941 exacerbated prejudice toward the Japanese community living in Oregon. In 1942, Executive Order 9066 was signed by President Franklin D. Roosevelt. This order granted the removal of any individuals on the West Coast who were considered a threat to national security – though the Japanese were not named explicitly, the order impacted them greatly and many lost their homes, businesses, and possessions as they were forced to move to so-called relocation centers. Today, Asian Americans

Eem, a popular Thai restaurant in Portland.

> *Matt Groening, the American cartoonist behind hit TV series The Simpsons and Futurama, was born in Portland.*

make up 5.4 percent of Oregon's population and, in Portland in particular, various aspects of Asian culture are celebrated. In the city, you will find both Chinese and Japanese gardens, Japanese bakeries and bubble teashops, and Chinese restaurants selling everything from *xiaolongbao* to noodles and Chongqing chicken.

OREGON'S RURAL COMMUNITIES

Oregon's agricultural and forestry industries, sustained by its rural communities, are large drivers of the state's economy. Across rural Oregon, ranchers, crop farmers, and lumberjacks work the land, as they have done for centuries. Today, it is estimated that Oregon has around 37,200 farms, which are spread over some 16 million acres, producing everything from grass seed and wheat to beef and milk.

Forest-related work employs more than 60,000 Oregonians, and the state is the largest softwood lumber producer in the country. Today, the lumberjack – typically caricatured as wearing plaid shirts and sporting a beard – is not just a vital component of Pacific Northwest industry, but also an emblem of popular culture. The name of Oregon's pro soccer team – the Portland Timbers – reflects the importance of logging in the state's cultural heritage. Their offbeat mascot, Timber Joey, is a real lumberman (Joey Webber) who saws a great round off a log every time the Timbers score a goal, awarding the spoils to the scorer.

OREGONIANS AND THE OUTDOORS

It is no exaggeration to say that Oregon is an oasis for nature lovers – hubs like Portland, Ashland, and Bend regularly top hotlists of the best places in the country for outdoorsy types. Oregon's cornucopia of natural wonders and recreational opportunities also encourages outsiders to move to the state. Californians are especially enamored: more than 11,000 people moved from the Golden State to the Portland metro area between 2015 and 2019. They're a green bunch too: Portland is tipped as having the largest number of bike commuters per capita of any major US city.

⊘ POLITICS AND POLICIES

Oregon is on the whole a left-leaning state, though, as is common across the USA, its rural and traditional communities tend to lean towards the conservative stance. The current governor is Democrat Tina Kotek, a lesbian woman with a liberal voting record, who formerly served as Speaker of the Oregon House of Representatives (2013–2022). Abortion remains legal in Oregon, after the repeal of Roe v. Wade in 2022 led to controversial bans across huge swathes of the USA. Oregon's ban on same-sex marriage was also overturned in 2014. Marijuana has been legal in the state since 2015.

All this means that many Oregonians place great importance on environmental issues and the management of outdoor spaces. According to a 2021 study by the Oregon Values and Beliefs Center, some 80 percent of Oregonians are in favor of the advancement of tree planting and renewable energy through government regulations, while almost three-quarters stand behind further restrictions on industrial emission and stricter fuel-efficiency standards. But as is common globally, tensions sometimes exist between loggers, who make a living harvesting Oregon's forests for timber, and environmentalists, who claim that their practices are harmful to these precious ecosystems. Over the years, various logging projects and enterprises have been blocked in court appeals, which have been spearheaded by campaigners concerned for wildlife and forest health. However, many in the logging industry say that, when carried out in a sustainable way, logging processes are vital for maintaining Oregon's forests, including preventing devastating fires by thinning the trees. There have been some landmark examples of cooperation between these two groups in the state. Loggers and environmentalists have reached peaceful agreements in logging towns, such as John Day in Eastern Oregon, in moves that protect both habitats and species and the livelihoods of people in the logging industry.

The state is a leader in renewable energy. According to the US Energy Information Administration, when it comes to states that produce the most total renewable energy, Oregon comes in at fifth place (measured by millions of megawatt-hours). Making the most of its abundant resources, Oregon's focus is on wind, water, and geothermal energy.

PORTLANDERS

Around 640,000 people live in Portland, Oregon's largest city. Portlanders are an eclectic – and often eccentric – bunch, and their diversity is precisely what defines them. The city's residents are renowned for their creative, rebellious spirit; alternative cultures; and generally open, liberal, and inclusive attitudes – so much so that *Portlandia*, an entire TV show parodying the city's hipster reputation, lasted eight seasons. Tech heavyweight Intel and sportswear giant Nike – founded around two hours south in Eugene – are major employers in the city. But Portland is also a mecca for small business owners, with independent

coffeehouses, boutique fashion stores, and artisanal gift shops on nearly every corner.

Portland is also hailed as an incredibly queer-friendly city. The Portland Gay Liberation Front was founded in 1970 and, in 1972, the state was the fourth in the country to repeal its sodomy laws. In the late 1980s, Portland's gay community faced further injustices as their rights were set upon by the conservative Christian group Oregon Citizens Alliance (OCA). In response to the views and actions of the OCA, Basic Rights Oregon was founded in 1996 and remains one of the state's

Portland Pride Parade.

premier LGBTQ+ rights organizations. In 2008, Sam Adams became the first openly gay major to be elected in a major US city. The area's vibrant Pride festivities also date back to the 1970s and now they manifest as a month-long event celebrating the area's LGBTQ+ community.

Like many large West Coast cities, Portland sadly has a sizable homeless population, with the city declaring a state of emergency on the issue back in 2015. The situation is complex, and it is thought that the crisis was principally caused by a lack of affordable housing, exacerbated by the Covid-19 pandemic. The City of Portland and Multnomah County have jointly pledged millions to aid the homeless population over the next decade. The money will go toward shelters and outreach programs.

Portland Farmers' Market is a locavore's dream.

Fresh
Oregon
Chinook $1...

B...
C...
$15

CULINARY CAPITAL

You are never far away from a good meal or a fine glass of Pinot Noir in Oregon. Deep-rooted agriculture heritage, fine growing conditions, and inventive chefs make it one of the best culinary states in the nation.

Oregon's distinct growing regions offer a cornucopia of produce. In fact, volcanic activity and floods over millennia have produced some of the most fructuous soil on the continent. In the Columbia River Gorge, weathered basalt enriches the earth, while in the Willamette Valley, Ice Age floods washed the land with fertile silt and sediments. That natural bounty has long been reaped by Native Americans who lived off the land for thousands of years before the arrival of non-Indigenous settlers.

Today, it is also a boon for the region's chefs, who turn out creative dishes in venues running the gamut from white-tablecloth spots to cool food trucks. Experiencing Oregon's food scene is less about ticking off a long list of "only-in-the-state" dishes, and more about appreciating meals made with zero-kilometer ingredients fished, foraged, and farmed yards from where you are sitting.

Tillamook Creamery.

> *Root Feast is a springtime event held by the Confederated Tribes of the Umatilla Indian Reservation, which celebrates traditional "first foods," including bitterroot (or pyaxi).*

The wine is some of the best in the country, too. So good, in fact, that the Beaver State keeps much of its spoils for itself: a very small portion of Oregon's wine is exported overseas, so leave room in your suitcase for a few bottles of Pinot Noir, the state's signature.

NATURAL LARDER

When it comes to growing, there is little that Oregonians won't turn their hand to – but there

are a few things that they do particularly well. Oregon produces about 99 percent of the country's hazelnuts and, unsurprisingly, it is now the official State Nut. Oregon is also a leading producer of blueberries.

There are around 350 growers in the state and farms cover over 15,000 acres (6,000 hectares). You'll find the blue fruit baked into pies, swirled into cocktails, and fashioned into drizzles for desserts at swish restaurants.

The diversity of produce born from the Willamette Valley – the state's premier agricultural region – is dizzying. More than 170 crops are grown in the region, including hops, wine grapes, various berries, and other fruits. Push eastward and the Hood River region is another of the state's fertile enclaves. This area is particularly well known for its pears and is the fruit's top growing region in a state whose pear orchards cover about 19,000 acres. The sprawling Columbia Plateau turns out root vegetables such as onions and carrots, as well as the state's largest supply of wheat.

As you drive through the rugged expanses of Southern and Eastern Oregon, herds of cattle framed against snow-crowned peaks is a common sight. Malheur County, which noses up to the border with Idaho in Oregon's far east, dominates when it comes to beef production.

The earthy marionberry is a special cultivar of blackberry developed by Oregon State University. You will find the fruit baked into pies across the state.

Meanwhile, there are more than 200 dairy farms scattered across the state and several coastal dairies have international recognition. Tillamook Creamery (4165 North Highway 101; tel: 503-815 1300; www.tillamook.com; daily 10am–

Oregon is an under-the-radar wine region home to 23 distinct AVAs.

⊘ PICK-YOUR-OWN FARMS

Oregon has an abundance of pick-your-own or "U-pick" spots, from orchards to vegetable patches. You will find them all over the state, but there is an especially great crop in the Hood River Valley area. Popular places include The Gorge White House (2265 Oregon Route 35; www.thegorge-whitehouse.com; seasonal hours), where you can pick strawberries in June, pears in August, and apples in September. In the Willamette Valley, Berkey's Blueberries (32589 Berlin Road; tel: 541-409 4558; www.berkeysblueberries.com) is a top stop. U-pick is available through the summer, alongside a farm stand.

6pm) is the most famous of all – this beloved cheese factory has roots back in 1910, when the Tillamook County Creamery Association was formed. In the 100-plus years since, the Tillamook Creamery has been producing its famous Cheddar to exacting standards (inspectors ensure quality and consistency). Since the late 1940s, the creamery has also produced incredibly popular ice cream. You can take a self-guided tour of the creamery, which includes a farm exhibit and a peek at operations in the viewing gallery, plus a shop and restaurant.

In Southern Oregon's Rogue Valley, the Rogue Creamery (311 North Front Street; 541-200 2353; www.roguecreamery.com; daily 10am–5pm) is another hotspot. The bijou Grants Pass dairy has won plenty of accolades for its organic offerings – prized varieties include the cave-aged Rogue River Blue and Bluehorn. You can come by to stock up on cheese at the shop, pick up a grilled cheese sandwich for lunch, or get a glimpse of the Cheddar production room.

SEA TO PLATE

Oregon offers some of the finest fish and seafood in the nation – no wonder, given its rippling 363 miles (584km) of Pacific coastline and ample inland waterways. Oregon's fishing herit-

Shack (155 1st Street SE; tel: 541-347 2875; www.tonyscrabshack.com; daily 10.30am–7pm) in coastal Bandon, has become famous for its offerings.

AN UNDER-THE-RADAR WINE REGION

Oregon wine is often criminally overshadowed by the titanic output of California to the south – however, it can more than match the Golden State's offerings when it comes to quality and variety. Oregon's varied terrain has created a series of "microclimates," meaning the wines on offer are wonderfully diverse – think Pinot Noir in the cool,

Pick-your-own farms are an excellent way to sample the bounty of the land.

age dates back thousands of years, when Native Americans milked the bounty of the state's rivers and ocean. Today, the practice still sustains communities up and down the coast.

For the finest meal, the trick is to order in season. Albacore tuna flies off fishing boats in the summertime, while oysters fare best from early fall through to spring. Salmon was a staple of Indigenous diets long before non-Indigenous settlers arrived, and it is still a gourmet signature in Oregon. Chinook salmon is best from April until October, while coho salmon has a slightly shorter season, from July to September.

Dungeness crab is another favorite, with the Pacific Northwest season running from around October to July. Local institutions, such as Tony's Crab

⊘ FOLLOW THE CULINARY TRAIL

Gourmands can get to the heart of a region's food scene by discovering the Oregon Food Trails program. The string of routes – ranging from the Central Coast Food Trail to the Great Umpqua Food Trail – joins together the finest restaurants, coffee shops, farms, winemakers, and distillers in a particular area, showcasing what a destination is famed for. Hop between dairy farms and ranches in the High Desert; feast in seafood shacks and chic harborside restaurants along the Wild Rivers Coast; or sample fine wines at the top wineries in the Mid-Willamette Valley. Download food trail brochures at www.traveloregon.com.

Hailed as the world's first queer wine festival, Queer Wine Fest debuted in Dayton in 2022, organized by local winemaker and mayor Remy Drabkin. The outdoor event aimed to celebrate queer-made and -grown wines from across the country.

moderate conditions of the Willamette Valley and bigger, bolder reds in the slightly warmer, drier climes of the Rogue Valley farther south.

When it comes to national reputation, California and Oregon were once on equal footing. However, an early Prohibition (in 1916) decimated Oregon's burgeoning wine industry – meanwhile, California would not ratify temperance laws until 1919. When Prohibition was finally overturned, the California wine industry quickly picked up where it had left off, but Oregon's was left in the dust. It was not until the 1960s that Oregon's wine industry was revived, when winemaker Richard Sommer – now dubbed "the father of Oregon wine" – began planting vines including Riesling, Chardonnay, and Pinot Noir in

The Knock Back bar in Portland's Alberta Arts District.

⊘ BEER, GLORIOUS BEER

It's not all about oenophiles in Oregon – beer lovers will be well sated, too. Brewing is written into the history of the area: the very first brewery, the Portland Brewery and General Grocery Establishment, opened even before Oregon became a state. Alongside 170 years of practice, there are several other reasons why Oregon beer is so good. The Willamette Valley is one of the top producers of hops in the country, while huge stores of malt are grown across the Pacific Northwest. Quality water from sources such as the McKenzie River create solid foundations for brews.

Today, most US states and cities have been gripped by the craft-beer craze, but Oregon was a frontrunner:

homebrewing was legalized in 1979 and brewpubs were sanctioned by 1985, meaning the state's first craft-beer wave was back in the 1980s. Now, Oregon is still considered one of the best beer states in the nation. You can find every type of brew here, from creamy stouts to blondes. But you cannot go wrong with a trusty Indian Pale Ale, the hoppy brew for which the state is best known. You will find fine examples at Deschutes Brewery (originally opened in Bend: 901 SW Simpson Avenue; tel: 541-385 8606; www.deschutesbrewery.com; Mon–Sat noon–6pm, Sun until 5pm) and pFriem Family Brewers (707 Portway Avenue #101; tel: 541-321 0490; www.pfriembeer.com; daily 11am–9pm) in Hood River.

the Umpqua Valley. Sommer bottled the first-ever vintage of Pinot Noir in Oregon in 1967. His winery, HillCrest Vineyard (240 Vineyard Lane; tel: 541-673 3709; www.hillcrestvineyard.com; daily 11am–5pm), is still operating and proudly bears the title of oldest estate winery in Oregon. In the decades that followed, other winemakers began to populate the Umpqua and Applegate valleys and the seeds of a wine industry were sown once more.

The Willamette Valley, arguably Oregon's best-known wine region today, burgeoned in the 1970s. Tualatin Estate Vineyard (10850 NW Seavey Road;

primarily for its Chardonnay and Pinot Noir (though creative winemakers turn their hand to all manner of varietals). Here, popular vineyards include the mammoth King Estate Winery (80854 Territorial Highway; tel: 541-685 5189; www.kingestate.com; tasting room by appointment), which offers expert-led tastings and a restaurant serving a European-inspired menu built on local produce. Willamette Valley Vineyards (8800 Enchanted Way SE; tel: 503-588 9463; www.wvv.com; Sat–Thu 11am–6pm, Fri until 8pm) is another big hitter. Food and wine pairings are on offer at the tasting room, which sits

Food trucks jostle for space alongside market stalls at Portland Mercado.

tel: 503-357-5005; www.wvv.com/Tualatin; Thu–Mon 11am–5pm) was established in 1973, making it a forerunner in the area. It is still known for its award-winning Pinot Noirs. By 1983, the Willamette Valley had become Oregon's first AVA (American Viticultural Area).

Today, there are 23 distinct AVAs – seven premiere AVAs, with 16 "nested" AVAs (the Willamette Valley AVA, for instance, has 11 smaller AVAs parceled within it, while the Applegate Valley AVA comprises part of the wider Rogue Valley AVA). Wineries range from boutique spots producing a few thousand cases per year, to sprawling estates with internationally recognized names.

Oenophiles could spend days (or even weeks) enjoying the fruits of the Willamette Valley, known

Sports Bra (www.thesportsbrapdx.com) in Portland's Sullivan's Gulch neighborhood is a forward-thinking drinking den that focuses on female brewers, winemakers, and distillers, and shows only women's sports.

on a scenic perch above the vines, or you can enjoy a private tour or blending experience.

Spreading out some 60 miles (97km) east of Portland, the Columbia Gorge AVA is a patchwork of distinct climates, sweeping from the Cascades to the High Desert, with elevations ranging from sea level to 2,000ft (610 meters). That means you can sip everything from Pinot Noir to Cabernet Sauvignon in this diverse AVA. Standout wineries include Phelps Creek Vineyards (301 Country Club Road; tel: 541-386 2607; www.phelpscreekvineyards.com; tasting room daily 11am–5pm), which is hailed for its ancient volcanic soils; excellent Pinot Noir, Chardonnay, and Pinot Gris; and views of Mount Hood from the vineyard.

Southern Oregon's Applegate Valley – part of the wider Rogue Valley – is one of the state's most up-and-coming wine regions. The growing area is characterized by hot days and cool

2123; www.quadynorth.com; Wed–Mon 11am–5pm), known for its flagship Syrah.

The easternmost AVA is Snake River Valley, which straddles the border with Idaho (where a larger concentration of wineries can be found). Vineyards cover the High Desert, where Syrah and Viognier thrive. Pay a visit to Copper Belt Wines' tasting room in Downtown Baker City (1937 Main Street; tel: 541-519 0949; www.copperbeltwinery.com; Sun–Tue noon–5pm, Wed–Sat 11am–6pm) to sample a selection. There is a cheese shop on site, too.

Coava Coffee Roasters is one of the vanguards of Portland's coffee revolution.

Oregon is serious about its coffee – there are more than 200 specialty shops in the state (of which more than a third are in Portland). The "fourth wave" movement focuses on education, sustainability, and brews inspired by the diverse backgrounds of their makers.

nights, making way for bold reds such as Syrah, Tempranillo, and Cabernet Sauvignon (as well as Oregon's trusty Pinot Noir).

Highly rated wineries here include Quady North (9800 Oregon Route 238; tel: 541-702

PORTLAND: A FOODIE'S MECCA

The Rose City's food scene is as wonderfully weird and eclectic as the city itself and you can dine in just about any restaurant you fancy – be it a Greek taverna, a taqueria, or an Italian trattoria.

There is a particularly strong crop of Asian outlets, especially in the Jade District, in Southeast Portland. Try Vietnamese-style soups at Ha VL (2738 SE 82nd Avenue, Unit 102; tel: 503-772 0103; www.mrgan.com/havl; Wed–Mon 8am–4pm); dim sum at HK Cafe (4410 SE 82nd Avenue; tel: 503-771 8866; www.hkcafetogo.com; Mon–Sun 9.30am–9pm); and Chinese pastries at King's Bakery (2346 SE 82nd Avenue; tel: 503-772 0955; Tue–Fri 9am–6pm, Sat, Sun until 6.30pm). Mama Dut (1414 SE Morrison Street; tel: 503-954 1222; www.mamadut.

com; Thu–Sun noon–7pm) in Southeast Portland's Buckman neighborhood is another fan favorite. The popular spot focuses on vegan banh mi, filled with everything from lemongrass tofu to fried chicken-style oyster mushrooms.

Sweet lovers will be satisfied, too. Voodoo Donut (22 SW 3rd Avenue; tel: 503-241 4704; www.voodoo doughnut.com; daily 5am–3am) – known for its giant and colorful confections heaped with bizarre toppings like bacon and bubble gum – has reached cult status, while popular ice-cream parlor Salt & Straw (838 NW 23rd Avenue; tel: 971-271 8168;

Tater tots were invented in Oregon in the early 1950s when the founders of frozen food company Ore-Ida discovered an imaginative way to use up leftover potato scraps. The delightful golden nuggets were in stores a few years later.

www.saltandstraw.com; daily 11am–11pm) doles out imaginatively flavored scoops from pear and blue cheese to marionberry coconut sherbet.

Portland boasts a particularly strong crop of Asian outlets, especially in the Jade District.

⊘ A FOOD CART REVOLUTION

One of the most unique things about Portland's dining scene is its huge concentration of food trucks. It is thought that the first food cart existed here as early as 1910 and was a horse-drawn produce wagon, operated by Italian immigrant Joseph Gatto. However, it would not be until the 21st century that the phenomena really took off in Portland – a few carts began to crop up in the early 2000s and then, perhaps surprisingly, the concept really boomed during and immediately after the recession from 2007 until 2009.

Today, there are more than 500 food carts around the city, often grouped into clusters called "pods" with alfresco seating areas. Popular pods include Cartopia (1207 SE Hawthorne Boulevard; www.cartopiafoodcarts. com) on Portland's Eastside, which is home to Latin American-inspired chicken cart Chicken and Guns and BKK Pad Thai.

At Southeast Portland's Cartlandia (8145 SE 82nd Avenue; www.instagram.com/cartlandia), you will find vegan barbecue, ramen, and poke. Individual stand-outs include Yoshi's Sushi (3530 SW Multnomah Boulevard; tel: 503-833 2940; www.yoshispdx.com; Tue-Sat noon–2pm, 4–7pm) in the Multnomah Village French Quarter and Erica's Soul Food (101 SE 12th Avenue; tel: 503-922 5519; www.ericassoulfood.com; Wed–Sat noon–2pm, 4–7pm).

NATURAL WONDERLAND

Oregon's endlessly varied terrain means it has natural drama in spades. Road trips reveal a hit list of thrusting mountains, desert plains, fir-filled forests, and wild rivers.

Perhaps no other state in the USA has the same volume of mind-bending natural wonders as Oregon. Snow-plastered mountains spike toward the sky; waterfalls tumble hundreds of feet by the roadside; and rivers chew through million-year-old basalt. The state's fabled landscapes shift as you move eastward. Temperate maritime forests and driftwood-strewn beaches out west give way to the thrusting peaks of the Cascade Range – and then great swathes of High Desert are undercut by complex cave systems.

Gangling fir trees are an emblem of the Pacific Northwest and dense forests are one of the state's great draws. Oregon has a total of 11 National Forests, gobbling up about 25 percent of the state and a whopping 16 million acres (6 million hectares). Lumbering Douglas firs, skinny ponderosa pines, and big leaf maples cover mountains, hug rivers, and give way to broad valleys carpeted with wildflower-flecked meadows.

There are rivers aplenty – 110,994 miles (178,627km) of them, in fact – from the mighty Columbia, which curls along the Washington–Oregon border, to the frothing Rogue River, known for its epic white water. Of these, nearly 2,000 miles (3,000km) are designated as "Wild and Scenic."

Tom McCall Preserve is carpeted with wildflower meadows and offers views of the Columbia River Gorge.

The Crooked River snakes through sheer rocky canyons in the belly of a fir-dotted valley at Smith Rock State Park in Central Oregon's High Desert.

Silver Falls State Park – the largest in Oregon – in the Cascades' foothills is dotted with waterfalls.

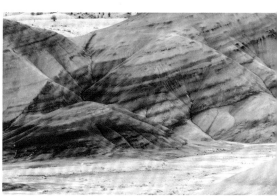

Oregon's fossil-sewn Painted Hills are a geological marvel.

Seven wonders of Oregon

Such is Oregon's natural bounty that the state has taken it upon itself to designate seven wonders. First, there is the Columbia River Gorge, a snaking basalt ravine formed over millions of years and sliced open by its namesake. Central Oregon boasts Smith Rock State Park, a wonderland of welded tuff that has become a veritable mecca for climbers. Out east, the color-striped Painted Hills are laced with trails and sewn with fossils that give evidence of some 40 million years of life.

Meanwhile, the Wallowa Mountains represent some of the most pristine and untouched wilderness in the state and are more than deserving of their "Alps of Oregon" nickname. The iconic Crater Lake National Park – comprising a sapphire-lake-filled caldera and acres of unbridled, forested backcountry – is another jewel in the state's gleaming crown.

Then there's the coast – all 363 miles (584km) of it – fringed with ocher sand and sheer cliffs. The Oregon Coast Highway beats a majestic path down the state's entire seaboard, joining up a postcard-perfect string of quaint lighthouses, traditional fishing towns, and stellar beaches.

Oregon boasts a whopping 11 National Forests, gobbling up around a quarter of the state and a staggering 16 million acres (6 million hectares).

Secret Beach, as its name hints, isn't easy to find but it's worth the effort: part of the Samuel H. Boardman State Scenic Corridor, it's between Brookings and Gold Beach.

Crater Lake National Park, the jewel in Oregon's crown.

Sand labyrinths scored into Face Rock Wayside at Bandon Beach.

CULTURAL LEGACY

Oregon is a hotbed for creativity. Find boundary-pushing artist-led spaces in buzzing cities and learn about Native American craft traditions that reveal millennia of heritage.

Oregon's creators have many muses – from natural wonders like the wild Pacific Ocean and the mighty Columbia River to political movements and pioneering people. The arts take on many forms here: Indigenous festivals are filled with dance and storytelling; fine paintings hang in galleries, and bold murals brighten the streets. Hit the road in Oregon and you might just be tempted to pick up a paintbrush (or a microphone, or a camera...).

NATIVE AMERICAN ART

Oregon's earliest art forms have been left behind by its First Peoples and both pictographs (painted forms) and petroglyphs (carved) have been found across the state. Styles and approaches varied between Indigenous tribes, from the peoples of the Willamette Valley to the Columbia Plateau. In fact, experts have divided Oregon's intricate rock art into broad categories, reflecting regional traditions. They include the Columbia Plateau Tradition, which is pioneered by Indigenous groups including the Nez Perce and Umatilla, and include depictions of human forms, hunting scenes, and spirit figures. Some of Oregon's finest Indigenous rock art can be found at Picture Rock Pass in Southern Oregon, near Summer Lake.

Beyond this, detailed sculptures made from basalt and elk antlers are characteristic of the Chinookan art style, made by Indigenous peoples along the lower reaches of the Columbia River. Many of these objects were collected from Sauvie Island, which noses up to the border with Washington, and you can see a selection at the Portland Museum of Art.

Basketry is an important craft for many Indigenous cultures. The Coquille tribe made detailed

Portland Pow Wow celebrating Native American culture.

⊘ NATIVE AMERICAN FESTIVALS

A defining piece of culture and heritage for many Indigenous tribes, Pow Wows are vibrant celebrations and expressions of Native American culture – they typically involve traditional dances, costume, arts and crafts, storytelling, and food. In Oregon, they include the Wildhorse Pow Wow, which is put on in July by the Umatilla Confederated Tribes of Eastern Oregon. The event is free and open to the public. The Annual Nesika Illahee Pow-Wow, hosted by the Confederated Tribes of Siletz Indians, also takes place in August. The three-day event includes Native American drumming and singing performances and Indigenous craft vendors.

baskets from spruce roots on the Southern Oregon coast, while intricate coiled basketry has been found at Oregon sites in Harney and Malheur counties, in Eastern Oregon.

Many highly regarded Indigenous artists are currently creating work in Oregon and the present curator of Native American Art at the Portland Art Museum (1219 SW Park Avenue; tel: 503-226 2811; www.portlandartmuseum.org; Wed–Sun 10am–5pm), Kathleen Ash-Milby, a member of the Navajo Nation, lays a strong emphasis on contemporary Indigenous art. The

Check out My People's Market, a pop-up market in Portland whose vendors are creators of color. You might find pieces by Indigenous maker Caroline Blechert, who creates art objects inspired by Inuit peoples and traditions, using techniques such as weaving and embroidery.

museum includes the Center for Contemporary Native American Art, which has showcased works by lauded Indigenous artists such as Sara Siestreem, a Hanis Coos tribal member from the Umpqua River Valley. Siestreem creates work based on the natural world and the ceremonial traditions of her ancestors, from acrylic and graphite pieces to woven basketry.

NORTHWEST SCHOOL ART MOVEMENT

The Northwest School has roots in Seattle, thought the art movement helped shape creativity across the Pacific Northwest, with its heyday in the 1930s and 1940s. The earliest major players in the movement included Morris Graves, who was born in Fox Valley, Oregon – the others were Kenneth Callahan and Guy Anderson (both from Washington state) and Mark Tobey (originally from Wisconsin). Their works – often oil on canvas – blended influences from Native American and Asian cultures, and used the Pacific Northwest's natural world as a muse. Many of Graves's art pieces hang in the Portland Museum of Art, including works of oil and tempera on paper and canvas. Callahan, Anderson, and Tobey are also represented.

CREATIVE HUBS: PORTLAND AND BEYOND

Many of Oregon's cities have thriving arts scenes – especially urban hub Portland, which is home to revered institutions such as the Portland Museum of Art, as well as many more diverse artist-run spaces and studios. In Portland's trendy Pearl District, you will find the cooperative-owned Blackfish Gallery (938 NW Everett Street; tel: 503-224 2634; www.blackfish. com; Tue–Sat 11am–5pm), which prides itself on having an artist present during business hours. Expect prints, oil paintings, and ink drawings by artists from a diverse range of backgrounds,

Stephany Smith-Pearson at the Shakespeare Festival.

⊘ SANDY SKETCHES

Such is the beauty of Oregon's wild, windswept coastline that some artists cannot resist using it as a blank canvas for their creations. That is true of Denny Dyke, an artist known for his elaborate sand labyrinths scored into Face Rock Wayside at Bandon Beach along Oregon's South Coast. Every summer, visitors can attend the Circles in the Sand Festival and view the intricate patterns carved into the sand. Each "drawing" has a theme – from the stars to the sea – and visitors follow a set path amid the dazzling creations. Details of upcoming festival dates are posted on the website www.sandy pathbandon.com.

tackling themes from gender identity to immigration and multiculturalism.

Oregon's smaller cities punch above their weight when it comes to top-notch galleries and public art. Bend's Old Mill District is home to a handful of fine art spaces and studios, including woman-owned Amejko Artistry (www.amejkoartistry.com) – creator and proprietor Anna Amejko Peterson focuses on woven works and wall hangings.

In Eastern Oregon, Pendleton – a place steeped in Old West history – is revered for its fine craftsmanship. Many of the city's makers have been operating in the city for generations, and the self-guided Makers Trail joins up the best of them. It includes the Pendleton Woolen Mills (1307 SE Court Place; www.pendleton-usa.com; Mon–Fri 11am–3pm), which are open for guided tours. Pendleton has been a wool-shipping center since the 19th century, and the mills opened in 1893 – today, they craft fine woolen blankets, clothing, and accessories. There are also milliners, boot and saddle makers, and chocolatiers working across town.

Southern Oregon's Ashland is another city that oozes creativity. Ashland Art Works (291 Oak Street; tel: 541-488 4735; www.ashlandartworksgalleries.wordpress.com; Thu–Sat 10am–5pm, Sun, Wed until 2pm) showcases a diverse collection of works by local makers, including fine Japanese raku pottery and intricate fiber art.

ON LOCATION

Given Oregon's natural beauty – not to mention its plethora of towns that look like ready-made sets – it is unsurprising that over 400 movies

Portland Open Studios takes place in October. For two weekends, around 100 artists open their studios, workshops, and creative spaces to the public. Visitors can see painters, jewelry makers, photographers, and sculptors in action on self-guided tours.

have been filmed in the state. Among the most famous is *Wild*, starring Reese Witherspoon and based on Cheryl Strayed's best-selling memoir.

Pendleton is famed for its saddle makers.

⊘ ART AS ACTIVISM

Art has long been used as a tool for protest, and Oregon is no exception. In Portland in particular, bold works of public art have often been used to express political messages, rally for change, and celebrate marginalized communities. *Never Look Away* is a striking mural in Portland's Pearl District, featuring eight prominent LGBTQ+ activists including Lynn Nakamoto, former Justice at Oregon Supreme Court, and gay rights advocate Marsha P Johnson. The mural is intended to honor the represented figures and reflect on the treatment of queer individuals across the country and the world. Art has also been used as a tool in the Black Lives Matter movement. Following the

murder of George Floyd at the hands of police in 2020, and as protests gathered momentum across the city of Portland, artist Emma Berger painted a giant portrait of Floyd on the plywood barricades protecting the Apple Store from riots at Pioneer Place (the artwork was later donated to Portland civil rights organization Don't Shoot PDX). In Northeast Portland, another mural honors Floyd, as well as Breonna Taylor (who was killed by police in Kentucky) and Ahmaud Arbery (who was murdered in a racially motivated hate crime while he was jogging in Georgia). Asian American artist Ameya Marie Okamoto is also well known for her memorial portraits of victims of police shootings.

The movie follows Strayed's 1,000-plus-mile (1,600km) hike along the formidable Pacific Crest Trail and Oregon's wild beauty is put on fine display. Featured locations in the movie include Central Oregon's Smith Rock State Park, the Mirror Lake Trail in the Mount Hood National Forest, and the Bridge of the Gods, which vaults over the Columbia River at Cascade Locks.

Another famous Oregon movie star is the Timberline Lodge, a storied, 1930s-built mountain inn that served as the exterior for the creepy Overlook Hotel in Stanley Kubrick's 1980 adaptation of psychological horror novel *The Shining* by Stephen King. Starring John Belushi, 1978 comedy *Animal House* included scenes filmed in the Willamette Valley town of Cottage Grove, while a giant mural downtown commemorates silent movie *The General*, which was also shot here.

Firm family favorite *The Goonies* (1985) has its roots in Oregon, too. Locations include the breathtaking Ecola State Park along the northern Oregon coast.

Visitors can learn more at the Oregon Film Museum (732 Duane Street; tel: 503-325 2203;

Colin Meloy of Portland band The Decemberists.

The iconic Powell's City of Books in Portland.

⊘ SHAKESPEARE FESTIVAL

A small Southern Oregon city might seem an unlikely place for one of the finest Shakespeare festivals in the country, but Ashland's event is revered across the nation and beyond. The 1935-founded non-profit theater – one of the oldest in the country – was borne out of the Chautauqua movement, which involved a push to bring education and culture to America's rural communities in the late 1800s and early 1900s. The first performance was of romantic comedy *Twelfth Night*. Fast forward 90-plus years and the Tony Award-winning festival remains a highlight of Oregon's cultural calendar. During each season, there are around ten plays across three stages, plus talks, workshops, and backstage experiences.

www.astoriamuseums.org; daily: Oct–Apr 10am–4pm; May–Sept until 5pm), which is housed in the historic Clatsop County Jail in Astoria (a setting for the movie *The Goonies*, among others). Museum exhibits share stories about the many movies that have been filmed in the state.

Of course, when it comes to TV shows, sketch comedy *Portlandia* – which teases the city's eccentricities – is the best-known Oregon export of all. It was filmed right across the city and fans of the show can spot landmarks such as Powell's City of Books and the iconic Keep Portland Weird sign before they even get past the opening credits.

With events across Portland, Eugene, and Bend, the Oregon Independent Film Festival is a celebration of moviemaking, featuring screenings and premieres. The festival has showcased the acting and directorial work of big names such as John Krasinski, Nicole Kidman, and Tom Hardy.

A MUSIC MEDLEY

There is no one musical genre that truly defines Oregon – but that is precisely its appeal. Oregon's modern music scene is built on an amalgamation of cultures and influences, and you can hear just about any kind of genre you could imagine in hubs such as Portland and Eugene.

Each year, the Oregon Festival of American Music, a summer cultural event held at The Shedd Institute in Eugene, explores the nation's eclectic musical output through a series of concerts, film screenings, and talks. Going strong since 1992, each event follows a particular theme, such as wartime music or movie soundtracks.

Timberline Lodge starred as the Overlook Hotel in Stanley Kubrick's 1980 film adaptation of The Shining.

Still, if one were to vault above the rest, it would probably be indie music. Portland has produced or nurtured a crop of indie artists, from The Decemberists to the late Elliott Smith. That is true of punk rock and grunge music, too. Portland's northerly sister, Seattle in Washington, is known as a pioneer of the genres, but the Rose City also played a part. Trailblazing punk rock band Wipers hailed from Portland in the 1970s, as were 1980s-formed Poison Idea.

Meanwhile, the Ashland Folk Collective nourishes the region's thriving folk scene, organizing shows fronted by local singer-songwriters and bands. Check out the website www.ashlandfolkcollective.com for details of upcoming events and concerts.

⊘ PORTLAND'S HIP-HOP SCENE

Rose City has a thriving hip-hop scene that visitors can tap into in various ways. Portland gave rise to a wave of prominent artists, including Vursatyl and HANiF, and there is an increasing crop of modern hip-hop musicians in the city too. You can hear them at the numerous showcases around town. Among the most popular are The Thesis at Kelly's Olympian and Mic Check at the White Eagle Saloon. Beyond the shows, there are hip-hop-themed venues in the city. Downtown, you can sip Pinot Noir while listening to a curated soundtrack at tasting room The Crick PDX, owned by Oregon's first Black winemaker, Bertony Faustin, or peruse displays of sneakers at Black-owned Deadstock Coffee.

Monkey Face at Smith Rock State Park is a climber's paradise.

OUTDOOR ADVENTURES

Sky-scraping mountains, alpine lakes, and labyrinthine caves make Oregon a veritable adventure playground. Travelers can ski, hike, bike, sail, and paddle in the Beaver State.

More than 50 percent of Oregon's land is public, with great swathes of it managed by the United States Forest Service and the Bureau of Land Management. This – coupled with the sheer diversity of Oregon's terrain – means that there are near endless ways to recreate in the state. You can scale volcanic mountains; scramble through caves; paddle rivers; and hike through maritime forests. There are lush river valleys, stark desert plains, yawning gorges, and craggy shorelines, all ripe for exploration. The state has a fantastic network of local expert guides who can help beginners navigate the state's wild rivers, or safely lead them through the backcountry.

BACKCOUNTRY SAFETY

Oregon's backcountry is a paradise for intrepid types. Whether you are snowshoeing little-trodden trails; hiking deep into pin-drop quiet forests or kayaking high alpine lakes, adventures in Oregon's vast wilderness offer an unparalleled sense of awe and wonder. However, trips into the backcountry should not be taken lightly and it is imperative that you are well prepared before you set off. If you are not experienced at navigating backcountry areas, there are many licensed guides who can help you safely explore. Guided excursions run the gamut from jaunts into Oregon's National Forests lasting several hours to multiday backpacking adventures. Take your pick from back-to-basics trips or deluxe experiences with creature comforts like bell tents, craft cocktails, and elevated campfire dining. If you are heading out to Oregon's mountain areas in winter, avalanches pose a real threat. Make sure you travel with a guide (or a companion) who has a minimum of AIARE 1 training and is equipped with beacons, probes, and shovels.

Mountaineering towards the Pearly Gates on Mt. Hood.

(Winter-hiking equipment such as polarized sunglasses, trail crampons, and of course gloves and waterproof shoes and clothing is important too.)

Oregon's weather can be unpredictable – always check the forecast but be prepared for every eventuality. Dress in layers and consider carrying a light emergency bivvy in case a turn in the weather means you need to take shelter. Do not rely on your cell phone for navigation: there may be scant reception in rural areas, so carry a map and a compass. Pay attention to the trail and always stop and retrace your steps if you feel as though you are getting lost.

Most important of all is to be constantly aware of your environment: pay attention to cliff edges, loose rocks, fallen trees, and wild animals.

Oregon's wildlife includes creatures such as black bears and mountain lions and though attacks are exceedingly rare, it is wise to be prepared. Always follow the National Park Service's bear safety advice: www.nps.gov/subjects/bears/safety.htm. Lightning can be dangerous, too. If you are caught in a thunderstorm while hiking, do not seek shelter beneath trees or rock hangings. Instead, stay low and, if you are in the mountains, try to descend from high ground as quickly as possible.

Do not forget the basics, either: wear good-quality wool socks and sturdy hiking boots, plus

RIVER SAFETY

Exploring Oregon's rivers and lakes is a thoroughly rewarding experience – but it is vital that you are adequately prepared for adventures on the water. As with overland trips, the best way to ensure your safety is to travel with a guide who is familiar with Oregon's waterways. If you are experienced enough to go it alone, study your preferred route carefully before you leave and check the weather forecast (keeping in mind that conditions can change quickly). Wear a well-fitting life jacket and carry a NOAA Nautical

Sparks Lake, cradled among the peaks of the Cascades, is a scenic spot for paddle boarding.

Swimming in Oregon's stretch of the Pacific Ocean is not advised. The water is typically chilly and can be rough, while dangerous riptides are also present.

sunglasses, a sun hat, and sunscreen in summer. Carry ample snacks, make sure you have plenty of water, and consider carrying a portable filter or purification tablets (note that the surest way to remove parasites from stream water is by boiling it). Other essentials include: a field repair kit, a first-aid kit, matches (in waterproof casing), a knife, and a headlamp or torch.

Chart for navigation. The NOAA Tide Predictions calendar is another useful resource. As with hiking, always be aware of your surroundings and potential hazards, including (where relevant) larger motorized boats (and their wakes), sand overhangs, and rocks. The Estuary Partnership organization has excellent safety guidelines on its website: www.estuarypartnership.org.

HIKING

When it comes to boots-on adventure, few states deliver more than Oregon. There are trails for all abilities and schedules, from short boardwalk hikes studded with interpretative panels, to epic backcountry odysseys that take hours or even days to complete. Trails skirt ocher cliffs on the

Pacific Coast; stripe through forests of Douglas firs; wiggle across High Desert, and scoop up thundering waterfalls. There are spectacular routes in all of Oregon's seven regions: the

---

Cyclists must follow the same laws as drivers on Oregon's roads. Plan your route ahead of time and conduct a basic ABC (air, breaks, chain) check on your bike before you set out.

Willamette Valley, Mount Hood and the Columbia River Gorge, the Oregon Coast, Southern Oregon, Central Oregon, Eastern Oregon, and even the Portland area.

Portland's urban trails are great for beginners. Forest Park is the city's green lung and the Wildwood Trail covers the length of it, beating a path across 30 wooded miles (48km). Meanwhile, the McKenzie River Trail is one of the most popular routes on the west side of the state and is well used by mountain bikers too. It whips out for 26 miles (42km), wending

Boots-on adventures abound in Oregon, with trails for every ability and timeframe.

⊘ PACIFIC CREST TRAIL

The most storied of all the trails on the West Coast (made famous by Hollywood blockbusters such as *Wild*, starring Reese Witherspoon), the Pacific Crest National Scenic Trail – better known as the Pacific Crest Trail (PCT) – runs for 2,650 miles (4,265km), wending its way from Mexico to Canada via the states of California, Oregon, and Washington. It is a bucket-list walking route for many long-distance hikers, and it takes most trekkers around five months to complete. Tackling the PCT is no small feat, and you will need to be an extremely fit and experienced backcountry hiker. The Oregon stretch totals 455 miles (732km) in length, but you can also dip into

sections of the trail on various day or as multiday hikes. One of the most epic (and challenging) stretches cuts through the Three Sisters Wilderness area for some 40 miles (64km), while another 33 miles (53km) slice through the backcountry of Crater Lake National Park. Some walking trails have brief brushes with the PCT – for example, the short but mettle-testing trek to the top of Pilot Rock in the Cascade-Siskiyou National Monument joins the PCT momentarily. Note that, given the high elevations, much of the PCT is snow-packed during the winter – the trail is best accessed through the spring and summer months.

past waterfalls, through old-growth forest, and beside gin-clear lakes – the McKenzie River Ranger Station is located along Highway 126.

When it comes to mountain routes, the Timberline Trail is one of Oregon's most iconic treks. It beats into the Mount Hood Wilderness and circles the peak itself, covering more than 40 miles (64km) and taking in meadows, waterfalls, and high alpine vistas. You can set aside several days to complete the whole route, or tackle a chunk of it on a day hike – such as the Paradise Park–Ramona Falls and Top Spur–Cloud Cap sections.

The Pacific Crest Trail is one of the West Coast's finest.

For wind-whipped, salty hikes, you can't beat the Oregon Coast Trail. It slinks out for more than 360 miles (579km) and it would take you a month to complete in its entirety. The route hugs the writhing Pacific Ocean, trekking across sandy beaches, through maritime forests, and over rocky peninsulas. The longer route can be broken down into 10 smaller sections, with spectacular stretches running between Otter Rock and Heceta Head (taking in a slew of landmark lighthouses) and scenic beach crossings between Bandon and Humbug Mountain State Park.

In Eastern Oregon, trails strike out into the rugged Wallowa and Blue Mountains. A standout hike is the West Fork Wallowa River Trail, which explores a portion of the sprawling Eagle Cap Wilderness. Colossal granite mountains, meadows, and fir forests reward the hiker amply on this 10-mile (16km) point-to-point route.

BIKING

Oregon's diverse terrain makes for white-knuckle bike trails that will suit seasoned pros, plus easy-going rides that are geared towards beginners. Trails range from dramatically undulating mountain routes to laid-back urban paths and paved Scenic Bikeways.

Cyclists are well served in all corners of the state. Splaying out in the foothills of the Cascade Range, the Sandy Ridge Trail System has paths for differing abilities – the Bureau of Land Management (www.blm.gov) has useful maps. You can access the network of trails 11 miles (18km) east of Sandy, which is on the Mt. Hood Scenic Byway.

⊘ STARGAZING

Oregon is a stellar place to gaze at the cosmos: the state's remote pockets of wilderness and clear, dark wide-open skies lend themselves perfectly to nights spent pondering the stars. The intrepid travelers who make it to the Alvord Desert – a stark, cracked plain in the southeast of the state – will be greeted with some of the most spectacular starry shows in Oregon.

Backpackers can pitch up a tent across Oregon's state parks and national forests and enjoy restful nights beneath inky skies unhindered by light pollution. Remote Summer Lake, an alkaline water body, in Southern Oregon is another fine spot for sighting stars and constellations.

Prineville Reservoir State Park in Central Oregon's high desert was certified as an International Dark Sky Park in 2021; you will need to download and print the stargazing permit from the state park website to visit just for the evening.

There is also a scattering of observatories from which to glimpse the cosmos, including Pine Mountain Observatory located near Bend; the Oregon Observatory in Sunriver; and the Dee Wright Observatory in the Willamette National Forest.

On clear nights free from fog and mist, the stargazing opportunities at Crater Lake National Park are spectacular, too.

The Columbia River Gorge is popular for windsurfing. Hood River is a great base camp for the watersport and has plenty of rental stores, plus tour operators offering lessons.

Best of all, these routes have been designed for downhill use, so you are guaranteed a thrill whatever your skill level. In nearby Welches, Mt. Hood Bicycle (68220 US-26; tel: 503-564 9086; www.mthoodbicycle.com; Apr–Oct Wed–Sun 10am–6pm; Nov–Mar Thu–Sun 10am–5pm) offers rentals.

The mountain town of Bend in Central Oregon is a base camp for many great cycling routes. Phil's Trail is a classic option, featuring a diverse network of single-track routes through ponderosa pine forest. Oakridge in the Willamette Valley is another biking hotspot, with various trails fanning out from the small city. The Cascades Outdoor Center (47365 1st Sreet; tel: 541-246 9007; www.cascadesoutdoorcenter.com) offers shuttle rides for various routes, including the popular Alpine Trail, an adrenaline-thumping track that whips through pine forest and meadows.

There are excellent road-biking options too, and an impressive network of Scenic Bikeways. Another jewel of Central Oregon, the Crooked River Canyon Scenic Bikeway is a moderately difficult 37-mile (60km) route that kicks off at Rimrock Park, before threading through a rugged canyon and eventually entering the Crooked River Wild and Scenic River Corridor – you turn around once you reach Big Bend Campground.

In Eastern Oregon, the 161-mile (259km) Painted Hills Scenic Byway connects the three units of the John Day Fossil Beds. Best for seasoned riders, this longer, strenuous route is broken down into a variety of sections, throwing up wonders such as the John Day River, the Ochoco Mountains, and the color-splashed Painted Hills along the way.

For something milder, try the Covered Bridges Scenic Bikeway in the Willamette Valley. This gentle, 36-mile (58km) ride joins together Lane County's pretty covered bridges on a route that is suitable for most cyclists and families. You can expect paved roads (shared with traffic) and, of course, wooden bridges. On its website, Oregon State Parks (www.stateparks.oregon.gov) breaks down each of the Scenic Bikeways and includes maps and cue sheets.

CAMPING

There are few better ways to get back to nature than to spend a night or two beneath the stars, and Oregon has myriad options for the camper. You can pitch up across Oregon's state parks and national forests, with sites everywhere from wooded coves and sweeping river valleys to canyon country and the mountains. There are different levels of luxury on offer: primitive sites dot the backcountry, or

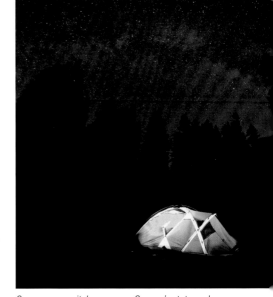

Campers can pitch up across Oregon's state parks.

there are RV parks with full hook-up and facilities. Some of Oregon's state parks also have yurts or cabins. The cabins are either "rustic" or "deluxe" and the latter usually has a refrigerator, TV with a DVD player, bathrooms with showers, and a barbecue outside (check with the individual park for details). Yurts typically have bunk beds and futon couches, and a little covered porch. In Umpqua Lighthouse State Park, along the southern Oregon Coast, you can stay in deluxe yurts with a covered deck and a bathroom with a shower.

There are plenty of privately owned campgrounds across Oregon too. Again, they run the gamut from basic tent sites in bucolic spots to glamping hubs with unique lodgings. The Willamette Valley's Vintages Trailer Resort (16205 SE

Kreder Road; tel: 971-267 2130; www.the-vintages. com) is a fun option. It is located in Dayton, in Oregon wine country, around a 45-minute drive from Portland. The site features more than 30 restored retro Airstream trailers alongside a swimming pool, a clubhouse, and an adults-only firepit area.

It is impossible to choose the best campground in Oregon – that depends on where in the state you want to be and the natural landscapes you're craving. However, standouts include the back-to-nature spots in Eastern Oregon's Cottonwood Canyon State Park, a wonderfully

Oakridge in the Willamette Valley is a biking hotspot.

⊘ GOING UNDERGROUND

The natural legacy of Oregon's long volcanic history is a fascinating subterranean world ripe for exploration. Guides take travelers underground on excursions ranging from easy boardwalk wanders to exciting trips including climbing, scrambling, and squeezing through extra-tight gaps. Central Oregon is a hub for caving, and Wanderlust Tours (tel: 541-389 8359; www.wanderlusttours.com) offers various underground trips through lava tubes in the Bend area. In Southern Oregon, the Oregon Caves National Monument includes a range of gentle interpretive tours and strenuous, expert-led off-trail activities.

You will need to display a State Sno-Park permit if you park in a designated winter recreation area (known as "Sno-Parks") between November 1 and April 30. Check www.oregon.gov for details. Passes are also available at Oregon Driver & Motor Vehicle Services offices.

rugged expanse of land chiseled out by the John Day River. There are fantastic opportunities for kayaking or rafting in the area.

Beverly Beach State Park, near Newport, is another popular spot and is a fantastic springboard for whale-watching at Yaquina Head. Meanwhile, farther north on the coast, Fort Stevens State Park has yurts, cabins, tent pitches, and RV hook-up sites, plus the haunting Peter Iredale shipwreck, which ran aground in 1906. If you want truly jaw-dropping natural wonders moments from camp, Silver Falls State Park and Smith Rock State Park deliver – Silver Falls has tent sites and cabins; Smith Rock has seasonal walk-in camping.

ON THE WATER

Oregon has more than 30 designated Wild and Scenic Rivers and over 1,400 named lakes. That means that taking to the water is an essential part of any Beaver State trip. As is the case with nearly all of Oregon's outdoor activities, the level of adventure is up to the individual traveler: the state offers up gentle paddles on calm, gin-clear lakes, or epic, multiday packrafting trips with jaunts on white water. Choose an adventure that suits your own skills and thirst for thrills.

A guided excursion is always a great way to uncover Oregon's wild waterways – you do not have to worry about kit or directions, so you can focus on drinking in the state's breathtaking watery landscapes. In Eastern Oregon, Go Wild: American Adventures (tel: 541-403 1692; www.gowildusa.com) offers multiday packrafting trips, including excursions in the Owyhee Canyonlands. You can expect days filled with paddling and hiking and nights in comfortable camps. In southwestern Oregon, the Wild and Scenic Rogue River is an oasis for water adventures. Indigo Creek Outfitters (tel: 541-282 4535; www.indigocreekoutfitters. com) leads day tours on the Rogue River's Class

III/IV rapids and multiday excursions. In four days, you can travel from the Southern Oregon town of Galice, all the way to the mouth of the Rogue.

For a more mellow experience, try the Fern Ridge Reservoir off Highway 126, around 30 minutes outside of Eugene – the Coyote Creek Nature Trail is a popular choice. Farther east, Waldo Lake in the Cascade Mountains is another peaceful option.

WINTER ADVENTURES

Come winter, Oregon's mountains are plastered in white powder, creating a hub for snowy adventures. Cross-country and downhill skiing, snowboarding, and snowshoeing are all on offer here.

Skiers should make a beeline for Mount Hood. The iconic pyramidal peak is home to multiple lauded ski resorts: Mt Hood Skibowl, Mt Hood Meadows, Timberline Lodge, and the Cooper Spur Mountain Resort come out on top. Timberline is touted as offering the longest ski season in North America, and has groomed beginner, intermediate, and advanced runs. The resort also offers snowcat rides on the glacial Palmer Snowfield, plus snow tubing at Summit Pass. When there's snow in the Columbia River Gorge area, the Mosier Twin Tunnels pathway is a great spot for cross-country skiing. Many ski resorts also offer guided snowshoe tours.

In Central Oregon and the Eastern Cascades, you will find Mount Bachelor – the sixth-largest ski resort in North America. The 9,065ft (2,763-meter) volcanic cone is crisscrossed with trails for all skill levels – in all, there are over 4,300 skiable acres (1,700 hectares) served by 11 lifts. You can take interpretive skiing tours with a ranger or try your hand at dog-sledding. There are also various Sno-Parks across Central Oregon, including groomed cross-country ski trails at Virginia Meissner Sno-Park. Tumalo Mountain is popular with backcountry skiers (note that beginners should not attempt to recreate in Oregon's backcountry alone in winter).

In Southern Oregon, the Mount Ashland Ski Area is a winter-adventure hub in the Siskiyou Mountains, while adventurous pros take to the backcountry in Crater Lake National Park.

Oregon's mountains are a dream for snowy adventures.

⊘ PEAK THRILLS

Given Oregon's abundance of soaring peaks, it is no surprise that thrill-seekers come from far and wide to scale the state's mountains. Smith Rock State Park in Central Oregon is the main pilgrimage site for devoted climbers, with the first recorded climb back in the 1930s.

Throughout the 20th century, interest in the area mushroomed, with its volcanic tuff posing a welcome challenge for the most adventurous of climbers. The saw-toothed ridges were further popularized by a pioneering climber named Alan Watts, who established and developed many previously untapped mountaineering routes in the area.

Now, sport climbers can choose from more than 1,500 routes carving through this otherworldly state park. What's more, relatively dry High Desert conditions means that it is pretty much a year-round destination for adventure sports. The sheer Morning Glory Wall is the pick of the bunch.

For beginners, the Smith Rock Climbing School offers guided climbs and lessons for various skill levels. Other popular climbing destinations include French's Dome in the Mount Hood National Forest and Trout Creek in Central Oregon. The latter is a favorite for crack climbing (ie using a natural crack in the rock to ascend).

Bald eagles perched above
Emigrant Lake.

WEIRD AND WONDERFUL WILDLIFE

Mist-cloaked maritime forests, rocky Pacific headlands, and volcanic caves provide a habitat for a fascinating world of wildlife, from Steller sea lions to black bear.

Oregon is home to endlessly diverse wildlife. Trail the coast and you might catch sight of a whale breaching in the ocean, while bald eagles and great blue herons fill the open skies. Black bears pad through quiet fir forests and Roosevelt elk nose through sprawling grasslands. Eight Wildlife Refuges manage Oregon's myriad species and their habitats, ranging from great parcels of the Pacific Coast to mountain retreats roamed by pronghorn and bobcats.

MARINE LIFE

Oregon's stirring coastline is a mecca for wildlife fans. Roaring Steller sea lions huddle on rocky ledges in the Pacific, while ten species of whale, dolphin, and porpoise frolic in the waters. Whale-watching is a popular activity, with boats

Black bears pad through Oregon's fir forests.

Whale Watch Week occurs twice a year, during peak migration periods in late December and late March. Experts and enthusiasts volunteer at the state's top whale-watching areas and are on hand to help you spot creatures of the deep.

departing from various points along the coast, including Depoe Bay and Newport. The former is a particular hub, with a busy Whale Watching Center (119 US-101; tel: 800-551 6949; www.stateparks.oregon.gov), which offers prime Pacific Ocean vistas from its vast viewing deck. Binoculars are available for use, and staff is on hand to answer your questions about the majestic marine mammals.

Whale-watching is virtually a year-round activity in Oregon. There are large migrations in winter (mid-Dec to Jan) and spring (Mar–June), while resident whales nudge toward Oregon's fish-filled shores to feed from June to mid-November.

Blue whale, minke whale, humpback whale, sperm whale, killer whale, and gray whales can all be spotted in Oregon's waters – the latter is the most prolific species, and it is estimated that as many as 18,000 gray whales journey past the state's rugged shores from late March through June. Most are heading toward Alaska, though some (typically around 200) prefer to stay put on the Oregon Coast. The winter migration generally peaks between Christmas Day and the

New Year. During this time, as many as 50 gray whales a day have been seen from Depoe Bay's Whale Watching Center.

There are myriad places to keep watch for the majestic mammals along Oregon's coast and the State Parks website (stateparks.oregon.gov) keeps maps and lists of the best spots. These include Fort Stevens State Park on the North Coast; Shore Acres State Park in Coos County; and Cape Ferrelo in Harris Beach State Park near Brookings, not far from the border with California. You will have the best chance of a sighting on a calm day. Typically, whales are not too difficult to spot – not least because of their immense size. Gray whales, for example, weigh around 80,000lbs (36,000kg) and they measure around 50ft (15 meters) in length. Keep watch for a telltale blow, or spout, which sees the whales shoot air up to a height of about 12ft (3.5 meters).

The killer whale is slightly more elusive than the gray whale – but you might catch sight of a dorsal fin slicing through the waves. Meanwhile, though they're usually farther away from

Ross's Geese pass through Klamath Basin on the Pacific Flyway migratory route between Alaska and Patagonia.

⊘ STELLER SEA LIONS

Steller sea lions are the celebrities of the Pacific seaboard. They are named for the botanist and zoologist Georg Wilhelm Steller, who wrote about the species as early as 1742. They have endearing, almost bear-like faces, small flippers, and ruddy hair and they collect in both rookeries (where they mate) and haul-outs (where they rest). The Sea Lion Caves near Florence is a very popular spot for viewing Steller sea lions – an elevator takes you down into a sea cave and deposits you on a viewing deck, where you can watch the wild mammals frolic on the rocks below. You might also see them from Cape Meares at Three Arch Rocks National Wildlife Refuge.

the shores, humpbacks are prone to breaching and slapping the water emphatically – if you are lucky enough to spot one, you're likely in for a spectacular show.

There's a bounty of marine life besides whales. On offshore charters, keep your eyes peeled for pods of playful bottlenose dolphin or, closer to the coastline and in shallow estuaries, look out for harbor porpoise. Oregon has three species of sea turtle in its waters: loggerhead, green, and leatherback.

Steller sea lions are also joined by the Northern fur seal and the California sea lion. You might spot the latter from late summer at Cascade Head in Tillamook County, or at Cape Argo in Coos County.

BIRDS

Oregon is a twitcher's delight. More than 500 species of bird have been spotted in the state, everywhere from coastal headlands to the lake-filled Klamath Basin. That means there are bird-watching hotspots in almost every region.

You need not stray too far from Portland to find some of Oregon's finest birding destinations. Mount Tabor Park (SE 60th Avenue and SE Salmon Street; tel: 503-823 7529; www.portland.gov/parks/mt-tabor-park) covers its namesake – an extinct volcano that thrusts over 630ft (190

> The dusky Canada goose loves to winter in the Willamette Valley – preserves including the William L. Finley National Wildlife Refuge protect the species.

meters) – and it sits within city limits in Southeast Portland. Many migratory birds make use of the park, which is carpeted with Douglas firs and big-leaf maples. You might catch a glimpse of any number of species, from orange-crowned warblers and dark-eyed juncos to song sparrows and winter wrens.

Also in the Portland region, Sauvie Island Wildlife Area sits at the confluence of the Willamette and Columbia rivers and supports some 275 bird species. Plenty of trails (including the popular Oak Island Trail) wiggle across the isle, where you will probably glimpse sandhill cranes and swans, plus a whole host of wintering waterfowl.

Oregon's epic coastline provides important habitats for a great number of species. Tillamook Bay on the North Coast is a standout. In winter, the waterfowl population here can creep up to 7,500. Key species include the northern pintail duck and western sandpipers, which appear in large numbers around September. Fort Stevens State Park is another sure bet for birdwatchers. Ranger-led hikes take enthusiasts in search of species such as snowy plovers and brown pelicans. Also on the North Coast is Yaquina Head Outstanding Natural Area – the rugged cape juts into the Pacific, where you might see a Brandt's cormorant diving for its fish dinner. There is also a 19th-century

lighthouse and an interpretative center with marine and birdlife exhibits here. Farther south, migrating waterfowl flock to the mudflats and marshes of the Coos River Estuary. Watch out for species like brown pelicans, great egrets, and dunlins.

In Southern Oregon and Northern California, the Klamath Basin National Wildlife Refuges offer some of the finest birding in the nation. Crossing Oregon and California, there are six refuges in total – Upper Klamath and Lower Klamath, Bear Valley, Tule Lake, Clear Lake,

Roosevelt elk can be seen in Jewell Meadows.

⊘ PACIFIC FLYWAY

The Pacific Flyway is a major migration route that sees myriad bird species swoop over Oregon on their journey from Alaska to South America's Patagonia. En route, Oregon's wetlands provide a critical habitat for visiting birds. Key birding sites include the Klamath Basin National Wildlife Refuges (of which there are six), plus bodies of water such as Summer Lake and Malheur Lake. A near-endless list of species passes through – these include the Ross's goose, snowy plovers, western and Clark's grebes, great blue herons, and egrets. There is both a springtime and a fall bird migration.

and Klamath Marsh – and each provides precious habitat for innumerable species. In Upper Klamath, the primary landscape is sprawling marsh and open waters, which support species such as American white pelicans.

Eastern Oregon – and Harney County in particular – is another fantastic destination. Head to the Malheur National Wildlife Refuge, which protects a swathe of the region's High Desert. A long list of species calls the refuge home, or at least home-from-home – they include various terns, night and great blue herons, California gulls, and great glossy ibises. Time your trip for the Harney County Migratory Bird Festival, which is typically held in April. The event generally includes van-guided tours, hiking and biking, family activities, and a wildlife-themed art sale.

MAMMALS

Running the gamut from lumbering black bear and mammoth elk to diminutive animals such as squirrels and skunks, Oregon's mammals represent some of its most fascinating wildlife.

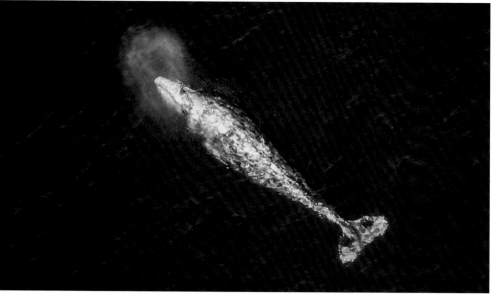

Up to 18,000 gray whales journey past Oregon's shores from late March through June.

◑ WILD HORSES

Northwestern tribes first acquired horses in the 1700s, revolutionizing their trading routes and offering access to previously inaccessible goods. In the centuries that followed, wild horses populated Oregon's vast plains and mountains. These figures declined as US and European settlers moved into the region, but a number remained free right into the 20th century.

By the 1970s, the Wild Free-Roaming Horses and Burros Act stipulated that "unclaimed horses" should be studied and protected, and Oregon made moves to protect its own wild steeds. This has had a positive impact on herd numbers.

Today, there are 19 wild horse herds in Oregon, mostly run by the Bureau of Land Management, with two run or co-run by the US Forest Service – it is estimated that more than 4,600 horses roam across these areas. One way to catch a glimpse of the enchanting creatures is to drive the Steens Loop Tour Route in Eastern Oregon.

The breathtaking drive is studded with viewpoints that might, if you're lucky, grant you vistas of herds of free-roaming horses grazing on the plains. Separate to this, the Big Summit Wild Horse Territory is contained within the Ochoco National Forest and is within easy reach of Prineville.

Elusive black bears are the only bear that exists in Oregon (the last grizzly in the state was killed back in the 1930s). These formidable animals – Oregon's largest carnivores

> Today, the beaver has the privilege of being the state animal. But Oregon earned its nickname because of the large rodents' prized pelts and a long history of fur-trapping, rather than their value or interest as a species.

– live in the mighty Cascades and in the Blue and Wallowa mountains and it is thought that they number round 25,000 to 35,000. Many of them are not black at all – they might be honey blonde or brown, so they are often mistaken for grizzlies. You might see them fishing in streams or browsing berries before they hibernate for the winter. Hikers in bear country need to be extra vigilant – the Oregon Department of Fish and Wildlife has detailed guidelines (http://dfw.state.or.us/wildlife/living_with/black_bears.asp).

Elk is another Oregon species that has the awe factor. Both Rocky Mountain elk and Roosevelt elk live in the state – the former east of the Cascades and the latter out west. The Jewell Meadows Wildlife Area is an excellent place to see these mighty mammals roam free. The refuge spreads out for over 1,100 acres (450 hectares) in the state's northwest corner, and protects forests thick with Douglas firs and hemlocks, plus open meadows and seasonal wetlands.

Roosevelt elk come here for winter, and it is not uncommon to see some 200 of the creatures grazing in the meadows in the right season. Come in fall, at the height of rutting season, and you might hear a male elk's bugling call. As its name suggests, the Dean Creek Elk Viewing Area on the Umpqua River is another great place to see these impressive mammals. A 60- to 100-strong herd makes the most of the riverside meadows, and a small interpretative display offers context for wildlife lovers.

In Southern Oregon, land is set aside to protect the Columbian white-tailed deer, a rare subspecies that only exists in the state. A long fluffy tail distinguishes them from other species, and the North Bank Habitat Management Area in the Umpqua River Basin is a great place to spot them.

Oregon is also home to three enigmatic cat species: the cougar (or mountain lion), the Canada lynx, and the bobcat. Biggest of all, cougars mostly roam west of the Cascades, though some are found in the far eastern Ochoco, Blue, and Wallowa mountains. Felids are notoriously elusive, and hikers are unlikely to encounter any of Oregon's big cats.

Sea lions can be spotted on rocky ledges in the Pacific.

⊘ BATS

Oregon is honeycombed with inky, volcanic caverns, and fifteen bat species make the most of these precious habitats, as well as seeking shelter among craggy cliff faces, forests, and even urban buildings. Species include the California myotis, which is found in most parts of the state; the Western small-footed myotis, which exists east of the Cascades; and the long-eared myotis, which loves Oregon's dense woodlands. When winter takes hold, some of the state's bats migrate south, while others brace themselves for the chill. As is common across the US, white-nose syndrome – a fungal disease – affects some of Oregon's bat populations.

The Goodpasture covered bridge is one of the best-known in Lane County.

GOODPASTURE BRIDGE
BUILT BY
LANE CO. 1938
A.C. STRIKER BRIDGE SUPT
NO. 16-2E-29

ONE WAY
TRAFFIC
FOR TRUCKS
AND BUSES

Red barn and vineyards in Mt Hood Valley.

Oregon Coast Highway near Cannon Beach.

St. Johns Bridge straddling the Willamette River in Portland.

INTRODUCTION

A region by region guide to the state of Oregon, with key sites cross-referenced by number to maps throughout.

Pinot Noir: Oregon's finest.

Travel the breadth of Oregon, be it east to west, or north to south, and you will find it hard to believe that you remain in the same state – such is the region's natural variety. Here, ancient volcanic mountains exist alongside pancake-flat river valleys, and damp, moss-filled forests are a drive away from cracked, dry desert. It is this diversity that defines the state.

Oregon can be roughly carved up into seven regions, each with its own distinct characteristics. The Portland region is centered on the state's biggest metropolis, and also includes smaller cities like Beaverton, where sportswear giant Nike is headquartered. Portland is an unwaveringly creative and entrepreneurial urban hub yet, this being Oregon, even the state's largest city has its own natural bounty, with giant parks and access to hiking trails.

Unfolding east of Portland is Mount Hood and the Columbia River Gorge, a region sculpted by the mighty waterway. The Columbia River Gorge National Scenic Area is the largest in the nation and all roads lead back to the river, with epic waterside drives, paddling trips, and panoramic viewpoints galore. Meanwhile, the snowy reaches of Mount Hood are a winter-sports paradise. This is one of the state's great growing regions too, and fruit and lavender farms pepper the landscape. The Willamette Valley, which inches between the Coast and Cascade mountains, also has agricultural prowess. More fruit farms await, plus acres of vine-striped land producing some of the nation's finest Pinot Noir and Chardonnay.

Nike HQ in Beaverton.

The Oregon Coast is a world all its own, rippling from northern Astoria – which all but kisses the Washington border – down to California. In between is a patchwork of dramatic headlands, sandy beaches, quirky towns, and wild rivers.

Southern Oregon lays claim to the state's shiniest jewel: Crater Lake National Park, which protects a mesmerizing lake-filled caldera and acres of trail-laced backcountry. North of here, Central Oregon's High Desert is an adventure playground, with world-class climbing, hiking, and skiing, plus funky mountain towns such as Bend. Out east, the state takes on a Wild West feel, with historic gold rush towns, cattle ranches, and The Blues – the oldest mountains in Oregon.

An extensive network of Scenic Byways reveals all corners of the state, alongside well-marked hiking and biking trails.

98

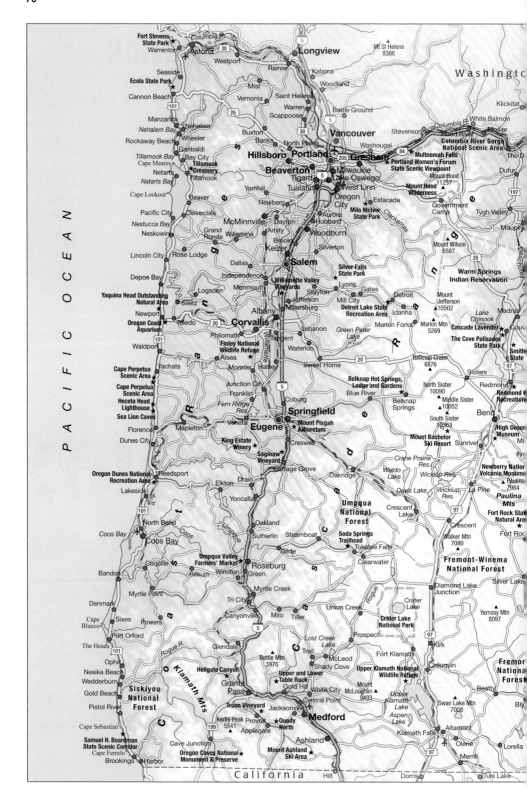

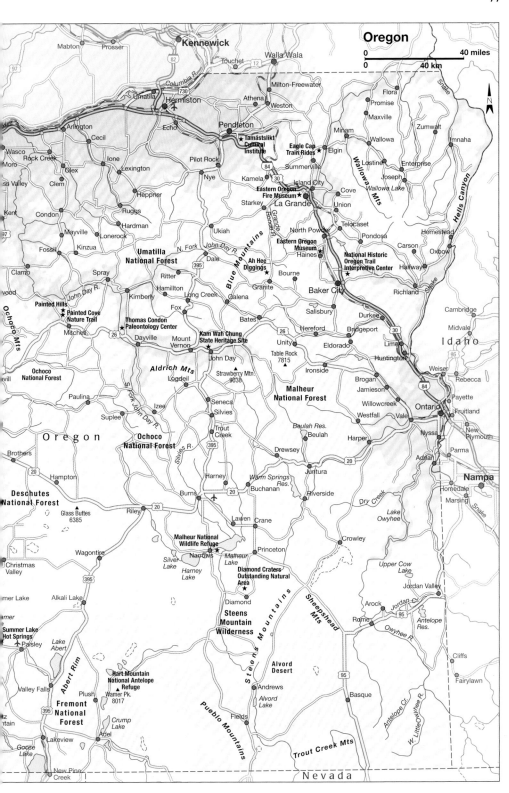

Oregon

0 — 40 miles
0 — 40 km

Mabton Prosser **Kennewick**
Walla Wala
Touchet
Columbia R.
97
82
12
Milton-Freewater
Umatilla Athena Flora
Hermiston Weston Promise
730 Maxville
Zumwalt
Arlington Echo Pendleton Minam Wallowa
Cecil Pilot Rock Tamástslikt Zumwalt
Wasco Ione Cultural Eagle Cap Imnaha
Rock Creek Lexington Institute Train Rides Enterprise
Moro Olex Nye Elgin
Clem Summerville Lostine
ss Valley Heppner 84 Joseph
Kamela 30 Wallowa Lake
Kent Condon Ruggs Eastern Oregon Island City
Hardman Fire Museum Cove
Mayville Lonerock Starkey La Grande Union
Fossil Kinzua Ukiah North Powder Telocaset Homestead
Clarno Umatilla N. Fork John Day R. Eastern Oregon Pondosa Carson
National Forest Dale Museum Haines Oxbow
97 Spray 395 Ah Hee National Historic Halfway
Ritter Diggings Oregon Trail
vood Hamilton Bourne Interpretive Center Richland
John Day R. Granite Cambridge
Painted Hills Kimberly Long Creek Galena Baker City Midvale
Painted Cove Fox Salisbury Durkee I d a h o
Nature Trail Bates Hereford Bridgeport 95
Mitchell Thomas Condon Kam Wah Chung 26 Eldorado 30
26 Paleontology Center State Heritage Site Unity Lime Weiser
Ochoco Dayville Mount John Day Table Rock Huntington Rebecca
National Forest Vernon 7815 Ironside Payette
Aldrich Mts Logdeil Strawberry Mtn. Brogan Ontario Fruitland
Paulina 9038 Jamieson New
O r e g o n Izee Seneca Malheur Willowcreek Vale Plymouth
Suplee Silvies National Forest Westfall Nyssa Parma
Ochoco Trout Harper Adrian Nampa
Brothers National Forest Creek Beulah Res.
20 Silvies R. 395 Beulah Homedale
Hampton Drewsey Marsing
Deschutes Harney Juntura Dry Creek Snake
National Forest Warm Springs 20 Lake
Riley 20 Res. Owyhee
Glass Buttes Buchanan Riverside
6385 Burns Crowley
Wagontire Lawen Crane
Christmas Silver Narrows Malheur National Princeton Upper Cow
Valley Lake Wildlife Refuge Lake
395 Harney Malheur Diamond Craters Jordan Valley
mer Lake Alkali Lake Lake Lake Outstanding Natural Arock Jordan Cr.
Area Rome Antelope
mer Diamond 95 Res.
Summer Lake Lake Steens Sheepshead Owyhee R.
Hot Springs Abert Mountain Mts Cliffs
Paisley Wilderness
Valley Falls Hart Mountain Andrews Fairylawn
National Antelope Alvord 95
Fremont Refuge Lake Basque
National Plush Warner Pk. Alvord
Forest 8017 Desert Antelope Cr.
Lakeview Adel Fields W. Little Owyhee R.
Crump Pueblo Mountains
Goose Lake Trout Creek Mts
Lake
New Pine N e v a d a
Creek

Mount Hood gazes over Portland.

PORTLAND AND AROUND

A distinctly rebellious and creative spirit defines Portland, which comprises a patchwork of neighborhoods filled with offbeat museums and attractions, indie shops, and imaginative restaurants.

It all started with a coin toss. In the 1840s, business partners Asa Lovejoy (hailing from Boston, Massachusetts) and Francis Pettygrove (of Portland, Maine) filed a land claim here, flipping a penny to decide whose hometown would become the site's namesake. Pettygrove won, and the area – previously known as "Stumptown," since thick fir and hemlock forest was cleared for passing immigrants and fur traders – earned its moniker.

That early whimsy feeds into the city's contemporary spirit. **Portland ❶** is a town of rebels and makers, free spirits, and founders, where self-expression is encouraged, and eccentricity nurtured. The city wears its "Keep Portland Weird" slogan as a badge of honor and you'll see it stamped in shop windows, painted onto walls, and emblazoned on T-shirts. Hit TV show *Portlandia* parodies the city's hipster streak – but it's the modern beatnik that gives Portland its flair.

The city's creative streak manifests in an abundance of independent businesses and you can't move for artisan coffee shops, alternative fashion stores, food carts, and concept restaurants. The great joy of exploring Portland is not in ticking off big sights or lingering too long in museums, but in diving into the city's distinct "quadrants" – North, Northeast, Northwest,

Pioneer Courthouse Square.

South, Southeast, Southwest – each made up of smaller neighborhoods with their own character. Most are wonderfully walkable – a boon in any US city – and there is an excellent network of cycling lanes.

The setting has star quality, too. Portland spreads out at the confluence between the Willamette and Columbia rivers, and the former slices the city in two: Old Town, Downtown, and the sprawling expanse of Forest Park unfurl to the west; creative havens such as the Alberta Arts District and

⊘ Main attractions

Portland Art Museum
Powell's City of Books
Washington Park
Portland Saturday Market
North Mississippi Avenue
Alberta Arts District

⊙ Maps on pages 102, 104

Montavilla to the east. The northern border is marked out by the Columbia, and a short hop east will take you to the Columbia River Gorge National Scenic Area, with heart-in-mouth views and miles of hiking trails. On a clear day, the hulk of Mount Hood is a visible beacon in the city.

The natural larder of the Willamette Valley, Oregon's prime agricultural region, is right on the doorstep, and it feeds an inventive food scene with global influences. World-class wineries dot the valley and make easy excursions from the city.

CENTRAL PORTLAND

Portland's Downtown is easy to explore on foot and the **Sentinel** hotel (614 SW 11th Avenue; tel: 503-224 3400; www.provenancehotels.com/sentinel-hotel) makes a luxurious central base. The grand entryway columns and exterior reliefs make a statement, and the refined rooms are accented with mid-century touches.

Begin your sightseeing at **Pioneer Courthouse Square Ⓐ**, an urban park lovingly known as the city's "living room." Portlanders gather on the red-brick steps, and food carts dish up lunch to hungry punters. It is also a hub for cultural events, from music concerts to open-air movie nights. On its eastern side, the plaza is flanked by its namesake, the 19th-century Pioneer Courthouse, which offers self-guided tours that take in the chambers and the cupola (700 SW 6th Avenue, Mon–Fri 9am–4pm).

A short walk southwest is the **Portland Art Museum Ⓑ** (1219 Southwest Park Avenue; tel: 503-226 2811; www.portlandartmuseum.org; Wed–Sun 10am–5pm). The largest art museum in the state, it dates to 1892 and is housed in a Georgian-style building designed by renowned Italian American architect Pietro Belluschi, who spent his defining years in the city. Here, you will find a 4,000-strong collection of Asian artworks, from Chinese ceramics to watercolors from Japan's Meiji era, plus works by Old Masters, including Rembrandt and Anthony van Dyck. Artists from the Pacific Northwest, such as Modern painter Morris Graves, are also well represented. Spread across the second and third floor of the Main Building's Hoffman Wing is the Confederated Tribes of Grand Ronde Center for Native American Art. Some 3,500 artifacts represent 200 cultural groups across what is now the United States (Portland itself was built upon land originally belonging to tribes, including the Multnomah, Chinook, and Clackamas). Expect to see everything from ceremonial masks, beads, and basketry to Modernist sculptures. There is a keen focus on contemporary work from Indigenous artists, too.

For a further dive into the past, head to the **Oregon Historical Society Museum** (1200 SW Park Avenue; tel: 503-222 1741, www.ohs.org; Mon–Sat 10am–5pm, Sun noon–5pm). The collection includes the very coin that was flipped in 1845 to decide the name

Portland and around

0   50 miles

0   50 km

of the city, plus logging artifacts and Native American relics like moccasins and canoes. Temporary exhibits explore everything from Oregon's musical heritage to its state parks.

A few blocks away is the **Keller Auditorium** C (222 SW Clay Street; 503-248 4335; www.portland5.com/keller-auditorium), a hub for the performing arts. You can catch Broadway shows, opera recitals, and dance performances at this versatile theater space, completed in 1917. It is part of **Portland'5 Centers for the Arts** (1111 SW Broadway; tel: 503-248 4335; www.portland5.com), a string of cultural venues including the **Arlene Schnitzer Concert Hall** and the snug, Edwardian-inspired **Newmark Theatre**.

Beyond the big-hitters, Portland's Downtown includes a warren of independent shops. Favorites include **Tender Loving Empire** (412 SW 10th Avenue; tel: 503-548 2925; www.tenderlovingempire.com; daily 11am–7pm), a record store (with its own record label) moonlighting as an artisan gift shop showcasing Oregon makers. **Wild Fang** (404 SW 10th Avenue; tel: 503-964 6746; www.wildfang.com; daily 11am–7pm) is another home-grown brand, with a mission to disrupt gender norms in fashion. **Amity Artisan Goods** (962 SW Morrison Street; tel: 503-954 3705; www.amitypdx.com; Wed, Thu noon–6pm, Fri, Sat until 7pm, Sun until 4pm) showcases a breadth of Portland designers, with a focus on underrepresented female, LGBTQ+, and BIPOC creators. Browse a treasure trove of prints, ceramics, handmade jewelry, and soft furnishings. Avid readers should swing by **Powell's City of Books** D (1005 W Burnside Street; tel: 800-878 7323; www.powells.com; daily 10am–9pm), the mother of all indie shops (see box).

PEARL DISTRICT

Immediately north of the main Downtown core is the achingly hip **Pearl District** E. Strung along the Willamette River, the area was known as the Northwest Industrial Triangle in the first half of the 20th century, due to its many warehouses and workers' homes, plus loading docks and railroad yards. Fast-forward several decades and industry

◎ Drink

Sample a dram or two at the Multnomah Whiskey Library (1124 SW Alder Street; tel: 503-954 1381; www.mwlpdx.com; Tue–Thu 4pm–10pm, Fri, Sat until 11pm). More than 1,500 spirits are on offer at this low-lit, wood-paneled whiskey lounge, and well-versed staff are on hand to help visitors choose the right tipple.

Trendy Pearl District.

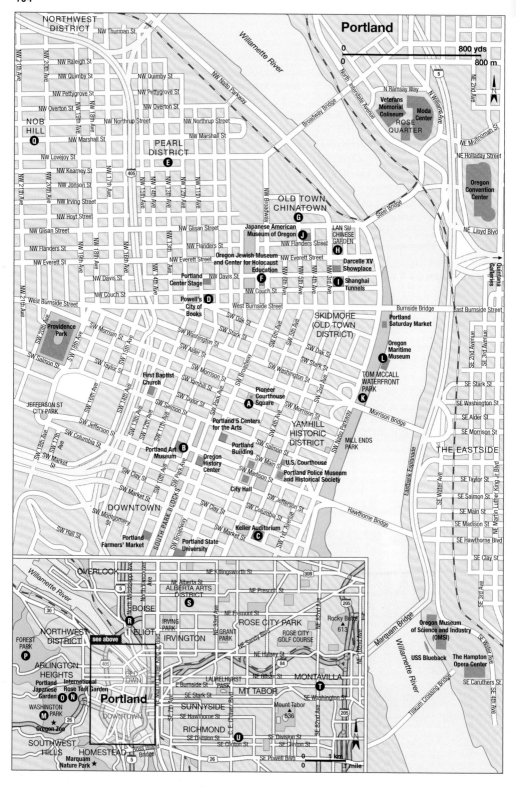

Portland

NORTHWEST DISTRICT
NW Thurman St
NW Raleigh St
NW Quimby St
NW Quimby St
NW Pettygrove St
NW Pettygrove St
NW Overton St
NW Overton St
NOB HILL **Q**
NW Northrup Street
NW Northrup Street
NW Marshall St
NW Marshall St
NW Lovejoy St
PEARL DISTRICT **E**
NW Kearney St
NW Jonson St
NW Irving Street
NW Hoyt Street
NW Glisan Street
NW Glisan Street
OLD TOWN CHINATOWN **G**
NW Flanders St
NW Flanders St
NW Flanders Street
Japanese American Museum of Oregon **J**
LAN SU CHINESE GARDEN
NW Everett Street
NW Everett Street
NW Everett Street
Oregon Jewish Museum and Center for Holocaust Education
H
Darcelle XV Showplace
NW Davis St
NW Davis St
Portland Center Stage
F
I Shanghai Tunnels
NW Couch St
NW Couch St
Powell's City of Books **D**
West Burnside Street
West Burnside Street
SKIDMORE (OLD TOWN DISTRICT)
Portland Saturday Market
Providence Park
SW Morrison St
SW Washington St
SW Stark St
SW Oak St
SW Oak St
SW Stark St
Oregon Maritime Museum **L**
SW Alder St
JEFFERSON ST CITY PARK
SW Taylor St
First Baptist Church
SW Morrison St
SW Yamhill St
SW Washington St
SW Stark St
TOM McCALL WATERFRONT PARK
SW Taylor St
SW Salmon St
Pioneer Courthouse Square **A**
SW Morrison St
K
SW Jefferson St
Portland Art Museum **B**
Oregon History Center
Portland Building
YAMHILL HISTORIC DISTRICT
MILL ENDS PARK
SW Columbia St
SW Clay St
SW Salmon St
U.S. Courthouse
Portland Police Museum and Historical Society
THE EASTSIDE
DOWNTOWN
SW Market St
SW Clay St
SW Jefferson St
City Hall
SW Montgomery St
SW Columbia St
Portland Farmers' Market
SW Hall St
Keller Auditorium **C**
SW Market St
Portland State University

Willamette River
Broadway Bridge
Steel Bridge
Burnside Bridge
Morrison Bridge
Hawthorne Bridge
Eastbank Esplanade

Veterans Memorial Coliseum
Moda Center
ROSE QUARTER
Oregon Convention Center
NE Lloyd Blvd
Quintana Galleries

OVERLOOK
NE Killingsworth St
NE Alberta St
ALBERTA ARTS DISTRICT **S**
NE Prescott St
30B
BOISE
NE Fremont St
ROSE CITY PARK
Rocky Butte 613
FOREST PARK
NORTHWEST DISTRICT
R
ELIOT
IRVING PARK
GRANT PARK
IRVINGTON
ROSE CITY GOLF COURSE
NE Sandy Blvd
NE Halsey St
Oregon Museum of Science and Industry (OMSI)
ARLINGTON HEIGHTS
see above
OLD TOWN
P
405
NE Glisan St
84
MONTAVILLA
205
USS Blueback
The Hampton Opera Center
Portland Japanese Garden **O**
International Rose Test Garden **N**
Portland
DOWNTOWN
LAURELHURST PARK
E Burnside St
SE Stark St
MT TABOR
T
SE Caruthers St
WASHINGTON PARK **M**
Oregon Zoo
SUNNYSIDE
SE Hawthorne St
Mount Tabor 636
SE Washington St
SOUTHWEST HILLS
RICHMOND
SE Division St
SE Division St
HOMESTEAD
Marquam Nature Park
5
U
SE Clinton St
SE Clinton St
26
SE Powell Blvd

Willamette River

0   800 yds
0   800 m

0   1 km
0   1 mile

was waning in the area: however, a creative scene sprouted in its place. Warehouses were reimagined as studios and gallery space and, by the 1980s, it was a thriving artists' enclave.

That creative energy remains today, and an eclectic crop of galleries showcases work by local and international artists. A top stop is the **Froelick Gallery** (714 NW Davis Street; tel: 503-222 1142; www.froelickgallery.com; Tue–Sat 11am–5.30pm), which has been a neighborhood stalwart since 1995. The gallery deals in cutting-edge contemporary works, in mixed media from 3D installations to prints and drawings. Just around the corner is the **Blue Sky Gallery** (122 NW 8th Avenue; tel: 503-225 0210; www.blueskygallery.org; Wed–Sat noon–5pm), also known as the Oregon Center for the Photographic Arts. Established in 1975, the space is the state's premiere photography gallery and displays works by emerging talent, as well as by renowned names. It shares a block with the **Oregon Jewish Museum and Center for Holocaust Education ⑤**

(724 NW Davis Street; tel: 503-226 3600; www.ojmche.org; temporarily closed due to construction), which is currently undergoing an expansion. Exhibitions explore systems of oppression and how they have affected Oregon's Jewish community, as well as the Jewish experience in the state, from the 19th-century Gold Rush era to the modern day.

Beyond art, the Pearl District is best known for beer. Breweries have operated here from as early as the mid-1800s, with the 19th-century red-brick **Henry Weinhard Brewery** (the complex is now a mix-used residential and retail space) serving as a hulking reminder of the era. Today, hotspots include **Von Ebert Brewing + Kitchen** (131 NW 13th Avenue; tel: 503-820 7721; www.vonebertbrewing.com; Mon–Sat 11.30am–10pm, Sun until 9pm), which specializes in German-inspired lagers, and elevated pub grub. There's the **Deschutes Brewery** (210 NW 11th Avenue; tel: 503-296 4906; www.deschutesbrewery.com; Mon–Thu 11.30am–9pm, Fri until 10pm, Sat 11am–10pm, Sun until 9pm),

⊘ **Tip**

Book a slot at the appointment-only Quintana Galleries (NE 29th & Prescott; www.facebook.com/QuintanaGalleries), where collections showcase the work of Native American artists. Expect everything from woodcarvings and sculptures to jewelry and contemporary paintings.

The 19th-century Henry Weinhard Brewery turned retail and residential space.

⊘ CITY OF BOOKS

Back in 1970, retired painting contractor Walter Powell was inspired after working a summer in his son Michael's Chicago bookstore, and upon returning to Portland opened his own used-books shop. It was an instant hit. Having quickly outgrown the original venue, Walter founded Powell's City of Books in an old car dealership in 1971. He was later joined by Michael and together they ran the business, selling used tomes on everything from psychology to history, plus the latest bestsellers. Fast forward more than five decades and it is still in the family, now run by third-generation Powell, Emily. At this point, it is nothing short of a city landmark, spreading out over an entire block. Onsite Guilder Cafe (daily 10am–8pm) is the perfect place to pore over your purchases. There are also regular author events.

Tip

Make the most of the Pearl District's First Thursday Street Gallery, which has been a tradition since 1986. As its name suggests, on the first Thursday of each month, art galleries in the area stay open late, often hosting receptions or debuting new exhibitions. You will also find artists selling their wares in the streets, plus live music performers and food vendors.

a Bend transplant that creates everything from IPAs to stouts and sours and serves them in laid-back industrial digs that were once an auto-body shop.

The neighborhood has a couple of great theaters. **Portland Center Stage at The Armory** (128 NW 11th Avenue; tel: 503-445 3700; www.pcs.org) is one of them, hosting classic Shakespeare plays and touring world shows in an 1891 Romanesque Revival-style building.

OLD TOWN CHINATOWN

To the immediate east of the Pearl District, **Old Town Chinatown** G collects in a bend in the Willamette River. This is Portland's original downtown area, and its oldest neighborhood. Gold was struck in Oregon in the mid-1800s and many Chinese people – mostly young men who worked as launderers, cooks, miners, and railroad laborers – migrated to this region. By the turn of the century, Rose City was home to one of the largest Chinatowns in the United States. However, life was tough for Chinese immigrants who, despite their sizable contributions to the economy

and labor force, suffered discrimination and violence. This also manifested in the Chinese Exclusion Act of 1882, which banned further Chinese laborers from entering the US. Many Chinese migrated farther north within the city in the 1920s and 1930s, but vestiges of this historical Chinatown remain today.

The most obvious nod to the community is the ornate **Chinatown Gateway**, which was proposed by the Chinese Consolidated Benevolent Association and opened in 1986. It is a worthy photo stop, flanked by a pair of bronze lions and adorned with ornate mythical creatures. Pass through the archway and the **Portland Chinatown Museum** (127 NW 3rd Avenue; tel: 503-224 0008; www.portlandchinatownmuseum.org; Fri–Sun 11am–3pm) is just a few minutes' walk away.

The space showcases work by Asian American artists, while a permanent exhibition dives into the experience of Oregon's early Chinese immigrants through black-and-white photography and dioramas, including a dry grocery store and medicine shop. Walk another block north and you will reach **Lan Su**

Ornate gateway at Old Town Chinatown.

Chinese Garden  (239 NW Everett Street; tel: 503-228 8131; www.lansugarden.org; daily 10am–4pm). The plot is based on traditional Ming Dynasty-style gardens and was designed by landscape artists from Suzhou in eastern China

Winding pathways lead to pavilions, koi ponds, and rock displays, while the traditional-style Teahouse in the Tower of Cosmic Reflections has an impressive and regularly changing menu of tea, plus lunch options including noodles and dumplings, and snacks like mooncakes.

Nearby is Old Town Pizza & Brewing (226 NW Davis Street; tel: 503-222 9999; www.otbrewing.com), which offers tours of the underground Shanghai Tunnels ❶. The tunnels are said to be among Portland's most haunted locations and tours focus on this ghostly lore, plus the somber history attached to them. It is thought that the subterranean passages were used to transport men who had been captured as slaves in order to be sold as crew to ship captains in need of workers – this practice was historically known as "shanghai-ing." Though legends abound, they have never been proved for sure.

Another neighborhood highlight is the Japanese American Museum of Oregon ❶ (411 NW Flanders Street; tel: 503-224 1458; www.jamo.org; Thu–Sun 11am–3pm). As Japanese migrants began arriving in Portland in the 1890s, a booming Japantown (or Nihonmachi) formed in what is now Old Town Chinatown, in the region south of West Burnside Street, and between Southwest Broadway and the Willamette River.

Japanese migrants labored at canneries and on the railroad but were exiled from their homes after President Franklin D. Roosevelt issued Executive Order 9066 in February 1942, during World War II. The order saw hundreds of thousands of Japanese immigrants confined to "relocation centers." The permanent exhibition "Oregon's Nikkei: An American Story of Resilience" covers this troubling part of history, as well as the wider experience of early Japanese settlers in rural Oregon and Portland.

The historic district is a gourmand's delight, and lines regularly snake from the original Voodoo Doughnut (22 SW 3rd Avenue; tel: 503-241 4704; www.voodoodoughnut.com; daily 6am–3am). The donuterie is known for its giant confections covered in eye-popping icing, sprinkles, and candy, in flavors from maple syrup to mango. Another revered institution is the Dan & Louis Oyster Bar (208 SW Ankeny Street; tel: 503-227 5906; Fri, Sat noon–9pm, Sun, Mon until 10pm), which has been dishing up excellent seafood dinners since 1907. The Pacific Northwest-style smoked salmon chowder is held up as a menu standout.

Toward the river, the Portland Oregon White Stag Sign has become a symbol of the city and a popular photo opportunity. It was first erected in the 1940s to advertise a sugar brand (with the wording "White Satin Sugar"), then later became an advertisement for

⊙ Tip

The Portland Streetcar joins together neighborhoods including Downtown, the Pearl District, and Nob Hill. It operates roughly every 15 minutes from early until late and costs $2 for a 2.5-hour ride. You can also get package deals that include journeys on light-rail trains and TriMet buses. Find maps and schedules at www.portlandstreetcar.org.

Portland Oregon White Stag Sign: a symbol of the city.

outdoor company White Stag. It took on its current form in 2010 when it was acquired by the city. Catch it glittering in neon by night and, if you're in Portland for the festive period, spot the stag's iconic red nose.

A quick pitstop at the White Stag Sign will place you by the Willamette River. Here, the paved, linear **Tom McCall Waterfront Park** , named for a former Oregon governor, runs beside the water. The park replaced a busy freeway when it opened in the 1970s and today it stretches for 1.5 miles (2.4km) from **Riverplace Marina**, northward to Northwest Glisan Street. It is popular with joggers and walkers, and the city's annual **Pride celebrations** are also centered here, alongside other festivals such as the **Waterfront Blues Festival** and the **Oregon Brewers Festival**.

Also along the river is the **Oregon Maritime Museum** (198 SW Naito Parkway; tel: 503-224 7724; www.oregonmaritimemuseum.org; Wed, Fri, Sat 11am–4pm). It's housed in a historic sternwheeler (the last operational steam-powered sternwheel tug in the country) and tours take visitors into the engine room and pilot house. The collection offers a deep dive into the state's maritime history through artifacts like replica cannons and model ships. On the other side of the river, to the south, the **Oregon Museum of Science and Industry** (OMSI; 1945 SE Water Ave; tel: 503-797 4000; www.omsi.edu; Sun–Fri 9.30am–5.30pm, Sat 9.30am–7pm) is a good spot for kids. In addition to its permanent exhibition, the immersive learning center has a planetarium and a working fossil preparation lab.

AROUND WASHINGTON PARK

The 410-acre (165-hectare) **Washington Park** spills out in Portland's northwestern corner and envelopes some of the city's top attractions. Chief among them is the **International Rose Test Garden** (400 SW Kingston Avenue; tel: 503-823 3636; daily 5am–10pm), home to over 10,000 roses in bloom from late May to October. The brainchild of *Oregon Journal* editor Jesse A. Currey, it dates to 1915 and offers fantastic views of the city and Mount Hood.

Portland Saturday Market: a local favorite.

⊙ MARKET DAY

Established in 1974, the beloved Portland Saturday Market spreads out beside the Willamette River and is the country's largest weekly open-air arts and crafts market, attracting around one million people a year. The market demands fine craftsmanship from its vendors, so potential sellers are vetted as part of a jury process before they can acquire a stall. The other criteria is that the product must be handcrafted and sold directly to customers by the person who made it. Typically, some 400 artisans hawk their wares at the market every season. Expect to see all manner of handmade goods from jewelry and clothing to watercolor paintings, pottery, and stained-glass ornaments. Food booths also dish up a variety of meals and snacks, from Indian delicacies to ice cream.

Immediately opposite is the **Portland Japanese Garden** ⊙ (611 SW Kingston Avenue; tel: 503-223 1321; www.japanese garden.org; Wed–Mon 10am–6pm), a serene oasis that begins with a steep and winding path through towering Douglas firs. At the trail top, the gardens unfold in a patchwork of ponds, bridges, rock displays, and waterfalls. An overlook grants heart-in-mouth views of Mount Hood, while the Pavilion Gallery hosts rotating exhibitions.

Kids will love the **Oregon Zoo** (4001 SW Canyon Road; tel: 503-226 1561; www.oregonzoo.org; daily 9.30pm–5.30pm), whose 64-acre (26-hectare) grounds provide a habitat for some 215 species, including Asian elephants, polar bears, American black bears, and the Black rhinoceros. Originally opened in 1888, the zoo is active in conservation efforts and has won awards for its work to reintroduce the Oregon spotted frog to its native habitat and help preserve the Oregon silverspot butterfly.

The **World Forestry Center Discovery Museum** (4033 SW Canyon Road, tel: 503-2281367; www.worldforestry. org; Wed–Sun 11am–4pm) is also well worth a visit. The wooden building blends seamlessly into its natural surroundings and is dedicated to sustainable forestry. An entire floor details the forests of the Pacific Northwest, including their management and wildlife. The museum's crown jewel sits just outside – a mammoth petrified Giant Sequoia stump, which is 5 million years old.

Once you have soaked up the formal gardens, museums, and zoo, hit the trails. **Hoyt Arboretum** (4000 SW Fairview Boulevard; tel: 503-865 8733; www.hoytarboretum.org; daily 5am–10pm) sprawls across 190 acres (80 hectares) and protects more than 2,300 species of tree and shrub. Wiggling amid the woodland are some 12 miles (19km) of hiking trails, passing through everything from magnolias and maples to bamboo and gingko trees.

Wild **Forest Park** ⊙ spools out to the north of Washington Park and is crisscrossed with around 70 miles (113km) of hiking and biking trails. You can explore the entire breadth of it with the 30-mile (48km) **Wildwood**

> ⊙ **Tip**
>
> A free shuttle services Washington Park, stopping at hotspots including the International Rose Test Garden, the Portland Japanese Garden, Oregon Zoo, and the World Forestry Center Discovery Museum. It runs year-round, every 15–30 minutes (Apr–Sept 9.30am–7pm; Oct–Mar 10am–4pm).

The 1915-founded International Rose Test Garden is home to over 10,000 roses.

⊙ BIKE TOURS

With miles of cycle lanes and ample green space, Portland is great for bikers. A guided bike tour is a top way to get to grips with the city – they range from urban excursions with themes such as food or beer to escapes into green lungs such as Washington Park. Cycle Portland Bicycle Tours (180 NW 3rd Avenue; tel: 844-739 2453; www.portlandbicycletours. com) is a frontrunner, offering a sightseeing jaunt around the Old Town and Pearl District, as well as a "foodie field trip" that delves into Portland's gourmet hotspots. Rentals are available if you would prefer to go it alone. Free guided rides around the city are typically also organized by the Portland Bureau of Transportation on select evenings during the summer months. Check www.portland. gov for details.

Trail, whose southern end begins at the **Vietnam Veterans Memorial** – look out for blue marker diamonds every quarter mile. Trail highlights include the **Pittock Mansion** (3229 NW Pittock Drive; tel: 503-823 3623; www.pittockmansion.org; Oct–May 10am–4pm; June to Labor Day until 5pm), tucked into the folds of Portland's West Hills. Finished in 1914, it was formerly the home of Henry and Georgiana Pittock, both of whom migrated west in the 1850s. Henry Pittock went on to become a wealthy magnate, best known for running the still-publishing newspaper *The Oregonian*. The elegant abode is built in a French Renaissance style, with rounded turrets and a tangle of sumptuous quarters, including a music room and a library. Self-guided tours are available and interpretive panels are dotted throughout the space, which is filled with heirlooms such as the Pittocks' own Steinway grand piano. More views of Downtown Portland and the Cascades await in the grounds. Another jewel hidden within Forest Park is the **Witch's Castle** or

Witch's Castle, a former restroom on the Macleay Park Trail.

Stone House. Though it looks like the crumbling remains of an enchantress's cabin, it's in fact the ruins of a former restroom. You can find it about one mile into the **Macleay Park Trail**.

A stone's throw from Forest Park is the well-heeled **Nob Hill** neighborhood. Quaint and charming, the district is characterized by Victorian-era buildings, which are filled with independent shops, art galleries, and sophisticated restaurants. Duck into the **Russo Lee Gallery** (805 NW 21st Avenue; tel: 503-226 2754; www.russoleegallery.com; Tue–Fri 11am–5.30pm) to see prints, tapestries, and paintings by Northwest artists, and don't miss the **New Renaissance Bookshop** (1338 NW 23rd Avenue; tel: 503-224 4929; www.newrenbooks.com; Mon, Tue, Thu, Fri 11am–5pm, Sat, Sun until 6pm), which focuses on spirituality.

MISSISSIPPI

Located in North Portland, **North Mississippi Avenue** is one of the most happening drags in the city. It's a mishmash of cool independent stores,

global restaurants, breweries, food carts, and buzzing nightspots.

Kick things off at **Blue Star Donuts** (3753 N Mississippi Avenue; tel: 971-254 4575; www.bluestardonuts.com; daily 7.30am–5pm) for a breakfast of French brioche-style donuts and coffee (the buttermilk old-fashioned flavor is a winner). Espresso joint **Albina Press** is another solid bet for a morning wake-up call. Walk a few minutes north of Blue Star and you will come to the progressive **Ori Gallery** (4038 N Mississippi Avenue; www.oriartgallery.org), which features changing artists in residence and serves as a platform for typically marginalized creators, focusing on works by trans and queer artists of color.

Close by, the **Q Center** is an LGBTQ+ community center that organizes public programming and art exhibitions.

This is also a shopping hotspot. Ten minutes up the road you will find beloved **Mississippi Records** (5202 N Albina Avenue; tel: 503-282 2990; www.mississippirecords.net; daily noon–7pm), which has a huge store of blues and soul albums, plus listening stations. **Rose City Comics** (3725 N Mississippi Avenue; tel: 503-282 5484; www.rosecitycomics.com; Sun 11am–7pm, Tue until 6pm, Wed–Sat until 8pm) is another must-visit, selling comic books and graphic novels (including the team's own original creations). **Sunlan Lighting** (3901 N Mississippi Avenue; tel: 503-281 0453; Mon–Fri 8am–5.30pm, Sat 10am–5pm) is a curious stop. Even if you are not in the market for a new lightbulb, this treasure trove of colorful and retro fittings feels almost like an art gallery.

Get into the Portland spirit and dine at Prost! Marketplace, the food cart pod at **Prost!** (4237 N Mississippi Avenue; tel: 503-954 2674; www.prostportland.squarespace.com), a German-style pub with a busy patio. Choose between Asian fusion dishes, burgers, or barbecue at this popular hangout. If you would prefer a sit-down dinner, try **Lovely's Fifty Fifty** (4039 N Mississippi Avenue; tel: 503-281 4060; www.lovelys5050.com; daily 5–10pm), known for its wood-fired pizza and ice cream.

Pittock Mansion on the Wildwood Trail in Forest Park.

There are plenty of places for a sundowner. **Ecliptic Brewing** (825 North Cook Street; tel: 503-265 8002; www.eclipticbrewing.com; Sun, Tue, Wed noon–8pm Thu–Sat until 9pm) is a favored spot, known for its creative barrel-aged pours and signature hoppy Starburst IPA. From here, a 4-minute walk north on the boulevard will bring you to **StormBreaker Brewing** (832 N Beech Street; tel: 971-703 4516; www.stormbreakerbrewing.com; Sun, Mon 11am–9pm, Tue–Thu until 10pm, Fri, Sat until 11pm), whose firepit-warmed patio is always buzzing. Oenophiles should make for chic **Stem Wine Bar** (3920 N Mississippi Avenue; tel: 503-477 7164; www.stemwinebarpdx.com; Mon–Thu 5–10pm, Fri 3–10pm, Sat 1–10pm, Sun until 9pm), which offers European-style small plates alongside an impressive global wine list. Owner Wei-En offers tarot card readings, too.

Round off your night with a live music session. Intimate **Mississippi Studios** (3939 N Mississippi Avenue; tel: 503-288 3895; www.mississippistudios.com) is a crowd-pleaser. The joint is owned and operated by musicians and hosts a wide variety of acts, from country rock artists to folksy singer-songwriters. Right around the corner is **The 1905** (830 N Shaver Street; tel: 503-460 3333; www.the1905.org), whose live jazz sets pull in the locals.

ALBERTA ARTS DISTRICT

Head east of Mississippi Avenue to Portland's Northeast quadrant and the creative **Alberta Arts District ❺**. The neighborhood is a historically Black area, though discriminatory city zoning laws throughout the 1900s caused a great amount of displacement. Now, a series of historical markers details the region's Black heritage.

Centered on Alberta Street, the artsy enclave is known for its many galleries, quirky shops, and eclectic restaurants. A visit to **Tin Shed Garden Cafe** (1438 NE Alberta Street; 503-288 6966; www.tinshedgardencafe.com; Mon–Fri 8am–2pm, Sat, Sun 7am–3pm) is a failsafe way to start the day. The cheerful blue-fronted restaurant has a top-notch breakfast menu featuring egg

The vine-combed slopes of the Willamette Valley.

⊘ URBAN WINE

The Willamette Valley wine-growing region is right on Portland's doorstep, but you can taste stellar wine without even having to leave town. Sleek winery Amaterra (8150 SW Swede Hl Drive; tel: 503-961 6057; www.amaterrawines.com; Fri, Sat noon–10pm, Wed, Thu, Sun until 9pm), in the West Hills neighborhood, has a 12-acre (5-hectare) vineyard within the city's boundaries, and includes a vast glass-clad tasting room and fine restaurant overlooking the lush surroundings. Meanwhile, Hip Chicks Do Wine (4510 SE 23rd Avenue; tel: 503-234 3790; www.hipchicksdowine.com; Fri 2–6pm Sat noon–6pm Sun noon–5pm), self-dubbed as the city's oldest urban winery, makes everything from rosé to Tempranillo in Southeast Portland, between the Reed and Brooklyn districts. Another great inner-city stop is Boedecker Cellars (2621 NW 30th Avenue; tel: 503-224 5778; www.boedeckercellars.com; Thu, Sun 2–6pm, Fri until 8pm, Sat until 7pm) in the Northwest Industrial Triangle. The urban winery specializes in Pinot Noir. There are plenty of fantastic tasting rooms scattered throughout the city. Head to Battle Creek Cellars (820 NW 13th Avenue; tel: 503-902 6636; www.battlecreekcellars.com; Sun–Thu noon–7pm, Fri, Sat until 8pm) in the Pearl District to sample varietals made by expert winemaker Sarah Cabot in the Willamette Valley.

scrambles, sourdough French toast, and a breakfast burrito.

Art lovers can then spend the morning drinking in murals and gallery hopping. Begin at the **Alberta Street Gallery** (1829 NE Alberta Street, Unit B; tel: 503-954 3314; www.albertastreet gallery.com; daily 11am–7pm), an artists' collective showcasing everything from ceramics and metalwork to paintings and sculpture. Heading east along the road, you will come to **Monograph Bookwerks** (5005 NE 27th Avenue; tel: 503-284 5005; www.monographbookwerks.com; Fri, Sat 11am–5pm), which is an Aladdin's cave of vintage posters and maps, rare art books, and one-off artworks. Another couple of minutes' east and you'll find **Flight 64** (2934 NE Alberta Street B; www.flight64.org), a printmaking studio that hosts monthly exhibits.

Once you have worked up an appetite, dine at **Bole Ethiopian Restaurant** (915 NE Alberta Street; tel: 503-719 6200; Mon–Sat noon–9pm), a mainstay for classic Ethiopian dishes, including traditional wot stews. Afterwards, the electric-blue **Alberta Street Pub** (1036 NE Alberta Street; tel: 503-284 7665; www.albertastreetpub.com; Mon–Thu noon–2am, Sat, Sun 11am–2am) is a popular watering hole, featuring live music, specialty cocktails, comfort food, and a lively patio. Another great after-dark option is the **Alberta Rose Theatre** (3000 NE Alberta St; tel: 503-719-6055; www.albertarosetheatre.com) – concerts, comedy, and dance shows are on the roster at this historic venue.

SOUTHEAST PORTLAND

Several distinct and colorful neighborhoods are tucked into Portland's Southeast quadrant. Among them is **Montavilla ❶**, a one-time farming community turned quirky hub filled with indie stores. Peruse the funky handmade clothing and jewelry in boutique **Union Rose** (8029 SE Stark Street; tel: 503-287 4242; www.unionrosepdx.com; Tue–Sat 10am–6pm, Sun until 4pm), then duck your head into the **Copper Moon Vintage Mercantile** (7910 SE Stark Street; tel: 503-877 2083; www.coppermoonvintage.com; Wed–Sun noon–6pm), whose rails are crammed with

The Oregon City Municipal Elevator.

patterned shirts, denim, and badge-covered jackets. Another highlight is the **Academy Theater** (7818 SE Stark Street; tel: 503-252 0500; www.academytheaterpdx.com), a 1940s-built cinema with craft beer on tap.

Immediately south of Montavilla, you will find the **Jade District**, known for its stellar Asian restaurants. Well-loved spots include **Mojo Crepes** (8409 SE Division Street; tel: 503-208 3195; www.mojocrepes.com; daily noon–10pm), for Japanese-style crepes, hot dogs, and bubble tea.

To the west is the **Division/Clinton** ⓤ neighborhood, which draws a stylish crowd to its boutiques, watering holes, and cafés. Favorite stops include the **Clinton Street Theater** (522 SE Clinton Street; tel: 971-808 3331; www.cstpdx.com), a quirky haunt that has been screening *The Rocky Horror Picture Show* every Saturday night since the 1970s. Make time to pop into **Books with Pictures** (1401 SE Division Street; tel: 503-841 6276; www.bookswithpictures.com; Mon, Tue 10am–6pm, Wed–Sun until 7pm), a progressive comic store

on a mission to prioritize inclusion and diversity. **Nuestra Cocina** (2135 SE Division Street; tel: 503-232 2135; www.nuestracocina.com; Tue–Sat 4–9pm) is one of the standout dinner spots in the area. The restaurant focuses on traditional Mexican dishes, from achiote-marinated steak to masa cakes filled with chorizo and chile.

The hip **Jupiter NEXT** hotel (900 E Burnside Street; tel: 503-230 9200; www.jupiterhotel.com) in the Central Eastside area makes a great base and offers an alternative to a Downtown stay. It's a buzzy spot with stylish common areas, plus it serves top-notch cocktails and imaginative Mexican and Asian fusion food at plant-filled **Hey Love** downstairs.

AROUND PORTLAND

While quirky Portland has enough to keep travelers busy for weeks, there are several smaller cities in the region that are worth a trip. Less than a 30-minute drive south of Portland is **Oregon City** ❷. This city has serious historical clout: it is best known as the final stop on the

Oregon State Capitol in Salem.

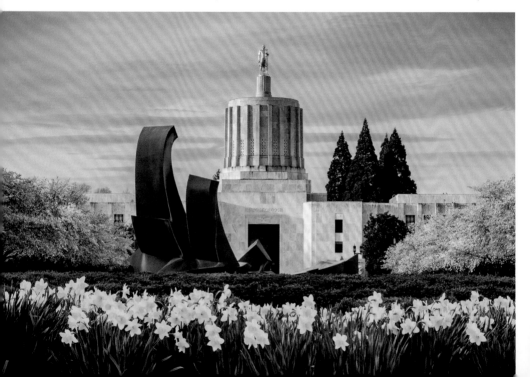

Oregon Trail and it served as the Oregon Territory's first capital. Today, the **End of the Oregon Trail Interpretive Center** (1726 Washington Street; tel: 503-657 9336; www.historicoregoncity.org; Mon–Sat 9am–5pm, Sun 10am–5pm) puts that heritage into context. The living museum brings the era to life with costumed interpreters, hands-on workshops (such as butter-making), and replica wagons, plus detailed information panels. Make time for a ride on the **Oregon City Municipal Elevator** (6 Railroad Avenue; tel: 503-496 1197; www.orcity.org; Mon, Tue 7am–7pm, Wed–Sat until 9.30pm, Sun 11am–7pm). The 1915-built contraption whisks visitors to a bluff affording fantastic views over town.

A short drive west of here, travelers will reach **Tualatin ❸**. The city is packaged into some 200 acres of green space, making it a haven for hikers and bikers – the **Tualatin River National Wildlife Refuge**, with its waterside trails and migratory birds, is right on the doorstep.

Some 15 minutes north of here (or the same distance west of Portland),

Beaverton ❹ is another worthy addition to your itinerary. It is home to the global headquarters of sports heavyweight Nike and as such, the city has a buzzy, cosmopolitan feel, with global dining options and a strong craft-beer scene.

Striking in the other direction, **Gresham ❺** is around 16 miles (26km) to the east of Portland. It is known for its fine **Japanese Garden** (124 S Main Avenue; tel: 503-969 4386; daily 6.30am–8pm) and the **Mt Hood Jazz Festival**, which celebrates the genre with local and national musicians each spring.

Farther afield, the Willamette Valley is a bucolic sliver of Central Oregon, filled with youthful university cities, historic towns, and fine wineries. State capital **Salem ❻**, home to the Oregon State Capitol, is rich with history, while **Albany ❼** is a jigsaw of architectural styles, from Italianate to Art Moderne and American Renaissance. Further south, **Eugene ❽** is one of Oregon's most happening cities, brimming with cultural centers, breweries, food halls, and indie stores.

Eugene is a cool city south of Portland.

KEEP PORTLAND WEIRD

In Portland, being "weird" is not an insult at all – instead, the city wears its quirks as a shiny badge of honor and has all manner of oddities for the visitor to discover.

Portland is undoubtedly weird. Revel in the city's wonderfully whacky nature by embarking on a whistlestop tour of all its curiosities. One of the must-visit photo stops is a bright Old Town Chinatown mural that shouts the motto "Keep Portland Weird" in towering yellow letters. Another offbeat hotspot is the Freakybuttrue Peculiarium (2234 NW Thurman Street; tel: 503-227 3164; www.peculiarium.com; Thu–Tue 11am–7pm), which houses a world of curios, from a giant Bigfoot statue to insect-infused cookies at the gift shop.

The weirdness continues with Portland's nightlife – there's everything from the Funhouse Lounge (2432 SE 11th Avenue; tel: 503-841 6734; www.funhouselounge.com), a wild theater with a clown room and a roster of karaoke and improv comedy shows, to the Wyrd Leatherworks and Meadery (4515 SE 41st Avenue; tel: 503-305 6025; www.wyrdleatherandmead.com), a fantastical medieval-themed spot that brews its own honey mead.

You can also swing by what is billed as the smallest 'park' in the world: the unbelievably dinky 452-sq-inch Mill Ends Park consists of a single scrubby tree and a miniscule circle of shrubbery on the median strip along SW Naito Parkway.

The iconic Keep Portland Weird sign in Old Town Chinatown is a must-stop on the weird and wonderful tour of the city.

The Freakybuttrue Peculiarium is crammed with curios and offers unusual experiences like photos with aliens.

Mill Ends Park, a single tree surrounded by a ring of shrubbery on SW Naito Parkway's median strip, is dubbed the smallest 'park' in the world.

Hawthorn Street Fair is a riot of food, art and shopping.

Quirky festivals

Offbeat attractions aside, the Portland region has a whole slew of unexpected and wonderfully weird festivals. For starters, there's the Portland World Naked Bike Ride, which sees thousands of people cycle through the city in their birthday suit come summertime. The stripped-bare ride in fact doubles as a peaceful protest against the world's dependence on oil and you can even rock up on a scooter, skateboard, or rollerblades.

If you prefer culture with your clothes on, Portland's Hawthorne Street Fair sees over 200 local businesses opening their doors against a backdrop of street vendors, food, music and entertainment. The event runs in a car-free zone from SE Cesar Chavez to SE 30th Avenue on Hawthorne.

Also on the curiosity calendar is the Portland Adult Soapbox Derby at Mount Tabor, which takes place in August. Imaginative teams assemble whimsical vehicles, which are then raced down the hulking cinder cone in the city's southeast. Expect wacky creations and loud, proud costumes. Another eccentric event worth the trip is the West Coast Giant Pumpkin Regatta, which unfolds in nearby Tualatin. Brave folks take to the waters of Tualatin Commons lake and race one another in enormous gourds each fall.

Race across a lake in a giant gourd, anyone? Only in Portland (at The West Coast Giant Pumpkin Regatta).

The Portland Adult Soapbox Derby sees all manner of whimsical vehicles race down Mount Tabor.

Odd sculptures and art abound in Portland, the undisputed champion of the weird and whacky.

WILLAMETTE VALLEY

A mecca for foodies, oenophiles, and outdoorsy types, this bucolic river valley cuts a fine figure between two of Oregon's major mountain ranges.

Parceled up between the rugged Coast and Cascade mountains, the Willamette Valley swoops 241km (150 miles) from the Columbia River southward to the Calapooya Mountains. It is no exaggeration to say that this bucolic slice of Oregon caters to every traveler. Hiking and biking trails beat into groves of towering Douglas firs; small towns are filled with listed buildings and curio shops; and university cities harbor fizzing live music, art, and craft-beer scenes.

Most of all, though, the valley is a gourmand's delight. Fertile silt laid down by ancient floods has created some of the best soils for growing in the country – the region is known for producing hordes of juicy fruits, hazelnuts, and hops that are conjured into tempting dishes and craft beers by imaginative chefs and brewers.

Willamette Valley is also one of the finest wine regions in the nation, celebrated for its Pinot Noir and Chardonnay, though inventive producers continue to push boundaries.

NORTH VALLEY

Strike out from Portland on Oregon Route 99W and you will eventually enter the northern portion of the Willamette Valley. Soon, lush vineyards begin to appear in pockets on either side of the road, and signs announcing

wineries invite drivers to turn down country lanes. The leafy city of **Newberg ❶** makes a wonderful gateway to the valley's 700-plus wineries. You would be hard pushed to find a bad spot to swill a glass of wine here, but **Rex Hill** (30835 OR-99W; tel: 503-538 0666; www.rexhill.com; daily 10.45am– 5pm; by appointment only), which has a focus on sustainability, is a frontrunner. Come by to sample the flagship Pinot Noir in the sleek tasting room, or take a behind-the-scenes tour, followed by a wine flight. The pint-sized

Main attractions

Oregon State Capitol
Silver Falls State Park
Brownsville
Eugene
King Estate Winery
Cottage Grove
  covered bridges
West Cascades
  Scenic Byway

Maps on pages 120, 122

Willamette Valley is a fine wine region.

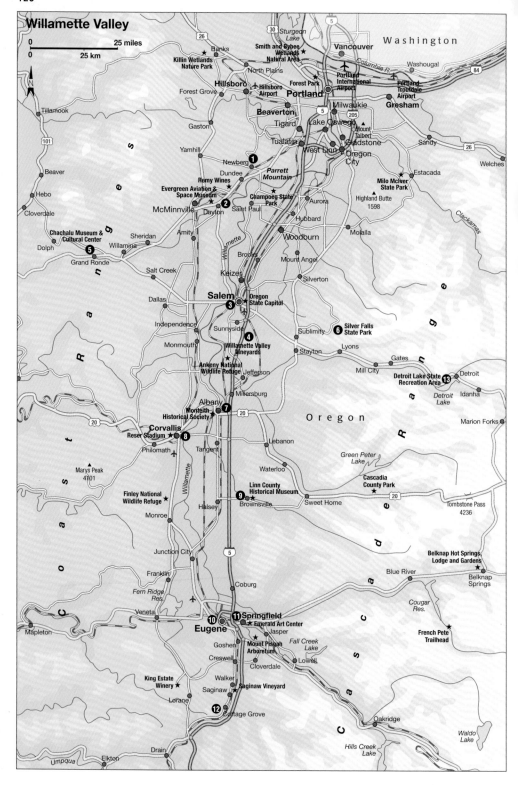

Willamette Valley

0 ————— 25 miles
0 ————— 25 km

Washington

Columbia R.

Oregon

Tillamook
101
Hebo
Cloverdale
Beaver

Banks
30 Sturgeon Lake
Smith and Bybee Wetlands Natural Area
Killin Wetlands Nature Park
North Plains
Forest Park
Vancouver
Washougal
Portland International Airport
Portland Troutdale Airport

Hillsboro
Forest Grove
Hillsboro Airport
Portland
Beaverton
Tigard
Milwaukie
Lake Oswego
Gresham
Sandy
Welches

Gaston
Yamhill
Tualatin
West Linn
Gladstone
Oregon City
Mount Talbert
26

Newberg ❶
Parrett Mountain
Dundee
Remy Wines
Evergreen Aviation & Space Museum
❷
McMinnville
Dayton
Saint Paul
Champoeg State Park
Aurora
Hubbard
Molalla

Milo McIver State Park
Estacada
Highland Butte 1598
Clackamas

Chachalu Museum & Cultural Center
❺
Willamina
Sheridan
Dolph
Grand Ronde
Amity
Willamette
Woodburn
Brooks
Mount Angel

Salt Creek
Keizer
Silverton

Dallas
Salem ❸
Oregon State Capitol
Sublimity
Silver Falls State Park ❻

Independence
Sunnyside
❹
Willamette Valley Vineyards
Ankeny National Wildlife Refuge
Lyons
Gates
Detroit Lake State Recreation Area ⓭
Detroit

Monmouth
Stayton
Mill City
Idanha
Detroit Lake

Jefferson
Millersburg
Marion Forks

Albany ❼
Monteith Historical Society
20

Corvallis
Reser Stadium ❽
Philomath
Tangent
Lebanon
Green Peter Lake
Cascadia County Park

Marys Peak 4101
Waterloo
20

Finley National Wildlife Refuge
Linn County Historical Museum
❾
Halsey
Brownsville
Sweet Home
Tombstone Pass 4236

Monroe
Willamette
5

Junction City
Coburg
Blue River
Belknap Hot Springs, Lodge and Gardens

Franklin
Fern Ridge Res.
Belknap Springs
Cougar Res.

Veneta
Eugene ❿
⓫ **Springfield**
Emerald Art Center
Jasper

Mapleton
Eugene
Mount Pisgah Arboretum
Goshen
Fall Creek Lake
Lowell
French Pete Trailhead

Creswell
Cloverdale

King Estate Winery
Walker
Saginaw Vineyard
Saginaw

Lorane
⓬ Cottage Grove
Oakridge
Waldo Lake

Drain
Hills Creek Lake

Umpqua
Elkton

town punches above its weight when it comes to restaurants, too. **The Painted Lady** (201 S College Street; tel: 503-538 3850; www.thepaintedladyrestaurant. com; Thu–Sat 5–10pm) is a fabulous special-occasion spot. It serves a seasonal and contemporary tasting menu, alongside an impressive selection of Oregon wine.

Push south and the next worthwhile stop is **Dayton ❷**. Here, the funky **Vintages Trailer Resort** (16205 SE Kreder Road; tel: 971-267 2130; www.thevintages.com) offers accommodations in retro Airstreams with creature comforts such as grills and soaking tubs, plus bicycles for your use. A must-visit winery in the Dundee Hills AVA (one of the valley's sub-AVAs) is **Remy Wines** (17495 NE McDougall Road; tel: 503-864 8777; www.remywines.com), run by lesbian winemaker Remy Drabkin – the founder of Queer Wine Fest, which is held in Dayton and tipped as a world first. The focus here is Italian-style varietals, including Lagrein and Dolcetto, and the charming tasting room is set in an old farmhouse.

Nearby, **Sokol Blosser** (5000 NE Sokol Blosser Lane; tel: 503-864 2282; www.sokolblosser.com; daily 10am–4pm) was the first winery in the country to achieve LEED certification.

Continuing southwest, drivers will eventually reach the town of **McMinnville**, a gateway to yet more fine wine and home of the family-friendly **Evergreen Aviation & Space Museum** (500 NE Captain Michael King Smith Way; tel: 503-434 4180; www.evergreen museum.org; daily 9am–5pm). Here, popular exhibits include the world's largest wooden airplane – known as the *Spruce Goose* – plus a launch system used in NASA's important Gemini program, which explored human spaceflight in the 1960s.

SALEM AND MID-WILLAMETTE VALLEY

Drivers can expect a scenic ride through yet more wine country and farmland to reach state capital **Salem ❸**. The city was founded in 1842 and became the territorial capital in 1851 (taking over from Oregon City), before

⊘ Tip

Big and little kids alike will love McMinnville's springtime UFO Fest (www.ufofest.com), which includes costume contests, concerts, fun runs, and a mini science-fiction film festival. The event also draws expert speakers from across the country.

South Falls in the Silver Falls State Park.

⊘ TRAIL OF TEN FALLS

You can take in the best of the Silver Falls State Park by striking out on the looping 12km (7.2-mile) Trail of Ten Falls. This route, as its name suggests, wends its way past a series of majestic cascades, including the famous 177ft (54-meter) South Falls (you will walk right behind this curtain of water). Craggy canyons, thick woodland, and a rippling creek add to the natural drama in this beautiful pocket of Oregon. This popular route forms part of over 56km (35 miles) of backcountry trails, which are shared by hikers, bikers, and horseback riders (along with elusive wildlife such as black bears). If you want to stay overnight in the park, the campground has both tent and RV sites, plus a handful of cabins. There is also a horse camp for riders.

statehood was eventually established in 1859. That means there is plenty to keep history buffs busy in the city today. The **Oregon State Capitol** (900 Court Street NE; www.oregoncapitol.com; Mon–Fri 8am–5pm) is a good place to begin. Built in the 1930s, it is a bold Modernist Art Deco confection covered in glittering white Vermont marble, and its striking ridged cupola is topped with the gold "Oregon Pioneer" statue. Tours of the building are free, and there are impressive views over the city and (on a clear day) out to Mount Hood if you climb the 121 stairs within the dome.

From the State Capitol, it is a 10-minute walk southeast to the **Willamette Heritage Center** (1313 Mill Street SE; tel: 503-585 7012; www.willametteheritage.org; Tue–Sat 10am–4pm). Mid-Willamette Valley history is explored across a campus of 14 buildings, including the 1841 Jason Lee House and Methodist Parsonage, considered to be the oldest standing wooden-frame house in the Pacific Northwest. The region's industrial heritage is traced at the 1896-built Thomas Kay Woolen Mill, once a major textile factory. Changing special exhibits also explore themes such as Chinese heritage in the area and winemaking.

Another 10-minute walk southward and you will reach the charming **Deepwood Museum & Gardens** (1116 Mission St SE; tel: 503-363 1825; www.deepwoodmuseum.org; tours Wed–Sat 9am, 10am, 11am, noon). Known for its impressive stained-glass windows and pretty turret, the Queen Anne Victorian mansion was built in the 1890s. Guided tours explore interiors filled with period fittings and furnishings. The 4.5-acre (1.8-hectare) grounds are beautifully laid out and include a Chinese garden.

After your historical deep dive, there are plenty of spots for a bite to eat. **Xicha Brewing** (576 Patterson Street NW, Suite 140; tel: 503-990 8292; www.xichabrewing.com; Tue–Sat 11am–9pm, Sun until 7pm) is well worth the trip west of the center (there is also a location to the north of the city center, and

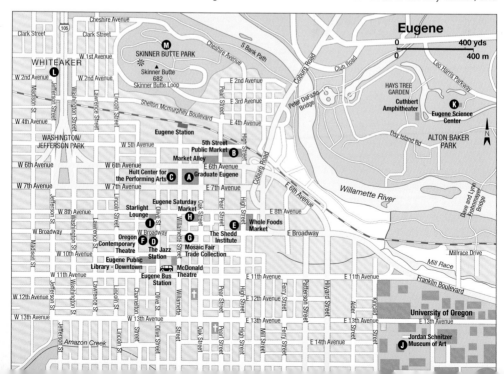

one in Eugene). The Latin brewery makes Mexican-style lagers and fruity sours, alongside a menu of tacos, empanadas, and Latin-inspired small plates. If you want to stay Downtown – and if you can't decide what's for dinner – opt for **Fork Forty Food Hall** (440 State Street; www.forkforty.com; Mon–Sat 11am–9pm, Sun until 3pm). The venue includes local favorite Slick Licks ice cream, alongside vendors selling bao, pizza, ramen, and more.

About 15 minutes south of the city (and right off I-5), the **Willamette Valley Vineyards** ❹ (8800 Enchanted Way SE; tel: 503-588 9463; www.wvv.com; estate tasting room: Sat–Thu 11am–6pm, Fri until 8pm) is one of the key wineries in the region, known for its stellar Pinot Noir. Try a glass in the tasting room overlooking the vine-combed landscapes. There is a patio and a 65ft (20-meter) viewing tower, too.

Meanwhile, the **Chachalu Museum and Cultural Center** ❺ (8720 Grand Ronde Road; tel: 503-879 2226; www.grandronde.org; Tue–Sat 10am–4pm) is worth the 48km (30-mile) trip west of Salem. The center is dedicated to telling the stories of the Confederated Tribes of the Grand Ronde Community of Oregon, a federally recognized coalition of tribes based in the foothills of the Coast Range. The reservation groups together Indigenous peoples whose homelands once spread across western Oregon and into southwest Washington and northern California. Exhibits cover tribal traditions and honor Indigenous elders and the sacred natural world. The Native American-owned **Spirit Mountain Casino and Lodge** (27100 Salmon River Highway; tel: 503-879 3764; www.spiritmountain.com) is also nearby, offering rustic-luxe accommodations and a giant gaming area. The cozy lobby has a giant stone fireplace and wildlife-inspired artworks.

Held up as one of Oregon's finest natural wonders (and there are a great many to choose from), **Silver Falls State Park** ❻ is located around a 30-minute drive southeast of Salem. OR-214 offers a scenic drive out, wriggling past Douglas firs, manicured

State capital Salem.

WILLAMETTE VALLEY WINE

With roots in the 1960s, the Willamette Valley wine region has blossomed from a young viticultural industry of just five winemakers to an established AVA peppered with 700-plus wineries.

The valley got its start as a wine region back in the 1960s, when winemaker David Lett – convinced that the temperate region offered perfect conditions for Pinot Noir and other cool-weather grapes – planted vines here. The Eyrie Vineyards, which Lett began all those years ago, are still thriving.

Willamette Valley is home to 700-plus wineries.

By the 1970s, the valley had five wineries, and that number would surge as the quality of the region's products was confirmed in blind tastings. Twenty years on, 70 wineries called Willamette Valley home. Over the decades that followed, the region's tourist offering would mushroom, with wine tours, luxury hotels, and tasting rooms popping up across the valley.

Today, the Pinot Noir-washed valley is home to more than 700 wineries, ranging from small family-run operations to mammoth estates producing hundreds of thousands of cases a year. The larger Willamette Valley now envelops eleven sub-AVAs: they include the Tualatin Hills, the Dundee Hills, the Chehalem Mountains, McMinnville, and Yamhill-Carlton. These smaller AVAs reflect subtle shifts in soil, elevation, and climate, making them distinct from one another, though they share common characteristics. For example, the Tualatin Hills, in the region's northwest, has a very high concentration of volcanic and fertile Laurelwood soil, a product of the ancient Missoula floods.

Meanwhile, the undulating peaks, and resulting elevation changes, of the Chehalem Mountains mean that this AVA is mostly characterized by its sheer diversity. The mountains also shelter the vines from cool winds. Pinot Noir still reigns supreme across the region, closely followed by Chardonnay, but you will also find many varieties such as Pinot Gris, Riesling, Sauvignon blanc, and Syrah.

Endless operators organize tours within the Willamette Valley, from casual bike excursions to luxurious chauffeured trips including fine dining. Good options include Sea to Summit's Willamette Valley Wine Tour (www.seatosummit.net), which explores the northern corner of the valley on easy jaunts from Portland. Wildwood Adventures (www.wildwoodtours.com) is another great option in the Portland area. Also highly commended is Embrace Oregon Tours (www.embraceoregon.com), based out of McMinnville and focused on small-group and private tours. Red Barn Rides' Combo Ride and Wine Tour (www.redbarnrides.com) is another winner. The trip involves a combination of cycling and bus rides as you travel between vineyards.

crop fields, and neat farmhouses. Once you arrive, the park envelopes 9,200 breathtaking acres (3,720 hectares) in the foothills of the Cascade Mountains and is named for the dazzling waterfalls that are sheltered within.

More historic treasures await in **Albany ❼**, which is well known for its wonderfully preserved architecture. The **Downtown Historic District** has a glorious mishmash of styles, dating from the mid-19th century – they include Queen Anne, Italianate, Art Moderne, and American Renaissance. In addition to the Downtown area, there are two other designated Historic Districts – **Monteith** and **Hackleman** – each as rich in centuries-old buildings as the next.

The **Monteith House** (518 SW 2nd Avenue; tel: 541-220 0421; www.monteithhouse.org; Sat 11am–3pm) – a restored 1849 colonial-era home – is a standout. It was the first frame house built in the city and now serves as a museum telling the story of the brothers (Thomas and Walter Monteith) who built and lived in it.

There is a different vibe in **Corvallis ❽** altogether, which is home to Oregon State University.

Catching one of the university's Oregon State Beavers football games is a fun introduction to the student-filled city – the team plays at **Reser Stadium** (660 SW 26th Street; tel: 541-737 2547; www.osubeavers.com). The city is also a fantastic jumping-off point for some regional hikes. Try the trek up **Marys Peak**, the highest point in Oregon's Coast Range at 4,097ft (1,249 meters). The most popular route is the 1.6km (1-mile) -long Summit Trail – from the top you will have sweeping views over the Willamette Valley and the Cascades (including Mount Hood and the Three Sisters).

Particularly if you end up traveling south on I-5, the little town of **Brownsville ❾** is a must-visit, with its quaint, stuck-in-time feel and its hodgepodge of antiques stores and small galleries. Stop in at the excellent **Linn County Historical Museum** (101 Park Avenue; tel: 541-466 3390; www.linnparks.com/museums/linn-county-historical-museum), which extends back much farther and holds

⊙ Where

Time your trip for Albany's Summer Homes Tour, held each year at the end of July. The self-guided events allow curious visitors inside a number of the city's 19th- and early 20th-century buildings. Past events have included transportation via horse-drawn carriage or trolley between the properties.

Oregon State University is based in Corvallis.

many more treasures than the exterior would suggest. The museum houses displays on the lifeways of the Kalapuya people; a recreation of a 19th-century Main Street featuring a barbershop and general store; and an authentic covered Oregon Trail wagon, used in 1865. **Randy's Main Street Coffee** (240 N Main Street; tel: 541-466 3900; www.facebook. com/randysmainstreetcoffee; Mon–Sat 7am–3pm) is a solid lunch option, offering sandwiches and soups.

A SCENIC DETOUR

Before continuing southward, make a detour on the **Over the Rivers & Through the Woods Scenic Byway** to take in some of the Willamette Valley's most gorgeous scenery. Striking out from Brownsville, the 106km (66-mile) road ripples through the Willamette Valley, opening out into the West Cascade Mountains.

As you push along OR-228, you are greeted with quaint towns such as **Crawfordsville**, with its pretty white covered bridge, and **Sweet Home**, known as a prime site for fossils. A star stop along the way is **Cascadia County Park** (48241 Cascadia Drive; tel: 800-551 6949; www.linnparks.com/parks/cascadia-state-park).

Formerly a state park, it sits at the confluence of Soda Creek and the South Santiam River, a historically important meeting spot for Indigenous tribes. Trails trace the river into old-growth forest and push toward wonders such as Soda Creek Falls, a curtain of water swaddled by fir, hemlock, and cedar trees. There are also RV and tent campgrounds.

As you continue along the byway, you will follow in the footsteps of historic travelers, who used the route to make their way toward gold-rush towns in Eastern Oregon and beyond. The road continues to wow as it snakes into the Willamette National Forest and eventually through the **Menagerie Wilderness**, known for its spiking rock formations, which attract professional climbers.

Another star of the route is the ominously named **Tombstone Pass**, which soars to 4,236ft (1,291 meters). Here,

The Oregon State Beavers play at Reser Stadium in Corvallis.

you will find the Tombstone Pass/Cone Peak Trailhead, which provides access to the gentle 2km (1.4-mile) **Tombstone Nature Trail**, whose meadows are bright with wildflowers in spring. The longer and more challenging **Cone Peak Trail** offers sweeping views over the Cascades.

EUGENE

Eugene ⑩, a hip city laced along the Willamette River, takes its name from Eugene Skinner, an early non-Indigenous settler who arrived in the region in 1846. This is the homeland of the Kalapuya people, who advised Skinner, born in New York State, to build his humble log cabin on high ground to protect it from flooding.

The city of Eugene was laid out a few years later, in the 1850s, and it mushroomed over the following decades, with the development of the railroad, and the establishment of the University of Oregon in 1876.

Now, second in size only to Portland, Eugene is one of the state's most happening cities. It has a thriving arts and culture scene, and a youthful vibe nurtured by its student population. This is also where mega sports brand Nike was founded, and that legacy is still alive in the city. It has world-class track and field facilities and was host to the World Athletics Championships in 2022.

Eugene's compact Downtown punches above its weight when it comes to cultural attractions, boutique shopping, and breweries. **Graduate Eugene** Ⓐ (66 E 6th Avenue; tel: 541-342 2000; www.graduatehotels.com) makes a great base for exploring. Shelves of vintage Nikes are built into the front desk, while in-room touches include desk lamps in the shape of waffle irons – Nike co-founder Bill Bowerman (see page 129) used a waffle iron to make soles when experimenting with early prototypes of the sneaker.

From here, it's a short walk to **5th Street Public Market** Ⓑ (296 E 5th Avenue; tel: 541-484 0383; www.5stmarket.com), which is packed with boutique clothing and jewelry stores, independent restaurants, and watering holes. The courtyard, with its elegant red-brick fountain, is a pleasant place to linger, while **Provisions Market Hall** (296 E 5th Ave; tel: 541-606 4563; www.provisionsmarkethall.com; daily 8am–7pm) is a foodie highlight. The speciality European-style grocer and deli shows off a bounty of Willamette Valley produce, with cheese, charcuterie, wood-fired pizza, and pastries.

There's a huddle of great live entertainment venues in the Downtown area. A short walk from the market is **Hult Center for the Performing Arts** Ⓒ (1 Eugene Center; tel: 541-682 5000; www.hultcenter.org), which hosts diverse dance and music shows. It's a treat for architecture buffs, too: the building rises in a series of glass-clad triangles, while the venue's **Silva Concert Hall** has undulating balconies and a ceiling inspired by weaved baskets. A few blocks south is **The Jazz Station** Ⓓ (124 W Broadway; tel: 458-205 1030;

Red poppies carpet the Willamette Valley.

⊘ Tip

Oakway Center (2350 Oakmont Way; tel: 541-485 4711; www.oakwaycenter. com) is Eugene's shopping hub, representing big-name brands and laid-back, family-friendly restaurants (plus Oregon favorites such as ice-cream parlor Salt & Straw).

www.thejazzstation.org). As its name suggests, the focus here is jazz, and you can catch live quartets, soloists, and jam sessions at the intimate venue. Also nearby is **The Shedd Institute** ⓔ (868 High Street; tel: 541-434 7000; www.theshedd.org), which hosts everything from orchestral performances to jazz ensembles. The **Oregon Contemporary Theatre** ⓕ (194 W Broadway; tel: 541-465 1506; www.octheatre.org) is well loved, too, known for its inventive plays with themes intended to challenge spectators.

Eugene is fiercely proud of its many independent shops. Jewels include the **Mosaic Fair Trade Collection** ⓖ (28 E Broadway; tel: 541-344 4000; www. mosaicfairtrade.com; Wed–Sat 11am–5.30pm, Sun, Tue until 4pm), which is stuffed full of colorful ornaments and home furnishings, jewelry, and accessories. You can also pick up one-off items at the **Eugene Saturday Market** ⓗ (126 E 8th Avenue and Oak Street; www.eugenesaturdaymarket.org; Apr to mid-Nov Sat 10am–4pm; holiday market Thanksgiving through Christmas

Eve). Artisans descend on Eugene's Downtown area, manning stands selling everything from watercolor paintings and macrame to crystals, wood carvings, and ceramics.

The high concentration of bars in Eugene's Downtown area has earned it the nickname "Barmuda Triangle." Get lost on a bar crawl joining up some local favorites, including the **Starlight Lounge** ⓘ (830 Olive Street; tel: 541-343 3204; www.starlightlounge. com; daily 4pm–2.30am), which is known for its happy-hour cocktails, pool room, and patio.

Just east of Eugene's Downtown core, the **Jordan Schnitzer Museum of Art** ⓙ (1430 Johnson Lane; tel: 541-346 3027; www.jsma.uoregon. edu; Wed 11am–8pm, Thu–Sun until 5pm) is the University of Oregon's art museum, opened in 1933. The original 3,000-object-strong collection mostly included Chinese and Japanese art objects, and Asian pieces still comprise a large proportion of the displays here. There is now also an impressive store of work by 20th- and 21st-century American artists, including Sally Haley, who spent her formative years in Portland, and Northwest School painter Morris Graves. Across the Willamette River, the **Eugene Science Center** ⓚ (2300 Leo Harris Parkway; tel: 541-682 7888; www.eugenesciencecenter.org; Tue–Thu, Sat, Sun 10am–5pm, Fri until 7pm) makes a great day out for families. Highlights include an alfresco solar system trail and a planetarium, plus exhibits on mechanics, fossils, and human biology.

Northwest of the center of town, **Whiteaker** ⓛ is the coolest and most bohemian neighborhood in the city, characterized by artisanal coffee shops, breweries and distilleries, and colorful houses and storefronts. Don't miss a trip to the **Ninkasi Better Living Room** (155 Blair Boulevard; tel: 541-735 9500; www.ninkasibrewing.com/ eugene; Tue–Thu noon–9pm, Fri, Sat

Cottage Grove: the "Covered Bridge Capital of the West."

until 10pm, Sun until 6pm), housed in a huge electric-blue building. The beloved brewery is a local stalwart, having been in the same location since 2007, and its signature menu includes a selection of imaginative IPAs, plus a popular pilsner and oatmeal stout. There is a giant rocket hanging inside: a reminder of a mission that saw Ninkasi send live yeast to space, then brew beer with it when it came back to Earth. The **Heritage Distilling Company** (10 Madison Street; tel: 541-357 4431; www.heritagedistilling.com; Mon–Thu noon–7pm, Sat 11am–8pm, Sun until 7pm) is another revered maker in the area. The brand offers imaginative concoctions such as "cacao bomb" whiskey, huckleberry, and sweet-ghost-pepper vodka, and corn-based gin, and you can come by to try a changing menu of specialty cocktails, plus tasting flights.

Immediately to the east (and just north of Downtown) is **Skinner Butte Park** Ⓜ (248 Cheshire Avenue; tel: 541-682 4800; www.eugene-or.gov), dedicated in 1914 and named for city founder Eugene Skinner. It opens out by the Willamette River and affords fabulous views over the city from its lofty perch. Highlights include rock climbing at an abandoned basalt quarry (known as the Columns), plus hiking trails and meadowed picnic areas. On the outskirts of the park is the eye-catching **Shelton McMurphey Johnson House** (303 Willamette Street; tel: 541-484 0808; www.smjhouse.org; Tue–Fri 10am–1pm, Sat, Sun 1–4pm), a Victorian mansion in a popping shade of turquoise that is now open as a museum.

SOUTH VALLEY

Immediately east of Eugene, quaint **Springfield** ⑪ has an altogether different vibe to its buzzy sister. It is famed as the inspiration for the setting of long-running cartoon TV series *The Simpsons*, whose creator Matt Groening was born in Portland. A giant mural featuring the beloved fictional family is emblazoned on the side of the **Emerald Art Center** (500 Main Street; tel: 541-726 8595; www.emeraldartcenter.org; Tue–Sat 11am–4pm), which also

Eugene embraces its rich sporting heritage.

Ⓞ TRACKTOWN USA

Eugene gained its TrackTown USA nickname in the 1960s when University of Oregon (UO) track-and-field coach Bill Bowerman and UO alum Phil Knight founded Nike, then Blue Ribbon Sports. Bowerman was a pioneer of the "waffle" sole on sneakers, which he tested out using a real waffle iron. Nike mushroomed over the decades and, though its headquarters are now in Beaverton (161km/100 miles to the north), the legacy of the iconic sport brand lives on in Eugene. Today, Eugene remains a leader in track and field athletics, even hosting the 2022 USA Outdoor Track and Field Championships at Hayward Field (named for coach Bill Hayward who nurtured many an Olympic champion at the UO). You'll find sneakers and sport memorabilia filling cafés, bars, and hotels all across town in honor of its heritage.

⊘ Tip

Explore the region with Best Oregon Tours (25330 Rice Road; tel: 503-572 5323; www.bestoregontours. com), which offers excursions into Willamette Valley wine country, plus history tours that join up the region's string of quaint covered bridges.

features works by local artists and has open studios on a Friday. Beyond the animated sitcom characters, Springfield has a plethora of treasure-filled antiques stores, a popular year-round farmers' market, and the **Washburne Historic District**, a collection of listed workers' homes built between the 1890s and 1940s. It is also worth venturing out to **Dorris Ranch** (205 Dorris Street; tel: 541-736 4544; www.willama lane.org/dorris_ranch; daily 6am–10pm), a living history farm and hazelnut orchard that has been operating for more than 100 years.

Around a 25-minute drive southwest of Eugene and Springfield, the vast and family-operated **King Estate Winery** (80854 Territorial Highway; tel: 541-685 5189; www.kingestate.com) is acclaimed for its Pinot Noir and Pinot Gris. It is also the biggest biodynamic-certified vineyard in North America. Tastings are available, and there is a restaurant serving seafood plates and elevated Contemporary American dishes.

Your next stop will be **Cottage Grove** ⓬, a cute-as-a-button town dotted with cafés and bookstores, and featuring a giant mural in homage to silent movie *The General* (1920), which was filmed here. It is also surrounded by biking trails: from here, the **Row River National Recreation Trail** ribbons out for 26km (16 miles), tracing an abandoned railroad line through forests and over covered bridges. A short drive from the center of town is the **Saginaw Vineyard** (80247 Delight Valley School Road; tel: 541-942 1364; www.saginaw vineyard.com; Sat–Thu 11am–5pm, Fri until 9pm). The winery features a charming tasting room housed in a red barn and hosts live music nights each Friday.

ADVENTURES ON THE WEST CASCADES SCENIC BYWAY

Road trips through the Willamette Valley provide ample opportunity for recreation, and the 346km (215-mile) **West Cascades Scenic Byway** (traveling on OR-22, FR-11, OR-126, and FR-19) serves some of the region's best outdoor adventures on a silver platter. Heading north, the byway

Shelton McMurphey Johnson House, a mansion turned museum in Eugene.

spools into Mount Hood territory, but the town of Detroit makes a great starting point for a Willamette Valley odyssey heading south. The picturesque drive beats through gangling fir forests and alongside rushing rivers, connecting trails and put-in points for activities on lakes and rivers. Spend some time at the **Detroit Lake State Recreation Area ⓭** (tel: 800-551 6949; www.stateparks.oregon.gov), which affords fabulous views of the Cascades' Mount Jefferson (the second-highest peak in the state), plus a vast campground and spots for wild swimming. From here, the byway continues a wiggling route south, slicing into the Willamette National Forest and hugging the Santiam River and, later, the Quartzville and Upper McKenzie rivers. If possible, carve out some time to spend at **Belknap Hot Springs** (59296 Belknap Hot Springs Road; tel: 541-822 3961; www.belknaphotsprings.com), a charming (and little-known) mineral-springs spa that features two swimming pools. Cabins, lodge rooms, RV sites, and tent pitches are available here.

Onward, the route pushes farther south, and it is worth finding the trailhead for the **Delta Old Growth Nature Trail** (located in the Willamette National Forest, at the west end of Delta Campground). The short 0.8km (0.5-mile) route plunges walkers into a jaw-dropping tract of towering old-growth Douglas firs, passing babbling creeks rushing off the McKenzie River. Afterward, continue south on Forest Service Road 19, past the popping blue Cougar Reservoir.

Along the way, you can park up and strike out into **Three Sisters Wilderness** (tel: 541-822 3381; www.fs.usda.gov), a 280,000-plus-acre (114,000-hectare) expanse that's part of the Willamette National Forest and crisscrossed with trails. These include the moderately challenging, roughly 14km (9-mile) **French Pete Trail**, which strikes along the French Pete creek and into a world of old growth firs, cedar, and maple trees.

Eventually, the byway curls toward **Oakridge**, which is loved by mountain bikers for its network of epic single-track trails.

Detroit Lake.

⊘ BUILDING BRIDGES

Cottage Grove has earned a reputation as the "Covered Bridge Capital of the West." There are six of the charming structures scattered across the small town, while Lane County boasts 20 in total (it has the highest concentration of any county west of the Mississippi). Early covered bridges were typically built by hand, and luckily, the region had a bounty of available timber. The bridges were covered to protect them from the elements: sea air and sometimes-heavy rain. Among the most significant are Mosby Creek Covered Bridge, a 90ft (27-meter) edifice from 1920 (the oldest in the county), and the 1925-built Chambers Railroad Covered Bridge, the only remaining covered railroad bridge in the state. You can check them out with a ride on the Covered Bridges Scenic Bikeway.

Ecola State Park.

OREGON COAST

Oregon's seaboard, revealed by the Pacific Coast Scenic Byway, is one of the nation's most dramatic. A road trip promises hikes on plunging clifftops, plus seafood feasts and Steller sea lions.

The Oregon Coast unfolds for 363 miles (584km), in a saga of lighthouse-crowned crags, trail-laced maritime forests, and quaint fishing towns. It was already richly populated when Euro-American settlers arrived: many distinct Indigenous tribes, from the Siuslaw to the Coos, have called the land home for time immemorial. But Captain James Cook sighted the Coast in 1778 and his later reports of the silky sea-otter pelts used by Native Americans triggered a "fur rush" that forever changed the region. Now, three federally recognized Indigenous tribes remain connected to the Oregon Coast, with its freshwater rivers, saltwater bays, and wind-carved dunes: they are the Confederated Tribes of Siletz Indians; the Confederated Tribes of Coos, Lower Umpqua and Siuslaw Indians; and the Coquille Indian Tribe.

Today, museums piece together the region's layered history, while wholesome seaside attractions draw in family travelers. This is prime road-trip territory: the region is stitched together by Highway 101, or the Pacific Coast Scenic Byway, an epic drive that traces the entire coastline.

ASTORIA

The coastal bolthole of **Astoria** ❶ is around two hours northwest of Portland, sitting at the mouth of the

Columbia River. Cross the mighty **Astoria–Megler Bridge**, an enormous truss structure that shoots over the river, and you will find yourself in Washington state. Astoria has as much history as it does stark coastal beauty. It is the oldest Euro-American settlement west of the Rocky Mountains, established as Fort Astoria in 1811 by fur traders, under the orders of magnate John Jacob Astor. Today, a small blockhouse serves as a replica of the fur-trading post and is accompanied by a historical panel.

⊙ Main attractions
Fort Stevens State Park
Ecola State Park/Cannon Beach
Tillamook Creamery
Sea Lion Caves
Heceta Head Lighthouse
Oregon Dunes National Recreation Area
Port Orford

Map on page 134

Astoria–Megler Bridge.

Now, the city's impressive store of Victorian architecture has earned Astoria the moniker "Little San Francisco" and the **Astoria Downtown Historic District** is packed tight with buildings on the National Register. Among them is the 1885-built **Flavel House Museum** (714 Exchange Street; tel: 503-325 2203; www.astoriamuseums. org; daily: May–Sept 10am–5pm; Oct–Apr until 4pm), a fine Queen Anne-style residence that once belonged to an affluent Columbia River Bar Pilot named George Flavel, one of Astoria's most noteworthy citizens of the period. The interiors are notable for their intricate woodwork and include a grand string of rooms from a formal parlor to a library. Just a block to the north is the **Oregon Film Museum**, which has exhibitions on the many movies filmed in the state, after which you can head to the riverside.

Spanning the length of the city's waterfront is the **Astoria Riverwalk Trail**. It forms part of the Lewis and Clark National Historic Trail and follows a section of the Astoria and Columbia River Railroad. Spectacular views of the river, Youngs Bay, and the vaulting Astoria–Megler Bridge unfold from the walkway, which stretches out for a total of 12.8 miles (21km). Along the way, the **Columbia River Maritime Museum** (1792 Marine Drive; tel: 503-325 2323; www.crmm.org; daily 9.30am–5pm) is a highlight. Exhibits explore the epic storms that have long pummeled the notorious Columbia River Bar, and the shipwrecks that have dubbed the region the "Graveyard of the Pacific." A star exhibit is the Lightship Columbia, a floating beacon that operated from 1951 to 1979.

You can stay and eat right on the water, too. The luxurious **Cannery Pier Hotel & Spa** (10 Basin Street; tel: 503-325 4996; www.cannerypierhotel.com) is, as its name suggests, housed in an old cannery, offering postcard views of the famous bridge. **Bridgewater Bistro** (20 Basin Street; tel: 503-325 6777; www.bridgewaterbistro.com; Mon–Sat 11.30am–3pm, 4–8pm, Sun 10.30am–3pm, 4pm–8pm) is a failsafe riverside dining option. Feast on delights such

Peter Iredale Shipwreck.

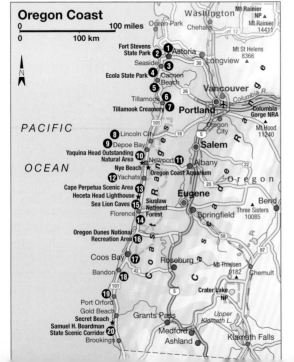

as savory Dungeness crab cheese-cake, cod fish and chips, and Willapa Bay oysters on the waterfront terrace. Farther inland, **Būsu** (www.instagram.com/busu_astoria; Tue–Sat 5–8pm) is Astoria's best-kept secret. It serves takeout Japanese delicacies like miso soup from a humble-looking window on 11th Street.

Just a 12-minute drive out of town is **Fort Clatsop National Memorial** (92345 Fort Clatsop Road; tel: 503-861 2471; www.nps.gov/lewi), a replica of the original structure, which served as the winter encampment for the Corps of Discovery group on the Lewis and Clark Expedition in the early 1800s. You can wander into the fort, and a tangle of walking trails unfurls beyond the building. There is a small museum at the visitor center.

Also a 15-minute drive west of Astoria is **Fort Stevens State Park ②** (1675 Peter Iredale Road; tel: 503-861 3170; www.stateparks.oregon.gov). The park wraps around the remains of Fort Stevens, which once guarded the mouth of the Columbia River. The original fort

was built toward the end of the Civil War and would have been an earthwork structure surrounded by a moat. It was eventually decommissioned after World War II. Now, visitors can explore the abandoned fort and learn more at a visitor center and small military museum. Beyond the fort, the park is a natural outdoor playground with 15 miles (24km) of hiking trails, campgrounds, and swimming and boating on Coffenbury Lake. Have your camera ready for the dramatic **Peter Iredale Shipwreck**. This four-masted vessel ran aground in 1906 and its eerie husk still protrudes from the sand.

SEASIDE

Strike south down the Oregon Coast Highway and **Seaside ③** will eventually emerge. This (as its name suggests) is the epitome of an old-school seaside resort town, which had established itself as a must-visit vacation hotspot by the turn of the 20th century. It takes its name from The Seaside House, the town's (now shuttered) first hotel, completed in 1904, and it soon

Fort Clatsop National Memorial.

had a buzzy beachfront promenade to boot. Today, Seaside is still a destination for wholesome fun, with cheerful restaurants, beachfront activities, and family-friendly attractions. The best way to pass an afternoon is to wander along the 1.5-mile (2km) "Prom," as the historic boardwalk is affectionately known, drinking in views of the Pacific Ocean and looking out for the bronze statue of Lewis and Clark. Classic fairground rides such as the bumper cars, carousel, and tilt-a-whirl will keep kids happy, and there is also the game-filled **Funland Arcade**.

ECOLA STATE PARK

Ecola State Park ❹ offers postcard views of the Oregon Coast. It is arranged around the dramatic Tillamook Head promontory, which soars above the Pacific Ocean, and protects 9 miles (14km) of dazzling coastline. Trails grant pinch-yourself views over Cannon Beach, with its iconic sea stacks, and involve peaceful treks through Sitka spruce forests and dramatic walks along tree-fringed cliff

Ecola State Park.

edges. An 8-mile (13km) portion of the fabled Oregon Coast Trail routes through the park – along the way, look out for the spur trail that diverts toward **Tillamook Rock Lighthouse viewpoint**. The quaint beacon, perched atop a wave-beaten rock out at sea, is a camera-worthy sight. Keep your eyes peeled for breaching whales at the various lofty lookout stops along the way. Before you head out, be sure to visit the park's **Indian Beach**, with its tide pools and excellent surf.

CANNON BEACH

Perhaps no view of the Oregon Coast is more iconic than that of sea stack-studded **Cannon Beach** ❺. It is dominated by Haystack Rock, a hulking monolith that looms over the sand and sea at 235ft (72 meters) high. The striking basalt formation is thought to have been formed from lava flows around 17 million years ago. It would be very easy to spend all your time on the sand here, but the town of Cannon Beach itself has some jewels, too. Browse galleries filled with art

⊘ OREGON COAST HIGHWAY

It is no exaggeration to say that US Highway 101 – which swoops all the way from northern Washington to southern California – is one of the most picturesque driving routes in the whole of the country. The Oregon segment – known as the Oregon Coast Highway – charms with dramatically placed lighthouses, plunging ocher cliffs, misty maritime forests, and rocky outcrops heaving with Steller sea lions. Funding for the road was first approved in Oregon in 1919 and work began in the early 1920s. Of course, the wild and winding Oregon Coast meant that the construction of the road posed problems – tunnels had to be blasted through rock, and bridges had to vault over creeks and bays. This led to pioneering engineering projects such as Ten Mile Creek Bridge, which spans its namesake – made from reinforced concrete, this 120ft (36-meter) tied-arch bridge was one of the earliest of its kind. Various updates were made to the road over the following decades, with a section near Florence becoming one of the most expensive examples of road construction in the country. Flash forward a century and the highway offers one of the most well-loved road trips in the nation. Take things slow, pulling out at overlooks; stealing down trails leading to isolated beaches; and stopping for seafood feasts in quaint fishing towns.

inspired by the Pacific Northwest – a highlight is **Images of the West** (224 N Hemlock Street #1; tel: 503-436 4113; www.randalljhodges.com; daily 10am–5pm), which comprises striking works by photographer Randall J Hodges. If timings allow, the town is well worth a visit during the **Earth & Ocean Arts Festival**, which is dedicated to both creativity and environmentalism and is typically held in September. The event includes nature-focused exhibitions, live art projects, folk music, and food with a farm-to-table focus.

A 10-minute drive south will bring you to **Hug Point State Recreation Site**, an underrated slice of the coast that you might just get all to yourself. Park up and wander to the sandy crescent, which opens out against a backdrop of Sitka spruce forest and ferns.

TILLAMOOK BAY

Rejoin Highway 101 and ease yourself into the hour-long journey toward **Tillamook** ❻. The drive is a reward in itself: skirting the Pacific Ocean and slipping past Nehalem Bay. Trailheads open out along the way – near Manzanita, you will find the **Elk Flats Trail**, which spikes through coastal meadows, affording gratifying views of the sea. Branch west to the **Devil's Cauldron** overlook to gaze down upon a dramatic rocky cove. **Neahkahnie Mountain** – a 1,680ft (512-meter) -high peak in the Oregon Coast Range – is another of the region's popular hiking areas. It is accessed via the challenging Oregon Coast Trail.

En route, you will pass family-friendly resort towns such as **Rockaway Beach**, known for its kite festival and long sandy strand.

Once you reach the Tillamook Bay area, the **Tillamook Bay Heritage Route** helps you to get to grips with the history of the region, joining Tillamook with other coastal communities, including Barview, Garibaldi, Bay City, and Cape Meares. Standout sights on the trail include the **Garibaldi Historic US Coast Guard Boathouse**, which keeps watch over glittering Tillamook Bay. In Tillamook proper, the route includes the **Tillamook County Pioneer**

Cannon Beach.

Museum (2106 2nd Street; tel: 503-842 4553; www.tcpm.org; Tue–Sun 10am–4pm), whose 55,000-strong collection (not including photographs) dives into North Coast history, from Native Americans to those who arrived on the Oregon Trail. Tillamook's **Air Museum** (6030 Hangar Road; tel: 503-842 1130; www.tillamookair.com; Tue–Sun: Oct–May 10am–4pm; June–Sept until 6pm) is another popular stop. Displays cover the Naval Air Station Tillamook that was in operation during World War II.

However, the city is best known for the historic **Tillamook Creamery** ❼ (4165 N Highway 101; tel: 503-815 1300; www.tillamook.com; daily 10am–6pm), which has been producing its award-winning sharp Cheddar since the early 1900s. Self-guided tours here include a farm exhibit and a viewing gallery looking over operations.

Meanwhile, the **Tillamook Forest Center** (www.tillamookforestcenter.org) is worth the half-hour drive northeast of town. The building (made of sustainably sourced timber and salvaged or recycled materials) blends seamlessly into the lush Tillamook State Forest and it houses exhibitions on forestry management, plus a theater and bookstore. There are sweeping views over the canopy from the top of a 40ft (12-meter) structure built to resemble a forest fire lookout tower.

THREE CAPES SCENIC ROUTE

Few sections of the Oregon Coast are anything but lovely, but there is something extra special about the **Three Capes Scenic Route**, a 40-mile (64km) drive that takes in **Cape Meares**, **Cape Lookout** and **Cape Kiwanda**, as it stretches out from Tillamook to Pacific City. Cape Meares juts out to the northeast of Tillamook and is known for its quaint 1890s lighthouse and ancient stands of Sitka spruce and hemlock trees. There is also a short trail to the **Octopus Tree**, so named for its dramatic display of splayed branches like the legs of an ocean creature.

Cape Lookout State Park unfolds farther south. Hike the 5-mile (8km) Cape Trail through more Sitka spruces and hemlocks to be rewarded with

Tillamook Bay.

⊘ CAPE FOUL WEATHER

This dramatic cape along Oregon's Central Coast is as steeped in history as it is in natural beauty, towering 500ft (152 meters) above the Pacific Ocean and affording far-reaching panoramas from its crest. It is the first slice of the coast that was spied by Captain James Cook on his voyage in 1778 – he named it for the stormy weather and the ferocious waves that battered the headland. Skip forward almost 250 years and the cape is now among the most popular tourist destinations along the Oregon Coast. It is a top spot for wildlife-watching, with thousands of gray whales passing its rocky expanse each year, and raptors like bald eagles soaring overhead. The Cape's lookout spot and tourist gift shop typically draw in the crowds.

sweeping ocean panoramas from the end of the headland. It is possible to camp year-round.

Eventually, your travels southward will land you at **Cape Kiwanda State Natural Area**, a fragile sandstone headland at the mercy of the Pacific Ocean. Scramble to the top of the sandy dunes for jaw-dropping sea views. The aptly named **Pacific City** is also a jumping-off point for this pocket of the coast. The little port city is known for its fleet of dory boats – these traditional vessels have been in use for centuries – and the current horde still goes out to fish for salmon and albacore tuna.

LINCOLN CITY AND DEPOE BAY

The beginning of Oregon's Central Coast, **Lincoln City ⑧** is hailed as the "Kite Capital of the World," and it is not uncommon to see the brightly patterned sails fluttering in the skies (though there are 7 miles/11km of sand so you should be able to find a quieter pocket if you'd prefer). There are also dedicated kite festivals in summer and autumn. Beyond this quirk, Lincoln City is a laid-back family vacation spot with down-to-earth restaurants, an outlet mall, and access to the outdoors – nearby **Cascade Head** is laced with trails, while **Devils Lake** is a haven for lovers of watersports. Outfitters rent kayaks, kiteboards, and jet skis. The lake is also popular for fishing. The Confederated Tribes of Siletz Indians own Lincoln City's **Chinook Winds Casino Resort** (1777 NW 44th Street; tel: 888-244 6665; www.chinookwinds casino.com), which has an enviable location overlooking the beach. The views from the property's Seafood Grill, with its giant windows, are unparalleled.

Around 12 miles (20km) south is **Depoe Bay ⑨**, which has earned a reputation as the best spot along the Oregon Coast for whale-watching. It is home to the **Depoe Bay Whale**

Watching Center (119 S Highway 101; tel: 541-765 3304; www.stateparks. oregon.gov; daily 9am–5pm), with its binoculars and vast viewing deck overlooking the Pacific. The winter migration period – which sees the majestic mammals travel from Alaska to Mexico from mid-December through to mid-January – offers the best chance of a sighting, though whale-watching is touted as a year-round activity here.

You will also be close to **Devil's Punchbowl State Natural Area** (US Highway 101 Otter Crest Loop; tel: 800-551 6949; www.stateparks.oregon.gov). It is named for the hollow rock formation that looks almost like an enormous punch bowl – the views of the Pacific Ocean bubbling up and frothing in the rocky crevice could have you transfixed for hours. The natural area is another popular whale-watching spot.

YAQUINA HEAD AND NEWPORT

The **Yaquina Head Outstanding Natural Area ⑩** comprises a rugged basalt headland that punches out into the

Lincoln City, the "Kite Capital of the World."

Pacific Ocean and is crowned by the **Yaquina Head Lighthouse**. The beacon, which is the tallest along the Oregon Coast at 93ft (28 meters), still operates after being first illuminated way back in 1873. Regular guided tours of the lighthouse reveal its history. Closer to the shore is a patchwork of tide pools that provides habitats for colorful marine life such as starfish and sea anemones – consider calling ahead to check the status of the tide for your best chance of viewing these fascinating creatures. Also venture inside the **Yaquina Head Interpretation Center** to see absorbing displays on birds and wildlife, including whales, plus human and maritime history.

A short hop south of the cape will place you in family-friendly **Newport** ⓫, laced by the wide sandy arc of **Nye Beach**. The waterfront is peppered with pavement cafés, seafood restaurants, ice-cream parlors, and hotels. The town is best known for the **Oregon Coast Aquarium** (2820 SE Ferry Slip Road; tel: 541-867 3474; www.aquarium. org; late May to Labor Day 10am–6pm;

Sept–Apr until 5pm), home to sharks, sea otters, and a giant Pacific octopus. You can visit the **Hatfield Marine Science Center** (2030 SE Marine Science Drive; tel: 541-867 0100; www.hmsc. oregonstate.edu; Thu–Mon 10am–4pm), which is based at Oregon State University. The visitor center includes hands-on exhibits covering everything from tsunamis and coastal erosion to marine life. Or if you have kids in tow, make for **Mariner Square**, where you will find a waxworks museum.

A stay in Newport will also be within easy reach of the **Agate Beach State Recreation Site** (tel: 541-265 4560; www.stateparks.oregon.gov), whose broad sandy sweep attracts both razor clammers and surfers. You can try the latter for yourself with lessons organized by the likes of **Ossie's Surf Shop** (4900 Oregon Coast Highway; tel: 541-574 4634; www.ossiessurfshop.com; daily 10am–6pm). If you are already a proficient surfer, rentals are available.

Long-running **South Beach Fish Market** (3640 S Coast Highway; tel: 541-867 6800; www.southbeachfishmarket.com), a market and casual restaurant, has a loyal following. The menu features wild-caught albacore tuna and chips, a Chinook salmon burger, and Dungeness crab with garlic butter.

YACHATS

A 30-minute drive south of Newport will land you in the charming seaside village of **Yachats** ⓬. The teensy town has a wonderfully bohemian feel, with a string of indie shops including **Perpetua Records** (373 Highway 101; www.facebook.com/perpetuavinyl), which sells vinyl records, books, and antique knick-knacks. Another favorite is the **Midtown Guitar Company** (357 Highway 101 N; tel: 831-247 9745; www. guitarsofmidtown.com), with its impressive store of vintage instruments. The quirky town is also a jumping-off point for the **Cape Perpetua Scenic Area** ⓭, a breathtaking 2,700-acre

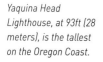

Yaquina Head Lighthouse, at 93ft (28 meters), is the tallest on the Oregon Coast.

(1,090-hectare) expanse of coastal land that forms part of the Siuslaw National Forest. Looming 800ft/meters over the Pacific Ocean, the Cape Perpetua headland is the highest point accessible by car along the Oregon Coast so, needless to say, it offers unparalleled views of the rugged surroundings. Some 26 miles (40km) of trails snake into great swathes of temperate maritime rainforest, while overlooking a series of coastal wonders.

Among them is **Devil's Churn**, a dramatic chasm where the frothing Pacific Ocean puts on a spectacular show. You can view it along the Restless Waters Trail, a mellow and paved 0.4-mile (0.6km) loop. **Spouting Horn** is another spectacle – a geyser-like rush of water that shoots above the rocks at higher tides. Drink in panoramas from the easy Captain Cook Trail – a one-mile (1.6km) route that also takes in Native American shell middens and **Thor's Well**. The latter is one of the most impressive water features along the coast, a vast rocky chasm that almost appears like a giant plughole, draining the great Pacific.

It is also well worth heading into the **Cape Perpetua Visitor Center** to learn about the Alsean-speaking peoples who have called this land home for many millennia before European settlers arrived. This Indigenous heritage is also honored with Amanda's Trail. A 3.7-mile (6km) segment of the Oregon Coast Trail, it pays homage to blind Coos tribe member Amanda De-Cuys who, in 1864, was forced to travel on foot from her Coos Bay home to Yachats, as Indigenous peoples were forcibly relocated to federal reservations.

FLORENCE

The Siuslaw River Bridge, with its graceful arches and Art Deco-style obelisks, is the standout sight in gorgeous coastal **Florence ⑭**. It has jutted over the waterway since the 1930s and it is loved by the camera. You can take in fabulous views of the structure from down by the water, on Bay Street, which is also home to an eclectic selection of gift stores, boutiques, cafés, and restaurants.

For prime water views, grab a coffee at **River Roasters** (1240 Bay Street

Oregon's Sea Lion Caves, said to be the largest sea cave in the USA, is packed with the lumbering mammals.

⊘ SEA LION CAVES

Part of the Cape Perpetua Marine Reserve, the privately owned Sea Lion Caves is touted as the largest sea cave in the USA. The wildlife preserve supports hundreds of the fascinating marine mammals. A short, paved trail leads from the kiosk and gift shop to an elevator that trundles down into the cave – from a lofty perch, you can look down toward the ocean, where a great number of sea lions may be barking and frolicking on the wave-lashed rocks. You have the best chance of seeing the wild animals during winter – in summertime, they typically move out to rookeries. If you can tear yourself away from this natural spectacle, detailed displays outline the region's various marine species and birdlife, as well as the history of the cave and Native heritage. Keep your eyes peeled for other curious critters such as bats, as well as peregrine falcons, and red-tailed hawks.

⚙ Eat

Fuel up at modern Nosh Eatery (1269 Bay Street; tel: 541-997 5899; www.nosheateryflorence.com; Tue–Thu 11am–8pm, Fri, Sat until 9pm), which has a great selection of vegetarian options, from a lentil-based "sloppy faux" to kung pao cauliflower and rice, plus a variety of seafood dishes. There is a fully stocked bar if you are partial to a cocktail.

#9648; tel: 541-997 3443; www.coffee oregon.com; daily 7am–5pm), a warm and welcoming café serving espresso drinks and flavored specialties.

Before Euro-American settlers arrived, this had long been the homeland and winter refuge of the Siuslaw people. You can learn about Indigenous lifeways, and see artifacts such as a dugout canoe, at the **Siuslaw Pioneer Museum** (278 Maple Street; tel: 541-997 7884; www.siuslawpioneermuseum.com; Wed–Sun noon–4pm), which chronicles the history of the area.

If you want to kick things up a gear, then make for **Sand Master Sandboarding Park** (4981 Oregon Coast Highway; tel: 541-997 6006; www.sandmasterpark.com; Jan–Mar Fri–Sun 10am–5pm; Apr–Dec daily 9.30am–6pm), where you can try your hand at a new sport. Sandboarding is exactly what it sounds like: you will ride the Oregon Coast's undulating dunes just as you would on a snowboard. Book in for a lesson at the store here. You can also rent sand sleds, boogie boards, surfboards, and paddleboards.

Cape Perpetua and Thor's Well.

Three Rivers Casino Resort (5647 OR-126; tel: 877-374 8377; www.three riverscasino.com), owned by the Confederated Tribes of Coos, Lower Umpqua and Siuslaw Indians, is a popular place to stay in the area. The resort includes a large gaming space, deluxe rooms and suites, and laid-back restaurants, and it also manages the **Ocean Dunes Golf Links** course (3345 Munsel Lake Road; tel: 541-997 3232). Just 10 miles (16km) north of Florence, the **Sea Lion Caves** ⑮ (91560 US-101; tel: 541-547 3111; www.sealioncaves.com; daily 9am–5pm) offers one of the best chances of sighting the North Pacific's Steller sea lions (see box, page 141). A five-minute drive up the coast takes you to **Heceta Head Lighthouse**, built in 1892 atop a moss-choked crag high above the ocean.

OREGON DUNES NATIONAL RECREATION AREA

Taking up 40 miles (64km) of the Oregon Coast, the otherworldly **Oregon Dunes National Recreation Area** ⑯ (tel: 541-271 6000; www.fs.usda.gov/siuslaw) protects what is dubbed as the largest expanse of temperate coastal sand dunes on the planet. The entire reserve sprawls across 31,500 acres (12,500 hectares) and forms part of the Siuslaw National Forest. The dunes were formed from grains weathered away from the Coast and Cascade mountains, which were then carried toward the ocean by rivers and glaciers. Eventually, the ocean would spil sand out onto the shore, and the wind would sculpt them into giant ridges.

The resulting phenomenon is a haunting sight: rippling sand mountains bleed into the Pacific Ocean, backed by mist-hung maritime woodland. Stand at certain points in this coastal desert and all you can see is golden sand – some dunes tower as high as 500ft (152 meters).

As you drive down Oregon's South Coast on Highway 101, you will see signs for various pockets of the Recreation

Area (note that some areas incur a fee of $5 per vehicle, per day). The 2-mile (3km) **Oregon Dunes Loop Trail** is a popular walk. It begins as a paved path that leads to a viewing area, then follows a hard-packed sand trail down to the beach. Rangers often lead hikes in the summer. Both the South Jetty and Siltcoos access points offer ATV trails, while you will share space with wildlife such as the threatened Western snowy plover (parts of the beach are off-limits to protect this species).

Many campgrounds are available, with some providing lake access for boaters and trail access for hikers. Find more information about camping and recreation at the **Oregon Dunes National Recreation Area Office** (855 US-101), located in Reedsport, around the midpoint of the area.

COOS BAY

Heading southward on Highway 101, the small city of **Coos Bay** ⓱ makes a great base for exploring the South Coast. Check in to **Bay Point Landing** (92443 Cape Arago Highway; tel: 541-351 9160; www.baypointlanding.com), scattered with chic glass-clad cabins and Airstream suites, plus space for RV camping. There is also a saltwater swimming pool, a fitness center, and a communal firepit.

In town, history buffs can check out the **Coos History Museum** (1210 N Front St; tel: 541-756 6320; www.cooshistory.org; Tue–Sat: Labor Day–Memorial Day 10am–4pm; Memorial Day–Labor Day until 5pm, also Sun noon–4pm). The center has exhibits on local industrial heritage such as logging and mining, plus displays covering natural history and Native American artifacts including a dugout canoe.

Best of all, though, the city is a launchpad for coastal hikes and adventures on the region's Wild and Scenic Rivers. A local highlight is **Shore Acres State Park** (800-551 6949; www.stateparks.oregon.gov), which is known as a prime whale-watching spot. It was formerly the estate of timber magnate Louis Simpson, and now gentle trails wend through formal gardens and along sandstone cliffs.

Oregon Dunes National Recreation Area.

Farther out but well worth the journey is the gloriously off-the-beaten track **Golden and Silver Falls State Natural Area**, reached via a looping road that hugs the Millicoma River. Here, hiking trails slice through craggy canyons to reach the misty 200ft (61-meter) -high Golden Falls and 130ft (40-meter) Silver Falls.

More outdoor adventures await at the **South Slough National Estuarine Research Reserve** (61907 Seven Devils Road; tel: 541-888 5558; www.oregon.gov/dsl/SS), which was established in the 1970s to protect the South Slough of the Coos River. This wildlife-rich estuary is the ancestral homeland of the Miluk-speaking Coos, who have long fished and hunted in the area. Now, 11 miles (18km) of hiking trails route through forests, and a visitor center features exhibits on the estuary's natural features and wildlife, including herons, river otters, beavers, and crabs. But the best way to experience the reserve is to get out on the water. **South Coast Tours** (300 Dock Road; tel: 541-373 0487; www.southcoasttours.

net) – the only outfitter with a special-use permit to operate in the reserve – offers guided paddling trips on the tidal estuary. Kayakers can expect a fairly challenging 4.6-mile (7.4km) trip that weaves through stunning wetland scenery – keep your eyes peeled for birdlife such as bald eagles and egrets.

Back on dry land, Coos Bay – and its sister cities of **North Bend** and **Charleston** – have some top spots to grab a bite. North Bend's **Wildflour** (1987 Sherman Avenue; tel: 541-808 3633; www.wildflourpub.com; Wed–Sat 3–8pm) is a great dinner option. It fills a stylish space decorated with mismatched vintage mirrors, exposed brick, and hanging mason jars, and it serves a modern menu featuring surf and turf, burgers, and imaginative small plates. Back in Coos Bay, the **Coach House** (604 6th Avenue; tel: 541-267 5116; www.thecoachhousecoosbayor.com; Mon–Sat 11am–9pm, Sun 4–9pm) is a local favorite. Beginning as a loggers' bar, the restaurant now serves a refined menu featuring steak, barbecue dinners, and seafood. For a waterfront spot, head to **7 Devils Brewing** (247 S 2nd Street; tel: 541-808 3738; www.7devilsbrewery.com), which pairs fruity IPAs, porters, and stouts with gratifying pub food such as poutine, po' boys, and mac and cheese.

CAPE ARAGO BEACH LOOP

The **Cape Arago Beach Loop** driving route takes in a series of scenic coastal spots, including three state parks. Leaving west from Highway 101 on Newmark Avenue in Coos Bay, the drive will lead you first to **Bastendorff Beach** (63377 Bastendorff Beach Road; tel: 541-888 5353), a quiet strand where you will likely see surfers in the ocean and colorful kites in the sky. More sand awaits at the **Sunset Bay State Park** (tel: 800-551 6949; www.stateparks.oregon.gov), where a sea cliff-backed crescent is a popular spot for picnics and tidepool walks. Ease a little

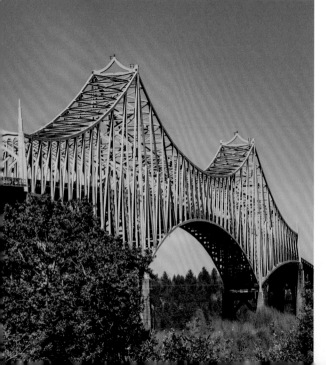

The Conde B McCullough Memorial Bridge, Coos Bay.

farther south and pull over for the **Cape Arago Lighthouse Viewpoint** – the neat-as-a-pin beacon stands at 44ft (13 meters) on a rocky slither that juts into the ocean. The road then swings into Shore Acres State Park, and on to the **Simpson Reef Overlook**, where you are likely to see a huge colony of seals and sea lions. The glittering finale is **Cape Arago State Park** (tel: 800-551-6949; www.stateparks.oregon.gov), another spot known for whale-watching. Choose between the North Trail for spectacular vistas of sea lion-covered Shell Island, or the South Trail, which leads down to the beach.

BANDON

As you continue to push south on Highway 101, the small town of **Bandon** 🅱, hooking around the mouth of the Coquille River, is a worthy stop-off point. The Old Town district is a charming place to wander and is filled with little cafés, gift stores, and art galleries. Lunch at the perpetually busy **Tony's Crab Shack** (155 1st Street SE; tel: 541-347 2875; www.tonyscrabshack.

com; daily 10.30am–7pm), known, as its name suggests, for its delicate and buttery crab meat, gloriously served on toasted sourdough bread with Thousand Island sauce. Less than a 10-minute walk east, you can sample fine Cheddar at the **Face Rock Creamery** – the café menu is filled with the likes of grilled paninis and mac and cheese. Bandon has also earned a reputation as Oregon's "Cranberry Capital," and visitors can take tours at working local farms such as **Bowman Bogs** (87303 McTimmons Lane; tel: 541-290 5530; www.facebook.com/GrandpaJacksCranberries). Tours are by appointment during the harvest season (typically October to December).

Bandon is a golfer's paradise, too. The **Bandon Dunes Golf Resort** (57744 Round Lake Road; tel: 877-652 2122; www.bandondunesgolf.com) has six separate links courses that nose up to the coastal sand dunes.

You can use Bandon as a base for adventures on the Coquille River. A scenic paddle trip is the route from Bullards Beach State Park upriver to

⊘ Tip

Keen cyclists should not miss the Wild Rivers Coast Scenic Bikeway, a 60-mile (97km) trail network – you could complete the whole route or enjoy one of the numerous out-and-back rides along the way. For example, a particularly scenic stretch strikes out from Port Orford's Battle Rock Park, while another beats across Cape Blanco State Park.

Cape Arago.

The region swooping south of Port Orford, towards the California border, is known as Oregon's "banana belt" for its unusually high temperatures and large quantity of sunny days. The distinct climate has to do with the region's unique topography in which the Coast and Cascade ranges fuse to form a single mass of high terrain (the Siskiyou Mountains). As air from the east and northeast travels down over these ranges, it compresses and warms.

Bandon Beach.

Randolph island and back (check the tides and the weather carefully before you set out if you are not traveling with a guide). Mountain bikers are spoiled by the region's **Whiskey Run trail system**. The network has 32 miles (51km) of single-track trails, including expert and beginner runs, and a total descent of 7,293ft (2,223 meters).

PORT ORFORD AND AROUND

The offbeat town of **Port Orford** ⑲ is around a 30-minute drive south from Bandon on Highway 101. The main drag has a handful of laid-back restaurants and watering holes, of which a favorite is **Mr. Ed's Espresso, Juice, and Underground Pub** (1870 Oregon Street; tel: 541-366 2295; www.mreds underground.pub; Tue–Fri 7am–9pm, Sat 8am–9pm). It hosts regular live-music sets and serves wood-fired pizza and local craft beer.

Spend a night or two at **WildSpring Guest Habitat** (92978 Cemetery Loop Road; tel: 541-332 0977; www.wild spring.com), where atmospheric cabins are tangled up among five acres of

forest. The cabins are cozily decked out with Persian rugs and quilted throws, and there is a hot tub overlooking the Pacific Ocean.

WildSpring is able to organize hikes with local tour leader Cathy Boden, who speaks of the human and natural history of the area on her guided excursions. Trails at **Port Orford Heads State Park** (Port Orford Heads Street Wayside; tel: 800-551 6949; www.state parks.oregon.gov) skirt soaring headlands laced with Oregon grape and Sitka spruce trees. Trails offer far-reaching views out to Cape Blanco, the westernmost point of the Oregon Coast, with its namesake lighthouse, and to Humbug Mountain, which rises to some 1,765ft (540 meters). The park is home to the **Port Orford Lifeboat Station Museum**, which tells the story of the US Coast Guard "surfmen," who were stationed here between 1934 and 1970. The brave men would be on guard to rescue sailors from the arms of the Pacific, putting their own lives at risk in the process. As you hike above Nellies Cove in the park, you can look

down at the remnants of the unit's old motorboat house, whose ocean-ravaged breakwaters remain.

A little farther south, **Humbug Mountain State Park** (tel: 541-332 6774; www.stateparks.oregon.gov) protects one of the highest headlands on the Oregon seaboard. A segment of the famous Oregon Coast Trail passes through the park, while many hikers tackle the 5.5-mile (9km) route to the summit, with its switchbacks and old-growth forest. The park's coastal waters are a hotspot for scuba diving.

SAMUEL H. BOARDMAN STATE SCENIC CORRIDOR

The **Samuel H. Boardman State Scenic Corridor** ㉟ is one of the Oregon Coast's final flourishes. It snakes down the coast for 12 breathtaking miles (19km), punctuated by tempting trailheads and scenic viewpoints. It is named for the first superintendent of the Oregon State Park system, serving in his role from 1929 to 1950. You cannot go wrong with any of the pullouts along this glittering stretch of the highway, but standouts include **Arch Rock**, a graceful rainbow-shaped hulk of ash-flow tuff. The overlook for the formation is accessed by an easy trail.

Just a few minutes down the road is **Secret Beach**, a boulder-strewn crescent where you'll likely be the only ones leaving footprints in the sand. Further south is **Natural Bridges**, a series of seven dramatic arches and blowholes that can also be viewed via a short hike to an overlook. Secluded **Whaleshead Beach** – named for a sea stack that resembles a whale breaching in the ocean, right down to a watery spray when the waves hit it just right – is a must-visit. There is a steep and bumpy trail directly down from the Whaleshead Trail Viewpoint parking area, or you can enjoy a forest hike or a drive down to the beach from Whaleshead Beach Road.

Eventually, Highway 101 curls into **Brookings** on the Chetco River, which is a good lunch spot. The **Chetco Brewing Company** (830 Railroad St; www.chetco brew.com) is a hip hangout offering craft porters, lagers, and IPAs, plus a truck dishing up vegan comfort food.

> ☉ **Tip**
>
> Once you have traversed the length of the Oregon Coast Highway, dip into Northern California and visit Jedediah Smith Redwoods State Park (30 minutes south of Brookings), which is characterized by soaring redwood groves.

Samuel H. Boardman State Scenic Corridor.

⊘ **WILD RIVERS COAST**

The southwestern corner of Oregon has earned the nickname Wild Rivers Coast, for its (you guessed it) high concentration of Wild and Scenic Rivers – there are more waterways here with this federal designation than anywhere else in the States. The most storied of them all is the mighty Rogue River, a haven for rafters, tubers, and white-water kayakers. The community of Gold Beach makes a great base camp for adventures on the waterway. The region is known for its jetboat rides and a popular operator is Jerry's Rogue Jets (29985 Harbor Way; tel: 800-451 3645; www.roguejets.com), which offers tours that follow a historic mailboat route used since the 19th century. For pure thrills, there is also the Express Whitewater Tour, which focuses on the river's churning rapids.

📷 LANDMARK LIGHTHOUSES

Once a vital part of the region's thriving maritime industry, Oregon Coast's lighthouses today tend to beckon tourists rather than sea captains to these shores.

The Oregon Coast is studded with lighthouses, and any Highway 101 journey should include at least one tour of a historic beacon. Though they now mostly serve as tourist attractions, lighthouses were once vital to mariners at the mercy of the Pacific Ocean. Whether steering a giant vessel heavy with lumber or a diminutive fishing boat, captains would surely relish the sight of a winking light guiding them toward the shore. A great number of Oregon's lighthouses were built in the second half of the 19th century by the US Army Corps, mostly in locations near major fishing, shipbuilding, lumbering, or other commercial operations. By the 1960s, automated systems had been installed up and down the coast and many of Oregon's historic lighthouses were left obsolete.

Today, nine of these original lighthouses remain, seven of which are open to the public. (On top of this, there are two additional privately built lighthouses, both of which are closed to visitors.) One of the most iconic is "Terrible Tilly," or the Tillamook Rock Lighthouse, which is poised on a rocky basalt outcrop off Tillamook Head. Treacherous weather hindered her construction (and one mason was killed as he surveyed the area), but "Tilly" was eventually lit in 1880. Though she protected the coast for decades, a ferocious storm in the 1930s smashed up the beloved lighthouse, and the last keeper visit occurred in the 1950s. Now, she is the domain of pelicans and cormorants. Though she is closed to the public, she can be seen from Ecola State Park.

Heceta Head Lighthouse has a picture-perfect setting.

Yaquina Head Lighthouse, the tallest on Oregon Coast.

Built in 1982, Heceta Head Lighthouse sits on a crag.

The abandoned "Terrible Tilly," off Tillamook Head.

Oregon's finest beacons

Around 12 miles (19km) north of Florence, the 1892-built Heceta Head Lighthouse is purportedly the most photographed on the Pacific Coast – no surprise, given its picture-perfect perch on a mossy crag, high above the ocean and backed by spruce trees. Best of all, the assistant keeper's former home – a neat, white gabled house with a red roof and wraparound porch – serves as the Heceta Lighthouse Bed & Breakfast (92072 US-101; tel: 541-547 3696; www.hecetalighthouse.com).

The oldest along the coast is the Cape Blanco Lighthouse (91100 Cape Blanco Road; tel: 541-332 2207; www.capeblancoheritagesociety. com; tour times vary, check website), which was built back in 1870. Visitors can take tours of the lighthouse, as well as the nearby Queen Anne-style Hughes House (91816 Cape Blanco Road; tel: 541-332 0248; www.capeblancoheritagesociety.com) – the home belonged to a landowning and dairy-farming family that included James Hughes, long-time keeper of the lighthouse.

Cape Blanco Lighthouse sits at Oregon's westernmost tip.

The former home of lighthouse keeper James Hughes.

Cape Blanco Lighthouse, the oldest on the Oregon Coast.

SOUTHERN OREGON

Artsy towns, creative winemakers, and dizzying natural preserves – including the extraordinary Crater Lake National Park – collect in the mountains and river valleys of this rugged region.

Nature reigns supreme in these lands, which are sliced open by wild rivers and undercut by labyrinthine caves. Southern Oregon is the ancestral homeland of the Cow Creek Band of Umpqua Tribe of Indians, most of whom were forcibly moved to the Grand Ronde area in the 1850s. Meanwhile, the lake-filled expanse that beats east of the Cascades is the domain of the Klamath Tribes. The region's waterfalls, lakes, and salmon-rich rivers have long been sacred to Native Americans and today, they are involved in efforts to heal waterways and bring back sustainable fishing practices.

Now, the area is also a playground for outdoor adventurers. To the north, Crater Lake National Park protects a volcanic caldera and the deepest lake in America – hiking trails swirl around the rim and into thickly forested backcountry. Southeast of the park, the Klamath Basin offers some of the best birding in the country, while the wild rivers out west promise world-class white water.

The Rogue and Umpqua valleys are up-and-coming wine regions that rival their northern counterparts when it comes to quality and diversity. More epicurean delights can be found in cool small towns and cities such as Grants Pass and Ashland, which has an arts and culture scene that punches well above its weight.

The river-threaded Illinois Valley.

ILLINOIS VALLEY

If you have made your way down the coast, with a quick pitstop in Northern California, then US-199 (Redwoods Highway) is a scenic entry point to Southern Oregon. The route hugs the Smith River in California then, after crossing the state line, spools into the Illinois Valley.

The **Illinois River** gives the valley its name. It flows without upstream dams and is an excellent white-water destination. Rapids range from Class III to IV and various tour companies (only

Main attractions

Oregon Caves National
  Monument and Preserve
Rogue Valley wine country
Jacksonville
Crater Lake National Park
Ashland
Upper Klamath Lake

Maps on pages
152, 158

experienced rafters should travel without a guide) offer excursions on the river, including highly rated **ARTA** (tel: 209-962 7873; www.arta.org; meeting location for Illinois trips is in Grants Pass). The river is also an important habitat for steelhead trout and wild salmon.

Push north on US-199 and you'll reach **Cave Junction**. This little gold-rush town is a springboard for **Oregon Caves National Monument and Preserve**  (19000 Caves Highway; tel: 541-592 2100; www.nps.gov/orca).

ROGUE VALLEY

From Cave Junction, continue north on US-199. You will pass pint-sized Illinois Valley towns such as **Wilderville** on the way to **Grants Pass** ❷, where the rustic **Weasku Inn** (5560 Rogue River Highway; tel: 541-471 8000; www.weasku.com) makes a great base for exploring the Rogue Valley. Opt for one of the quaint lodge rooms or a cabin overlooking the Rogue River. It is also well worth making a jaunt out west to the **Rogue Creamery Dairy Farm** (6531 Lower River Road; tel: 541-471

7292; www.roguecreamery.com; Wed–Sun 10am–5pm). Free guided tours (10am and 2pm) offer the chance to meet the dairy herd and take a peek at the robotic milking room.

Jet-boat tours on the **Wild and Scenic Rogue River** are popular in this area. **Hellgate Jetboat Excursions** (966 SW 6th Street; tel: 541-479 7204; www.hellgate.com) is one of the original operators and one of the best – guides will take you on a thrilling high-speed ride in the Hellgate Canyon and offer narration on the waterway's wildlife and history. Some tour options include brunch and dinner.

Grants Pass also has a neat downtown core with several great spots for craft drinks. Sup IPAs and blondes at **Climate City Brewing** (509 SW G Street; tel: 541-479 3725; www.climatecitybrewing.com; Tue–Sun 3–8pm) or try house-made vodka and gin at adjacent steampunk-themed **Steam Distillery** (505 SW G Street; tel: 541-236 4459; www.facebook.com/SteamDistilleryGP; Tue–Sun 4–10pm). Also on this main drag is the **Glass Forge Gallery and Studio**

(501 SW G Street; tel: 541-955 0815; www.glassforge.com; Mon–Fri 8am–5pm, Sat 10am–4pm), where professional glass-blowers chat to visitors in their workshops, and an exhibition space showcases fine examples of the craft. You can get involved with make-your-own sessions, too. Just along the road is the **Grants Pass Museum of Art** (229 SW G St 2nd Floor; tel: 541-479-3290; www.gpmuseum.com; Tue–Sat 10am–5pm; free), which has changing exhibits by local and international artists, with mediums ranging from pottery and fabric to paintings and photography. The museum also hosts regular art workshops and live-music events.

The table to book is at **River's Edge Restaurant** (1936 Rogue River Highway; tel: 541-244 1182; www.riversedge restaurant.net; daily noon–8pm). As its name suggests, it has a prime location right on the banks of the Rogue River, with a patio offering water views. Its kitchen milks the Pacific Northwest's bounty of produce, with a menu that includes blackened Oregon steelhead and Rogue Creamery blue cheese.

WINE COUNTRY

From Grants Pass, OR-238 beats a scenic path through the Applegate Valley, passing squat red barns, cattle-speckled fields, and an abundance of wineries. Sitting within the larger **Rogue Valley AVA**, the **Applegate Valley AVA** sprawls across 275,000-plus acres (110,000 hectares) and spools 50 miles (80km) northward from the California border to the Rogue River. It's parceled into the Siskiyou Mountains, which shelter the land from cooling Pacific Ocean breezes and create a climate that's altogether warmer than popular Willamette Valley to the north. The undulating hills and valleys produce a series of microclimates that make for an extremely diverse growing region: more than 70 varietals can be found here. The region's hot, dry days and cool nights lend themselves particularly well to bold Rhone and Bordeaux-style wines. Standouts include Cabernet Sauvignon, Syrah, Tempranillo, and Merlot, plus the Pinot Noir and Chardonnay that is also commonly grown in the northern reaches of the state.

Grants Pass.

Tourist offerings vary between the wineries in the area. **Troon Vineyard** ❸ (1475 Kubli Road; tel: 541-846 9900; www.troonvineyard.com; daily 11am–5pm) is a leader in sustainability and has met strict criteria for its Regenerative Organic certification. The vineyard grants unrivaled views of the lushly forested Siskiyou Mountains and has a tasting room where you can sip varietals from Vermentino to Tannat. Continue traveling southeast along OR-238 and you will reach **Red Lily Vineyards** (11777 OR-238; tel: 541-846 6800; www.redlilyvineyards.com; Thu–Sun 11am–5pm), a pretty boutique winery that deals in Tempranillo and Syrah. The venue offers tasting flights in little test tubes and a menu of light bites, including a tapas platter with local cheese and charcuterie, and home-made soup. Also close by is **Quady North** ❹ (9800 OR-238; tel: 541-702 2123; www.quadynorth.com; Wed–Mon 11am–5pm), whose offering draws inspiration from France's Rhône and Loire valleys. Attached to the winery, the tasting room offers five-wine flights,

Applegate Valley AVA is dotted with vineyards.

showcasing thoughtful Rhône blends, plus Viogniers and Syrahs.

JACKSONVILLE

Arrow north on OR-238 toward the historic small town of **Jacksonville** ❺ – one of the oldest in the state. It sprouted up when gold was struck in the region in 1851, some eight years before Oregon was admitted into the union. The setting is spectacular, tucked into the foothills of the Siskiyou Mountains, surrounded by the vine-striped Rogue Valley.

Its Historic District was listed on the National Register in 1966, so its 19th-century Western-style architecture has been mercifully preserved, and a walk down the atmospheric Main Street will make you feel as though you're on a movie set. It has indeed been the setting for several Western movies, including *The Great Northfield Minnesota Raid,* shot here in 1972. And it has its own bona-fide Wild West history, too. The criminals behind what's tipped as "the last great train robbery in the West" were tried at the **Historic**

⊘ GOING UNDERGROUND

Tucked away in the Siskiyou Mountains, the caverns of the Oregon Caves National Monument were formed as acidic water ate away at the region's marble rock over many millennia. Ranger-led tours take visitors into the maze of marble passageways and book up quickly in summer. The 90-minute Discovery Cave Tour and the Candlelight Cave Tour are popular options, but there are also tours geared toward kids, plus more strenuous off-trail excursions that involve crawling and scrambling. Above ground, the Cliff Nature Trail offers hikers sweeping views across the Illinois Valley. The Illinois Valley Visitor Center (201 Caves Highway; tel: 541-592 5125; Mon–Sat 8.30am–4pm) is right in town – you can buy tour tickets and peruse a small exhibition about the history of the caves. From here, the site entrance is around 20 miles (32km) east on OR-46.

Jackson County Courthouse (206 N 5th Street). Twins Ray and Ron DeAutremont and their younger brother Hugh held up a Southern Pacific Railroad train thought to be carrying some $40,000. The robbery was unsuccessful but, in their attempt, the brothers killed several workers including the brakeman and the mail clerk. The siblings fled the scene and weren't tried until 1927. The event became known as the Siskiyou Massacre.

Begin your tour of Jacksonville by drinking in the facade of the courthouse, an elegant Italianate building completed in 1883. In summer, from June to September, the **Jacksonville Farmers Market** is hosted outside on the lawn. Next, wander down to California Street, Jacksonville's main artery, which is filled with Western false-front architecture and red-brick buildings stamped with fading ghost signs. Today, those protected 19th-century relics have been reimagined as upscale boutiques, independent restaurants, coffee shops, and wine bars. Favorites include **Bella Union**, a pizza parlor with

a buzzy, tree-shaded patio and regular live-music sets, and **Umi Sushi**, a modern Japanese spot. Also on this street is the **Beekman Bank Museum** (110 W California Street; temporarily closed). It's the oldest financial institution north of San Francisco, built circa 1863, and also the only wooden commercial building to have survived the multiple fires throughout Jacksonville's history. It has been preserved as a museum since 1915, the year in which entrepreneurial bank owner Cornelius C. Beekman passed away. Historic Jacksonville (tel: 541-245 3650; www.historicjacksonville.org) usually offers tours of the bank, though these are temporarily paused.

Just off the main drag, **South Stage Cellars** (125 S 3rd Street; tel: 541-899 9120; www.southstagecellars.com; Feb–Apr Wed–Sun 1–7pm; May–Dec daily 1–7pm) is a tasting room offering wines made with grapes grown at Quail Run Vineyards, a string of 13 vineyards in the Rogue Valley that supports some 31 varieties. It is housed in a red-brick building dating back to 1864 and features a pretty shaded garden; live

Winery near Ashland.

music; and rotating exhibitions featuring local artists.

Head west along California Street and you will reach the entrance to **Britt Gardens**, which is the location for the **Britt Music & Arts Festival**, an annual summer event showcasing orchestral performances, comedy and film screenings, and live concerts headlined by big names such as American singer-songwriter Kelsea Ballerini. The garden is named for local hero Peter Britt, a photographer and horticulturalist who documented 19th-century Jacksonville history and planted early grape vines here. His homesite was destroyed by fire, but a reconstruction of the foundations was added in 1976.

DRIVING THE ROGUE-UMPQUA SCENIC BYWAY

Once you've explored Jacksonville, you can either head immediately north toward Crater Lake National Park or first strike farther south and east. If you take the first option, you will find yourself on the **Rogue-Umpqua Scenic Byway**, a picturesque driving route dominated by two of Oregon's Wild and Scenic Rivers (the Rogue and Umpqua) and the verdant Cascade Range.

Push north from Jacksonville on the bucolic Old Stage Road and within 20 minutes you will reach **Gold Hill** and the entry point to the Scenic Byway. From here, the road follows the Rogue River's wiggling route upstream, passing through **Shady Cove ❻**, a great jumping-off point for adventures on the water. **Rapid Pleasure Rafting Company** (125 Chaparral Drive; tel: 541-878 2500; www.rapidpleasurerafting.com) operates from the town and offers raft, kayak, and stand-up paddleboard rentals. Make sure you familiarize yourself with river best practice and safety before heading out on any self-guided trip.

The byway follows the OR-62 north and skirts **Lost Creek Lake**, a sprawling mountain reservoir popular for water-skiing, boating, and fishing. Boat rentals are available at the marina. Push farther north along the fir-lined road and you'll come to **Prospect**, a

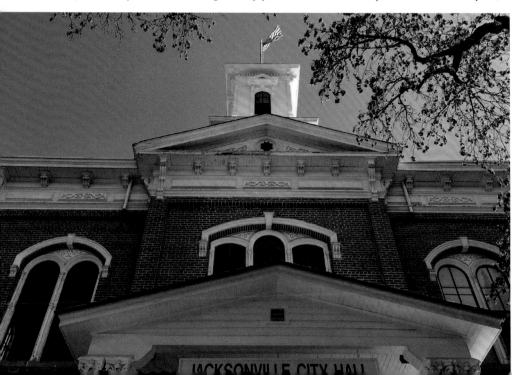

Jacksonville City Hall.

blink-and-you'll-miss-it town that makes a good base for exploring **Crater Lake National Park** ❼. Book into the **Union Creek Resort** (56484 OR-62; tel: 866-560 3565; www.unioncreekoregon. com), which offers lodge rooms with wood-clad country decor and a series of rustic log cabins.

It would be criminal not to detour eastward on OR-62 to explore the national park, but the northern stretch of the Rogue-Umpqua Scenic Byway, which continues on OR-230, is not to be missed either. **Diamond Lake Resort** (350 Resort Drive; tel: 541-793 3333; www.diamondlake.net) is an adventure-lover's paradise. In summer, it is a hub for hiking, fishing, and equestrian activities, while in winter, the focus is snowshoeing, tubing, and skiing.

Next, the Byway curls west on OR-138, snaking toward **Toketee Falls** ❽ (tel: 541-957 3200; www.fs.usda.gov/ umpqua). The trail to reach the cascade is relatively short at 0.4 miles (0.6km), but it does involve around 200 stairs – a bench positioned halfway along the route offers a welcome reprieve

from the climbing. It is well worth the calf-shredding ascent, though: the hike slices through thickets of old-growth Douglas firs and Western red cedars and opens to a lookout point that offers spectacular views of the cascade. The waterfall plunges a total of 120ft (37 meters) over two drops and its name comes from the Chinook word for "graceful."

The northern stretches of the byway are a mecca for hikers. The region's **North Umpqua Trail** takes in 79 scenic miles (127km), hugging the densely forested banks of its namesake. Thirteen trailheads stud the route, offering tempting diversions.

At this point in your journey, you'll be within easy reach of the **Jessie Wright Segment**, accessed by the **Marsters** or **Soda Springs Trailhead** ❾. Named for an early homesteader, it extends for 4.1 miles (7km), slicing through peaceful Douglas fir and maple forests.

Continuing west, OR-138 ambles west toward **Roseburg** ❿, gateway to the wine-rich **Umpqua Valley**.

Toketee Falls.

158

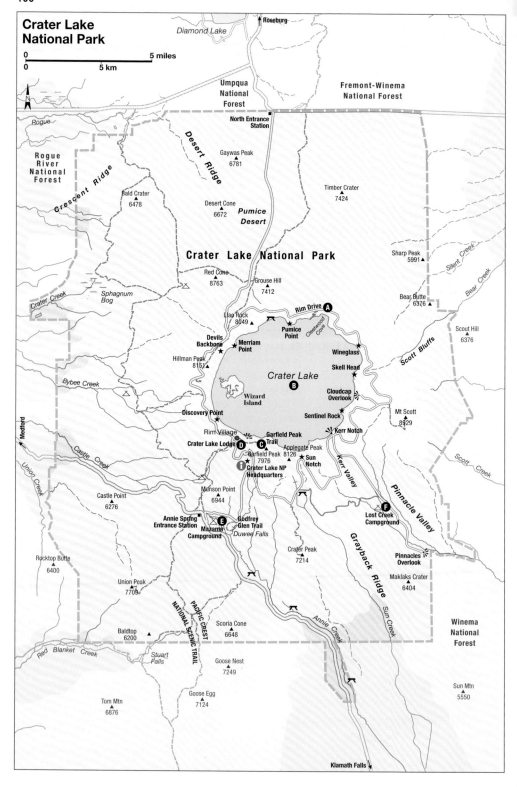

Crater Lake
National Park

0 _____ 5 miles
0 _____ 5 km

N

Diamond Lake

↑ Roseburg

Umpqua
National
Forest

Fremont-Winema
National Forest

Rogue

North Entrance
Station

Rogue River
National Forest

Crescent Ridge

Desert Ridge

Gaywas Peak
6781

Timber Crater
7424

Bald Crater
6478

Desert Cone
6672

Pumice
Desert

Sharp Peak
5991 ▲

Silent Creek

Crater Creek

Sphagnum
Bog

Crater Lake National Park

Red Cone
8763

Grouse Hill
7412

Bear Butte
6376

Bear Creek

Scout Hill
6376

Llao Rock
8049

Rim Drive Ⓐ

Pumice
Point

Cleetwood Cove

Devils
Backbone

Merriam
Point

Wineglass

Skell Head

Scott Bluffs

Hillman Peak
8151 ▲

Bybee Creek

Crater Lake

Ⓑ

Wizard
Island

Cloudcap
Overlook

Mt Scott
8929

Medford

Castle Creek

Discovery Point

Sentinel Rock

Scott Creek

Union Creek

Rim Village

Garfield Peak
Trail

Kerr Notch

Crater Lake Lodge Ⓓ Ⓒ

Garfield Peak 8126
7976

Applegate Peak

Kerr Valley

Pinnacle Valley

Ⓘ Crater Lake NP
Headquarters

Sun
Notch

Ⓕ

Castle Point
6276

Munson Point
6944

Lost Creek
Campground

Rocktop Butte
6400

Annie Spring
Entrance Station

Ⓔ
Mazama
Campground

Godfrey
Glen Trail

Duwee Falls

Grayback Ridge

Pinnacles
Overlook

Crater Peak
7214

Maklaks Crater
6404

Union Peak
7709

PACIFIC CREST NATIONAL SCENIC TRAIL

Scoria Cone
6648

Annie Creek

Sun Creek

Winema
National
Forest

Red Blanket Creek

Baldtop
6200

Stuart
Falls

Goose Nest
7249

Sun Mtn
5550

Tom Mtn
6876

Goose Egg
7124

Klamath Falls ↘

UMPQUA VALLEY

It is worth lingering in Roseburg. The city is home to the **Douglas County Museum**, which focuses on the region's natural history, from the mountains to the river valley. Exhibits also display relics such as basketry and weaponry from the Umpqua, who have been residing in the area for more than 10,000 years. You will find several locations on the **Great Umpqua Food Trail** in Roseburg.

Among them is the **Umpqua Valley Farmers' Market** (1771 W Harvard Avenue; tel: 541-530 6200; www.uvfarmersmarket.com), which takes place on Saturdays and celebrates the region's producers. Other favorites include **Old Soul Pizza** (525 SE Main Street; tel: 541-672 3513; www.oldsoulpizza.com; Tue–Wed 3–8pm, Thu–Sat noon–8pm) for artisan wood-fired pies, and the **Takelma Roasting Company** (2048 NE Airport Road; tel: 541-492 6248; www.takelmaroasting.com; Mon–Fri 9am–4.30pm), a specialty coffee roaster run by the Cow Creek Band of Umpqua Tribe of Indians. Those who prefer beer over beans should try **Two Shy Brewing** (1308 NW Park Street #100; tel: 541-236 2055; www.twoshybrewing.com; Mon–Thu noon–8pm, Fri, Sat until 9pm). The highlights here are a crisp Czech/German style pilsner and citrusy IPAs, plus it has plenty of outdoor space and offerings from a rotating roster of food trucks. (There's another location on the coast at Reedsport.)

The Umpqua River Scenic Byway provides further opportunity for exploring the valley. Drive north from Roseburg on the I-5 until you reach **Sutherlin**. From here, you can follow the Scenic Byway to **Oakland ⑪**. The main calling card of this quaint town is its historic core, which is protected on the National Register of Historic Places: upward of 80 sites are preserved here, many dating from the 1880s and 1890s.

Lose yourself in the tangle of antiques stores and art galleries, then make a pitstop at the **Oakland Museum**, which gives an insight into local history and industry, from peach canning to logging.

⊙ Tip

In winter, due to the snow, the road from the Park Headquarters to Rim Village at the south entrance may be closed. Rim Drive and the North Entrance to the park always close for the winter season (typically mid-October through to mid-July). Check the alerts page on the NPS website (www.nps.gov/crla) for updates before you travel.

Umpqua Valley is one of Oregon's oldest wine regions.

⊘ UMPQUA VALLEY WINES

The fertile banks of the Umpqua River form one of Oregon's oldest wine-producing regions. The Umpqua Valley AVA is incredibly diverse given that it is flanked by the Cascades on its eastern side and the Coast Range to the west, plus the Willamette Valley to the north and the Rogue Valley to the south. This lends the region a series of microclimates, from cooler, more rain-prone climes in the western area around Elkton, to warmer, drier conditions as you swoop south toward the Rogue Valley. A short drive northwest of Downtown Roseburg is the Cooper Ridge Vineyard (1389 Old Garden Valley Road; tel: 541-671 2373; www.cooperridgevineyard.com; Thu–Sun noon–7pm). Come by the tasting room to try bold Syrahs and Tempranillos, plus crisp Rieslings and Viogniers. Another hotspot is the Henry Estate Winery (687 Hubbard Creek Road; tel: 800-782 2686; www.henryestate.com; daily 11am–5pm), a short drive north. Here, you'll taste the traditional German variety Müller-Thurgau, as well as excellent Pinot gris and Pinot noir. Farther north, the Elkton AVA is a sub-appellation. Bradley Vineyards (1000 Azalea Drive; tel: 541-584 2888; www.bradleyvineyards.com; Wed–Sun 11am–5pm) is well worth a stop. It deals in Pinot Noir, Gewurztraminer, and Riesling, and has fantastic views of the Coast Range.

Crater Lake in winter.

CRATER LAKE

Depending on where your Southern Oregon adventures have taken you, you might approach **Crater Lake National Park** from various entry points. From the southwest (Jacksonville, Medford, Ashland) or the immediate south (Klamath Falls), you'll approach on the OR-62 – the section of OR-62 routing north from Klamath Falls overlaps with the **Volcanic Legacy Scenic Byway**, making for a spectacular introduction to the park. From the north (Sutherlin, Roseburg), you'll come in on the OR-138, which also eventually morphs into the drama-filled byway.

There are various ways to explore the park and in summer, the most popular way is by car or bike along the 33-mile (53km) **Rim Drive** Ⓐ (open seasonally). As its name suggests, it skirts the rim of the caldera, affording epic views over the deep blue **Crater Lake** Ⓑ. Besides being closed in winter, the park sometimes operates car-free days, when Rim Drive is only open to cyclists – check the NPS website for upcoming dates.

Beyond the scenic drive, some 90 miles (145km) of hiking trails beat into Crater Lake's wilderness. Among them is the popular **Garfield Peak Trail** Ⓒ. It spills out for 1.7 miles (2.7km), gaining around 1,000ft (305 meters) in elevation as it strikes toward the rim. Your uphill efforts are rewarded with more pinch-yourself views over the lake. Conveniently, the trailhead is next to **Crater Lake Lodge** Ⓓ (70 Rim Village Drive; tel: 866-292 6720; www.nps.gov/crla), a charming historic inn built back in the early 20th century.

There are also camping options within the park – both **Mazama Campground** Ⓔ (OR-62; tel: 866-292 6720) and **Lost Creek Campground** Ⓕ (Rhododendron, OR 97049; tel: 541-328 0909) typically open in July and close in the fall.

The latter is tent only, while the former has space for RVs with some electric hook-ups available.

You can get out on the water, too. Throughout the summer months, daily tours run by **Crater Lake Hospitality** (www.travelcraterlake.com) take to

⊘ WINTER AT CRATER LAKE

Crater Lake is an altogether different beast in winter – but the landscapes are impossibly beautiful when carpeted in blindingly white snow. If all the roads to the rim are closed, you can tackle the strenuous Raven Trail as a snowshoe hike. It is a 2-mile (3.2km) round trip that should take around 3 hours out-and-back and involves blazing a path through heavy snow, gaining 610ft (186 meters) in elevation. You will pass two avalanche zones so it is advisable to hire a guide who is trained in avalanche safety and is equipped with shovels, probes, and beacons. Main Street Adventure and Wine Tours (tel: 541-625-9845, www.ashland-tours.com) is a fantastic option.

Make sure that you dress in warm layers, with waterproof boots, thick socks, gloves, and sunglasses to counteract the snow glare. The chance to have a snowy, fir-filled wilderness to yourself is the hike's great appeal, as are the sweeping views of Crater Lake from the rim. Be aware that low-hanging clouds can often obscure lake views in winter – various live cams allow you to check visibility before you head out. Conditions shift quickly, though, so it is worth lingering if the lake is clouded when you arrive. Beyond hiking, there is the opportunity for downhill skiing (there are no lifts, and the ungroomed trails are best left to pros), cross-country skiing, snowmobiling, and sledding. As always, only venture into Oregon's backcountry in winter if you are experienced and prepared, or with a guide.

the lake. A short but steep trail – the **Cleetwood Cove Trail** – leads to the lakeshore and the boat docks. Narrated **Crater Lake Trolley tours** also run through the season.

MEDFORD

The largest city in the area, **Medford ⑫** may be characterized by urban sprawl, but that is not to say it lacks charm – not least because of its bucolic Rogue Valley setting, which means ample opportunity for ventures into wine country. Within easy reach are local favorites **RoxyAnn Winery** (3283 Hillcrest Road; tel: 541-776 2315; www.roxyann.com) and **2Hawk Vineyard & Winery** (2335 N Phoenix Road; tel: 541-779 9463; www.2hawk.wine).

Highlights in the city proper include 1740-acre **Prescott Park** (3030 Roxy Ann Road; tel: 541-774 2400; www.medfordoregon.gov). Here, hiking trails wind to the summit of Roxy Ann Peak, sitting a sky-piercing 3,571ft (1,088 meters) above sea level. On the cultural front, the beloved **Craterian Theater** (23 S Central Avenue; tel: 541-779 3000; www.craterian.org) sets the stage for musicals, family-friendly plays, dance recitals, and orchestral performances.

Meanwhile, just outside of town, **Upper and Lower Table Rock** – a pair of dramatic, lava-topped mesas – beckon to hikers. Take the 2.5-mile (4km) Upper Table Rock Trail or the 3.5-mile (6km) Lower Table Rock Trail, each with epic vistas of the Rogue Valley and the Cascade and Siskiyou mountains.

ASHLAND

A cultural haven at the base of the Siskiyou and Cascade mountains, the college town of **Ashland ⑬** has a bounty of theaters, galleries, and festivals with a focus on the arts, and is the home of Southern Oregon University. The **Allen Elizabethan Theater** (15 S Pioneer Street; tel: 541-482 2111; www.osfashland.org), which has been remodeled several times over the decades, is America's oldest, and home of the beloved **Oregon Shakespeare Festival**, established back in 1935. Each season, the long-running

◉ Tip

Mount Ashland's lofty terrain lends itself best to intermediate and advanced skiers: the 1st to 5th Chutes is a series of double black diamond runs, while single black diamond routes include the Upper Tempest and Balcony Trails. There are lessons available for beginners, and the area around the Learning Center also has a couple of easier and gentler runs. Gear rentals are available here, too.

Ashland is sheltered at the foot of the Siskiyou and Cascade mountains.

⊙ Eat

Ashland's elevated culinary offerings and artistic delights are celebrated with multiple festivals throughout the year. These include the springtime A Taste of Ashland (www.atasteof ashland.com), which organizes tastings from the region's top restaurants and wineries, alongside local gallery openings.

Allen Elizabethan Theater in Ashland.

theater company puts on a program of the Bard's most revered comedies, tragedies, and histories. The **Oregon Cabaret Theater** (41 Hargadine Street; tel: 541-488 2902; www.oregoncaba-ret.com) is another highlight, hosting everything from Broadway shows and murder mysteries to contemporary plays. On the gallery front, do not miss **Art & Soul Ashland** (247 E Main Street; tel: 541-880 4100; www.artand-soulashland.com; Tue–Sat 10am–6pm), which showcases everything from oil paintings to pottery.

Ashland has fine restaurants aplenty. Book a table at **Alchemy** (35 S 2nd Street; tel: 541-488 1115; www.alchemyashland.com; Tue–Sat 5–10pm), an experimental restaurant known for its upscale French-inspired dishes such as duck leg confit or curried moules frites. **Irvine & Roberts Vineyards** (1614 Emigrant Creek Road; tel: 541-482 9383; www.irvinerobertsvine-yards.com; daily noon–6pm) produces fabulous Pinot Noir, Chardonnay, and sparkling wines at a breathtaking site 2,100ft (640-meter) in elevation. Just

30min outside the city, the **Mount Ashland Ski Area** ⓮ (11 Mt Ashland Ski Road; tel: 541-482 2897; www.mtashland.com) has been running since the 1960s and spreads out in the Siskiyou Mountains, soaring to 7,533ft (2,296 meters).

KLAMATH BASIN

Around 64 miles (103km) east of Ashland, **Klamath Falls** ⓯ can be found within the breathtaking Klamath Basin, a vast and scenic area drained by the Klamath River. This is the ancestral land of the Klamath, Modoc, and Yahooskin-Paiute, who now form the federally recognized Klamath Tribes and have been living in the region for many millennia.

In town, the **Favell Museum** (125 W Main Street; tel: 541-882 9996; www.favellmuseum.org; Tue–Sat 10am–5pm) centers on Indigenous culture, showing more than 100,000 Native American artifacts, from ancient stone tools and arrowheads to beads and basketry. There is also a collection of Western art, including works by painters such as Charles Marion Russell.

Klamath Falls is the perfect jumping-off point for adventures on the **Volcanic Legacy Scenic Byway**, which reveals more of the astonishing Klamath Basin area. The byway follows OR-140 along the western edge of **Upper Klamath Lake**, first sweeping past sprawling cattle ranches and pine forests, and soon affording sweeping views of the water. Upper Klamath is the largest freshwater lake in Oregon, offering ample opportunities for paddling on the surface and hiking on the shores. Keen kayakers can follow the **Upper Klamath Canoe Trail**, which snakes through freshwater marshes for 9.5 miles (15km) – there are boat launches at the Rocky Point and Malone Springs day-use areas. Keep your eyes peeled for beavers, otters, and muskrats, plus ducks and geese.

A detour west will lead you to some of the area's best hiking. From the **Summit Sno-Park** (tel: 541-885 3400; www.fs.usda.gov/recarea/fremont-winema/recarea), you can trek a portion of the fabled **Pacific Crest Trail**. Head south on the haunches of Brown Mountain,

through epic volcanic scenery, and you will be rewarded with views of Mount McLoughlin. The **Upper Klamath National Wildlife Refuge** ⑯ is a must-visit for birders. The refuge supports an abundance of species, from the American white pelican to bald eagles and osprey, and provides critical habitat for birds traveling on the Pacific Flyway migration route, from Alaska to South America's Patagonia.

Farther north on the Byway, **Fort Klamath** ⑰ (51400 OR-62; tel: 541-381 2230; www.klamathcountymuseum; June–Sept Thu–Mon 10am–6pm) is a top stop for history buffs. This old military outpost was established in 1863 and, today, museum exhibits tell the story of the Modoc War, a bloody conflict between the Modoc people and the federal government that raged on from 1872 to 1873. The war was sparked when the Modocs resisted forced removal from their homeland to the Klamath Reservation, and the colonizers responded with violence. The site includes the graves of four members of the Modoc tribe.

The Klamath Basin, a pitstop for migratory birds on the Pacific Flyway.

⊙ OREGON OUTBACK

A portion of the Oregon Outback Scenic Byway routes through the South, before bending into Central Oregon. The region is characterized by vast and starkly beautiful swathes of High Desert, soaring lakes – from Goose Lake to Lake Albert – and little towns such as Paisley, which has a palpable Old West feel, right down to the Pioneer Saloon (327 Main Street; tel: 541-943 3289; Wed–Sun 11.30am–9pm). The oldest human feces to have been found in North America were discovered in nearby Paisley Caves (currently closed). Nearby, Summer Lake Hot Springs (41777 Oregon 31 Mile Marker; tel: 541-943 3931; www.summerlakehotsprings.com) are revered for their healing waters and a resort provides lodging in cabins. Lakeview touts itself as "Oregon's Tallest Town," sits at an elevation of 4,798ft (1,462 meters), and proving popular with hang-gliders.

📷 CRATER LAKE

A cataclysmic eruption more than seven millennia ago created one of Oregon's most awe-inspiring natural wonders.

Crater Lake National Park offers heart-in-mouth views like no other place in the state. A pool of sapphire water is cradled among volcanic walls, its otherworldly blue hue gaining an extra pop when its surroundings are caked in snow. It was formed some 7,700 years ago when ancient Mount Mazama – once a sky-scraping 12,000ft (3,656 meters) tall – erupted violently, shooting columns of searing hot gas and rock into the air. Some 12 cubic miles (50 cubic km) of matter streamed out of the volcano, which then collapsed in on itself, leaving a gaping caldera.

Following this major event, smaller eruptions continued to shake the aching chasm, creating formations such as Wizard Island, the tree-blanketed cinder cone that spikes out of the lake's glossy surface today. Then, over the centuries, the caldera filled up with rain and snow until it formed what is now the nation's deepest lake, at a mind-boggling 1,943ft (592 meters). Mount Mazama has remained dormant for the past 5,000 years, though experts think some kind of volcanic activity is a possibility in the future.

The national park was formed in 1902, protecting the ancient mountain and its caldera, plus great tracts of old-growth forest, home to black bears, mountain lions, and deer. It is laced with some 90 miles (145km) of hiking trails, plus scenic drives studded with overlooks and interpretive panels.

Cleetwood Cove bites into the shoreline of Crater Lake.

Wizard Island, the result of volcanic activity.

Vidae Falls in Crater Lake National Park.

Crater Lake Lodge, a good base for the Garfield Peak Trail.

Mount Mazama and the Llao spirit

Though there is little evidence to suggest that Mount Mazama was ever settled permanently, it is of great importance to the Klamath people, who are descendants of the Makalaks. According to oral histories, the mountain was inhabited by a spirit named Llao, who was Chief of the Below World. Llao would regularly come up from below ground to the summit of Mount Mazama and look out across the land; on one of these occasions, he caught sight of the Makalak chief's beautiful daughter and was instantly besotted by her. He promised her eternal life if she would return with him to the Below World. When she rebuffed him, he flew into a rage and launched fire down toward the Makalak village. That's when the spirit Skell, Chief of the Above World, who lived atop Mount Shasta, took pity on the victimized humans and waged his own war against Llao. The powerful spirits fought until two local holy men sacrificed themselves by jumping into the pit of fire between the raging gods to appease them. Emboldened by the men's bravery, Skell ultimately drove Llao into the ground and when the sun rose the next morning, the mountain had collapsed on top of him, sealing him inside forever.

Serene views await hikers in Crater Lake National Park.

The endangered Sierra Nevada red fox roams the park.

The 400,000-year-old Phantom Ship pierces the lake.

Bend cityscape against a backdrop of Mount Jefferson.

CENTRAL OREGON

Swathes of sage-scattered High Desert, volcanic peaks, and the rushing Deschutes River have created a natural arena for hiking, biking, rafting, and kayaking.

You can see the evidence of eons of volcanic activity at every turn in Central Oregon. Brawny peaks, from Mount Jefferson to Black Butte to craggy Three Fingered Jack, shoot toward the skies; inky black lava flows twist across the ground. By the time you reach Central Oregon, the Cascades have squeezed the rain from the clouds, leaving acres of stark, dry High Desert and dust, scattered with sage and juniper, and threaded with ponderosa pines. The other life force here is the Deschutes River, which writhes through the region, providing a playground for rafters, kayakers, and boaters. This is the homeland of the Confederated Tribes of Warm Springs – including the Wasco, Paiute and Warm Springs peoples – who make efforts to preserve their traditional culture and lifeways.

All roads lead to Central Oregon. Depending on your route through the state, you might strike south from the Columbia River Gorge region on US-197, the great hulk of Mount Hood rising out to the west. Or you could approach from the coast, snaking through the Cascades on US-20 and skirting the Santiam Pass as you beat toward Bend. Coming up from Southern Oregon, you will travel on the US-97, which hugs the Deschutes River as it pushes north, passing La Pine and Sunriver.

Old Mill District in Bend.

BEND

The mountain town of **Bend** ❶ is at the region's heart and makes an ideal springboard for outdoor adventures in Central Oregon. Do not be tempted to escape into the mountains as soon as you arrive, though – this dinky city has plenty to offer in its own right, from award-winning craft beer to galleries and live entertainment. Bend's Downtown is compact and easily walkable, and most of the action is centered on Wall Street and Bond Street, as well as on Minnesota and Oregon avenues.

Main attractions

Bend
High Desert Museum
Newberry National
  Volcanic Monument
Prineville Reservoir
  State Park
Mount Bachelor
  Ski Resort
Three Sisters Wilderness
The Museum at
  Warm Springs

**Maps on pages
168, 170**

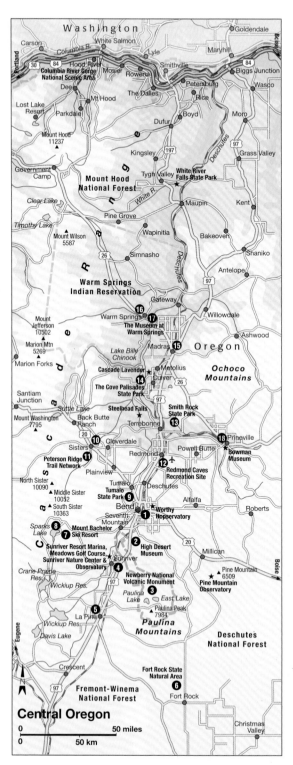

The **Oxford Hotel Bend (A)** (10 NW Minnesota Avenue; tel: 541-382 8436; www.oxfordhotelbend.com) makes an ideal base. The decor takes cues from the great outdoors with plenty of dark wood and nature-inspired artworks, and the property anchors you on Minnesota Avenue. Immediately opposite is the Downtown location of **Thump Coffee (B)** (25 NW Minnesota Avenue; tel: 541-388 0226; www.thumpcoffee.com; Mon–Fri 6am–5.30pm, Sat 7am–5.30pm, Sun 7am–4.30pm), a local favorite for a morning brew, bagels, and baked goods. Just around the corner, on Wall Street, **Tower Theater (C)** (835 NW Wall Street; tel: 541-317 0700; www.towertheatre.org) has earned the nickname "Bend's Living Room." The schedule here runs the gamut from comedy shows and live theater to movie screenings and concerts. A few doors down, by way of a couple of boutique clothing stores, you will find the **Mockingbird Gallery (D)** (869 NW Wall Street; tel: 541-388 2107; www.mockingbird-gallery.com; Mon–Sat 10am–6pm, Sun 11am–4pm). Fine artists from across the country are represented here, and the collection is dominated by rural landscape and wildlife paintings in a variety of mediums. It is also a participating venue in Bend's First Friday Art Walk.

Continue southwest down Wall Street and you will eventually come to the **Deschutes Historical Museum (E)** (129 NW Idaho Avenue; tel: 541-389 1813; www.deschuteshistory.org; Tue–Sat 10am–4.30pm). It's housed in the attractive 1914-built Reid School, which operated until the 1970s, and is constructed from locally quarried pink volcanic tuff. Displays cover the Native Americans who traditionally owned these lands, and the early history of Bend and Central Oregon, including homesteaders and logging.

The Downtown area has some fabulous eating spots. **Wild Rose (F)** (150 NW Oregon Avenue; tel: 541-382 0441; Sun–Thu 11am–8.30pm, Fri, Sat until 9.30pm) is rightfully popular, specializing in dishes from Northern Thailand such as fragrant khao soi curry. (Right opposite, **Smith Rock Records**  (117 NW Oregon Avenue; tel: 541-389 6116; www.facebook.com/SmithRockRecords; Tue–Thu 11am–6pm, Fri, Sat until 7pm, Sun noon–5pm) is the best place to buy new and used vinyl and CDs, as well as band T-shirts and posters.)

For old-school vibes, try **The Pine Tavern** ⑭ (967 NW Brooks Street; tel: 541-382 5581; www.pinetavern.net; Tue–Sat noon–8pm, Sun 2–8pm), which sits on Mirror Pond and has a ponderosa pine tree growing right up through the dining room. You can expect standard American dishes executed to a high standard and made from thoughtfully sourced ingredients. For something casual, visit **The Podski** ⑪ (536 NW Arizona Avenue; www.thepodski.com). This fun food cart lot is filled with trucks dishing up everything from tacos and Thai food to pierogi (dumplings) and barbecue.

Immediately south of Downtown, **Box Factory** ⑯ (550 SW Industrial Way) has plenty more restaurants and drinking holes, plus a variety of shops.

As its name suggests, the venue began as a box factory, built in 1916 as part of the Brooks-Scanlon mill complex, and operating up until 1994. Renovations began in 2013 and it is now a well-loved local hangout. Shop for one-off art pieces, outdoor gear, and home furnishings and feast on deli sandwiches, ramen, or pub food. There are myriad spots to sup cider, beer, and wine.

Bend's wider neighborhoods also have a few jewels. The **Old Mill District** ⑯ is the best place for shopping. The area is essentially an open-air mall with stores selling everything from clothing and jewelry to gifts and home decor. It is home to the **Hayden Homes Amphitheater** ⑫ (www.bendconcerts.com), a live-music venue that's hosted big names from Bob Dylan to Ringo Starr.

The funky **Midtown** ⑭ neighborhood is home to the world's very last **Blockbuster** ⑭ store (www.bendblockbuster.com; 211 NE Revere Avenue), plus a cluster of great spots to sink a pint on the West Side: the **Boss Rambler Beer Club** ⑭ is a firm favorite (1009 NW Galveston Avenue; www.bossrambler.com;

⊙ **Tip**

Time your trip to Bend for August when the Art in the High Desert Festival (www.artinthehighdesert.com) kicks off around 15 minutes north of the Downtown area. International artists – from sculptors and painters to jewelry makers – descend on the region to showcase and sell their works.

High Desert Museum near Bend.

☉ Tip

Located close to Bend, Phil's Trail Complex is one of the region's most popular mountain-biking areas. A vast network of trails exists here, from beginner to expert, routing through the Deschutes National Forest and the foothills of the Cascades.

Mon–Thu 1–8pm, Fri, Sat noon–9pm, Sun until 8pm).

SOUTH OF BEND

Heading south from Bend, the US-97 throws up plenty of volcanic marvels and a few towns worthy of a pitstop. Just off the highway, the **High Desert Museum ②** (59800 US-97; tel: 541-382 4754; www.highdesertmuseum.org; daily: Apr–Oct 9am–5pm, Nov–Mar 10am–4pm) is an excellent primer. Shifting exhibits showcase artwork from Indigenous artists, educate on High Desert wildlife, and share tales from fur-trappers and Oregon Trail travelers.

Pushing south, you will eventually come to the **Newberry National Volcanic Monument ③** (58201 US-97; tel:

541-383 5300; daily 9am–5pm), in the **Deschutes National Forest**. Central Oregon owes much of its dramatic landscapes to this volcanic marvel, which began a period of eruption some 400,000 years ago. The hulking volcano is one of the largest by volume in the Cascades Range. Among the monument's features are the cinder cone of **Lava Butte,** whose eruption some 7,000 years ago created the otherworldly **Lava Lands** area. Visit the **Lava Lands Visitor Center** (58201 US-97; tel: 541-383 5300) to learn about this volcanic wonderland. Here, the **Trail of the Molten Land** offers a great introduction to the area's geological history. It is a short one-mile (1.6km) hike that beats through the twisting basalt

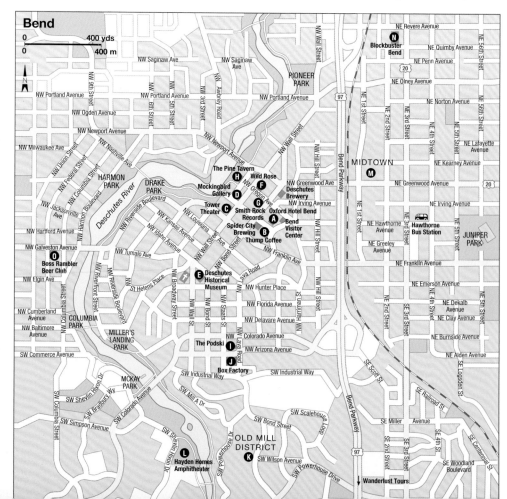

expanse with interpretative panels along the way. Just five minutes south of the Newberry National Volcanic Monument is the small community of **Sunriver** ❹. The **Sunriver Resort Marina** is a jumping-off point for activities on the **Deschutes River**, and you can rent canoes, rafts, stand-up paddleboards, and tubes from here. The 6-mile (10km) trip between the marina and Benham Butte is a popular one.

There is a strong craft-beer scene in Sunriver, and you can sample offerings from the **Sunriver Brewing Company** at the **Sunriver Pub** (57100 Beaver Drive, Building 4; tel: 541-306 5154; Sun–Thu 11am–9pm, Fri, Sat until 10pm). It is also a hotspot for golfers with several acclaimed courses. Tee off at sites including **Crosswater Golf Course** (17600 Canoe Camp Drive; tel: 541-593 3428; www.crosswater.com) or **Meadows Golf Course** (17600 Center Drive; tel: 541-593 4402; www.sunriverresort.com).

A little farther south, the pocket-sized town of **La Pine** ❺ is a gateway to the rugged **Oregon Outback Scenic Byway**, a portion of which slices into Central Oregon. The landscape dries as you thread eastward, with pine forests giving way to great sweeps of sagebrush and juniper. Around 40 minutes southeast of La Pine, you will reach **Fort Rock State Natural Area** ❻ (Co Road 5-11A; tel: 800-551 6949; www.stateparks.oregon. gov). Hulking Fort Rock cuts a fine figure, rising as if from nowhere in the middle of the High Desert – its circular shape makes it look almost like a man-made fortress, hence its name.

The old tuff ring was in fact formed by volcanic activity around 100,000 years ago. Nearby is **Fort Rock Cave**, which you can explore with tours run by the Oregon State Parks service (tel: 541-536 2428). It was here that a pair of sagebrush sandals were discovered in 1938 – at more than 9,000 years old, they are considered the oldest footwear in the world (now on display in the Museum of Natural and Cultural History at the University of Oregon in Eugene).

CASCADE LAKES SCENIC BYWAY

The **Cascades Lakes Scenic Byway** is a great way to get to grips with Central

⊙ **Tip**

Based out of Bend, Wanderlust Tours (61535 S Highway 97 #13; tel: 541-389-8359; www.wanderlusttours.com) offers excellent excursions into some of Central Oregon's epic wilderness. Join them on snowshoe adventures in the Cascades; kayaking on the region's high-elevation lakes; or on hard-hat tours of inky lava tubes, such as Boyd Cave, just a 25-minute drive from the city.

Newberry National Volcanic Monument.

⊙ BEND'S BEER

Bend takes its beer very seriously. In fact, though craft-beer fever has spread across the nation in the past decade, the small town has long been a frontrunner. The region's quality "soft water," a result of snowmelt, makes for ideal brewing conditions. Over 30 craft breweries are connected by the Bend Ale Trail. Highlights include the 1980s-born Deschutes Brewery (1044 NW Bond Street; tel: 541-382 9242; www. deschutesbrewery.com; daily 11.30am–9pm), known for its Black Butte Porter, and the women-owned Spider City Brewing (1177 SE 9th Street; www.spidercitybrewing.com; Tue–Thu 3–8pm, Fri until 9pm, Sat 2–9pm, Sun 1–7pm), which turns out hoppy pale ales. Pick up the Ale Trail from the Visitor Center (50 NW Lava Road #160; www.visit bend.com; Mon–Sat 10am–4pm, Sun until 12.30pm, 1–4pm) or download the app.

STARGAZING

After dark, stars splash over Oregon's skies like a Pollock painting. And the region's high elevation, lack of light pollution from giant cities, and clear skies all help to make Central Oregon one of the best places to gaze at the cosmos.

Prineville Reservoir State Park (tel: 800-551 6949) was recognized as Oregon's first International Dark Sky Park back in 2021, certified for its inky nights and the thoughtful and responsible installment of lighting throughout the site. The park is approximately a 50-mile (80km) drive northeast of Bend and free, 90-minute, ranger-led stargazing sessions run from Memorial to Labor Day from Friday through Sunday.

There are several observatories spread throughout the region. The Sunriver Nature Center & Observatory (57245 River Road; tel: 541-593 4394; www.snco.org) is a highlight. Visit after dark and you can pore over the stars using state-of-the-art telescopes with the help of astronomers and see educational presentations and exhibits about the cosmos (program hours change with the season, so check the website). The Pine Mountain Observatory (Pine Mountain Road; tel: 541-382 8331; www.pmo.uoregon.edu) is another solid option. It sits high on a mountaintop perch at 6,300ft (1,920 meters) and allows seasonal public visits on clear nights (observatory staff recommend that you arrive after sunset, but well before 10pm – you can call ahead to check conditions).

In Bend, the Worthy Hopservatory (495 NE Bellevue Drive; tel: 541-647 6970; www.worthy environmental.org/hopservatory) offers a particularly unique way to see the stars. Tipped as the only brewery-cum-observatory in the world, the "hopservatory" is attached to the Worthy Brewing Company, with its upper deck offering panoramas of the Cascade Mountains. The deck also has a 16-inch research-grade telescope for drinking in the cosmos, plus a resident astronomy docent to help you make sense of the galaxy.

For the best stargazing experience, check the weather before you head out – needless to say, the less cloud cover the better. Bring bug spray to ward off mosquitos if you are out for long periods after dark and don't forget a couple of torches to be able to find your way through Oregon's preserves by night.

The Sunriver Nature Center & Observatory is a stargazing hotspot.

Oregon's mountainous terrain and volcanic wonders (note that some sections are closed during the snowy winter months). You can head south from Bend, or north from Crescent, just under 50 miles (80km) south.

Easing west out of Bend, you will join OR-372, traveling over the Deschutes River and shooting into the Deschutes National Forest. The road is the destination here. You will see twisted volcanic landscapes and acres of ponderosa forest as you skirt around the eastern Cascades. When the fir and hemlock trees begin to pepper the pines, you know you are beating toward **Mount Bachelor Ski Resort ❼** (13000 SW Century Drive; tel: 541-382 1709; www.mtbachelor.com).

Continuing west, the mesmerizing necklace of lakes that gives this Scenic Byway its name begins to reveal itself. **Sparks Lake ❽** smooths out for a glassy 250 acres, fringed by craggy lava shores and sky-piercing mountains, including the South Sister and Broken Top peaks. The gentle waters are ideal for a relaxed paddle ride amid jaw-dropping scenery – the day-use area has a boat launch, plus spots for picnicking. If you would prefer to stay on dry land, the short Ray Atkeson Memorial Trail fringes the water body, providing equally epic vistas.

Push onward and more glittering water bodies emerge, including Elk, Hosmer, and Little Lava lakes. The latter forms the beginnings of the mighty Deschutes River, which beats all the way to the spectacular Columbia River farther north. The byway follows the curves of the river, before winding up at **Crane Prairie Reservoir**, another watery hotspot for boating and kayaking. The reservoir is also a top place for birding, home to osprey, bald eagles, and many waterfowl.

TUMALO

More adventures await north of Bend, where **Tumalo** is a springboard for **Tumalo State Park ❾**. The park provides access to the Deschutes River, the wriggling waterway that defines Central Oregon, and countless campgrounds are draped across riverbanks

Mount Bachelor Ski Resort is threaded with 35 miles of cross-country trails.

and tucked within groves of ponderosa pines and junipers. Hikers can also access the 12-mile (19km) **Deschutes River Trail** from the park's day-use area – the Tumalo segment runs for 2.4 miles (3.8km). There are put-in areas for float rides here, too.

SISTERS

The little town of **Sisters** ❿ takes its name from the trio of dramatic peaks that spikes toward the sky out west, and the opportunities for outdoor recreation are abundant. You can hike, bike, climb, and boat all within easy reach of town – the **Sisters Ranger District Office** (201 N Pine Street; tel: 541-549 7700; www.fs.usda.gov/recarea/deschutes; Mon–Fri 8am–4.30pm) has information on the many activities available in the Deschutes National Forest and offers passes and permits where necessary.

Around 14 miles (23km) northwest, glacier-hewn **Suttle Lake** is a hotspot for kayakers and stand-up paddle-boarders, while campgrounds dot the shores. It is reached via the **McKenzie Pass–Santiam Pass Scenic Byway**, which is replete with showstopping mountain views as it swerves west toward the Willamette Valley.

Meanwhile, the **Peterson Ridge Trail Network** ⓫ (Three Creek Road; www.sisterstrails.org) is one of the region's top-rated mountain-biking areas, encompassing around 25 miles (40km) of runs. The 38-mile (61km) **McKenzie Pass Scenic Bikeway** also routes out of Sisters, flowing into the Cascade Mountains and through thickets of ponderosa pines and Douglas firs.

Back in town, in true Central Oregon style, a top-notch pint is never far away. **Three Creeks Brewing** (721 S Desperado Court; tel: 541-549 1963; www.threecreeksbrewing.com; daily noon–8pm) is known for its hoppy IPAs and its brewpub serves a crowd-pleasing menu of pizzas, burgers, and tacos. Mexican restaurant **Rancho Viejo** (150 E Cascade Avenue; tel: 541-549 3594; www.ranchoviejosistersoregon.com; 2–9pm) is another local favorite.

If you can, time your trip for the **Sisters Folk Festival** (www.sistersfolkfestival.

Black Butte Ranch in the shadow of the Three Sisters peaks.

org) in fall. The quirky and welcoming event is a joyful celebration of American roots music, from bluegrass to blues.

Less than 10 minutes outside of town, Black Butte Ranch (13899 Bishops Cap; tel: 866-901 2961; www.black butteranch.com) makes a fine base in the region. The former cattle ranch is now a sprawling resort offering chic yet rustic vacation rental homes enveloped by forest. There is also golfing, swimming pools, and dining at the swish Lodge Restaurant (with far-reaching mountain views) and the laid-back Robert's pub. It is named for **Black Butte**, a dramatic cinder cone whose summit can be reached via a moderate 1.9-mile (3km) hike that climbs around 1,600ft (488 meters) in elevation.

REDMOND AND TERREBONNE

Highway 97 carries you north from Bend towards **Redmond**, a small town that sits pretty between the Deschutes and Ochoco national forests, with a plethora of natural sights on its doorstep. Make a trip to the **Redmond Caves Recreation Site** ⓬ (SE Airport Way;

tel: 541-416 6700; www.blm.gov/visit/redmond-caves-recreation-site), a volcanic wonderland that features five caves with various access points for public exploration. Inside, the caves are in their natural state, so be aware of rocky rubble and bring several lights.

Push northward and you will eventually pull into **Terrebonne**, jumping-off point for the popular **Smith Rock State Park** ⓭, which is often hailed as the birthplace of sport climbing in the USA. Great steeples of ocher rock rise toward the skies and are crisscrossed with almost 2,000 climbing routes, of which over 1,000 are bolted. Popular climbing areas include the 350ft (107-meter) -high Monkey Face, so named as it resembles a simian countenance, and the rumpled Dihedrals. If you would prefer to stay on the ground, the park is also laced with hiking trails. Keep your eyes peeled for prairie falcons and golden eagles.

Terrebonne is always within easy reach of **Steelhead Falls**, a camera-loving cascade that is reached via a straightforward 0.5-mile (0.8km) hike

Sisters, a tiny town peppered with antique and vintage stores.

⊘ THREE SISTERS

A world of wonders awaits in the Three Sisters Wilderness, which spreads out for over 285,000 acres (115,000 hectares) in the Willamette and Deschutes national forests. Its namesake trio of peaks – the North, Middle, and South Sisters – is joined by other big-hitters, such as Broken Top, a craggy stratovolcano, and Collier Glacier, the largest in the state. Beyond the hulking mountains, the landscape is contoured by lava fields, Alpine meadows, and forests thick with fir trees, mountain hemlock, and pines. Various trailheads are easily accessible from Bend (Cascade Lakes Scenic Byway/Forest Route 46) and Sisters (via Highway 242 and Forest Service Roads 15 and 16). They include the Broken Top Trail, Todd Lake Trail, and the Park Meadow Trail. Note: all visitors require a permit between June 15 and October 15 (www.recreation.gov).

⊙ Tip

Terrebonne-based Smith Rock Trail Rides (20890a NW Butler Road; tel: 541-604 6769; www.smith rocktrailrides.com) offers guided horseback rides through dramatic Smith Rock country, on routes that wiggle through the Crooked River Canyon.

(watch out for one fairly steep section). It is best visited in spring when wild-flowers brighten the route.

CULVER AND MADRAS

Central Oregon becomes ever wilder as you push north on US-97 and curl toward **Culver**. The miniscule town is a springboard for **The Cove Palisades State Park** ⓮ (tel: 800-551 6949; www. stateparks.oregon.gov), which is just a 15-minute drive from the center of town. The gloriously rugged park wraps around both the Deschutes and Crooked River canyons, and is a hotspot for camping, kayaking, boating, and tubing. There are stellar vistas of **Lake Billy Chinook** from the popular (and fairly mellow) **Tam-a-láu Trail**. House-boating is also popular on the lake, and you can organize rentals through **Lake Billy Chinook Houseboats** (tel: 541-815 1644; www.lakebillychinook.com). A ten-minute drive to the southeast of Culver, **Haystack Reservoir** – which affords views of Three Sisters and Mount Jefferson – is another popular spot for watersports and swimming.

Travel another 10 miles (16km) north and you will reach the small city of **Madras** ⓯, the county seat of Jefferson County. Madras began as a ranchers' town, and farming is still the area's life-blood. The ever-popular **Madras Saturday Market** (112 9th St; www.madras saturdaymarket.com) runs throughout the summer season, with vendors hawking fresh produce and artisanal crafts, alongside live-music performances. Also worth a visit is the **Cascade Lavender** (5000 SW Feather Drive; tel: 541-550 0385; www.cascadelavender.com), which explodes in a sea of purple in mid-summer – visitors can come by the farm to pick their own fragrant bunches and peruse the gift shop.

Outdoorsy highlights here include the **Madras Mountain Views Scenic Bikeway**, which is exactly what it sounds like: it ripples out for 29 miles (47km), traveling past bright lavender fields and into High Desert scrub, hugging Lake Billy Chinook and offering cinematic views of peaks including Mount Hood, the Three Sisters, and Broken Top.

Monkey Face, a jutting rock so named for its simian countenance.

WARM SPRINGS

The **Warm Springs** ⑯ area is centered on the 644,000-acre (260,000-hectare) reservation of the Confederated Tribes of Warm Springs, which is made up of the Wasco, Paiute, and Warm Springs peoples. The land is bounded by Mount Hood, Mount Jefferson, and the roaring Deschutes River. Be sure to pay a visit to **The Museum at Warm Springs** ⑰ (2189 US-26; tel: 541-553 3331; www.warmsprings-nsn.gov; Tue–Sat 9am–5pm), one of the finest centers of its kind. It holds an extensive collection of Native American artifacts, from fine art and sculpture to ceremonial attire and historic photographs. There are also life-sized models of traditional dwellings.

Also in the area is the Indigenous-owned **Indian Head Casino** (3236 US-26; tel: 541-460 7777; www.indianheadcasino.com; Fri, Sat 9am–2am, Sun–Thu 9am–1am), whose laid-back **Cottonwood Restaurant** is a popular eating spot.

PRINEVILLE

Historic **Prineville** ⑱ was the first city in Central Oregon, having been established in 1870. Today, the Main Street feels like stepping back in time, with decades-old brick structures and the **Bowman Museum** (246 N Main Street; tel: 541-447 3715; www.crookcounty historycenter.org; Tue–Fri 10am–5pm, Sat 11am–4pm), which houses displays on regional history, including logging.

Prineville is also known as a rock-hounder's paradise, as the area surrounding the city is rich in gemstones such as agates and thunder eggs. Always make sure you are in a designated rockhounding site – it is prohibited to take material from many natural areas. A good spot is the **White Fir Springs Collection Site** (www.fs.usda.gov/detail/ochoco/recreation), which is rich in jasper thunder eggs and has dedicated rockhounding pits.

Hikers should also make time for the **Steins Pillar Trail**, which strikes out from the city. The 4-mile (6km) round-trip sees walkers wend through old-growth woodland and meadows, before reaching the trail's namesake: a 350ft (107-meter) -high tuff crag that was formed some 40 million years ago.

⊙ WHITE RIVER FALLS

The teensy town of Maupin is an excellent jumping-off point for exploring the White River Falls State Park (White River Road; tel: 800-551 6949; www.stateparks.oregon.gov), named for a dramatic 90ft (27-meter) cascade that rushes over hunks of craggy basalt. The hiking trail that leads to the foot of the falls – where you will be granted with epic views – is short (0.7 miles/1km) but relatively steep and its challenging nature demands a level of fitness. The route also takes walkers past an old hydroelectric power plant that operated until the 1960s. Pretty picnic spots pepper the trail, but note that there are no campgrounds located in the park for overnight stays. Swimming in the area is also not advised because the fierce river currents can prove dangerous.

Crook County Courthouse, Prineville.

The color-splashed Painted Hills.

EASTERN OREGON

A road trip in Oregon's cowboy country reveals the state's most otherworldly landscapes, from rainbow-hued hills filled with fossils to sweeping tracts of desert.

Nowhere is the spirit of the Wild West more alive than in Oregon's great southeastern swathes. This is a land of cracked, crumpled desert; sprawling ranchlands; treasure-sewn fossil beds and dusty towns. The jewel of the region is the John Day Fossil Beds National Monument, whose rocky stratas conceal evidence of millions of years of life. Meanwhile, plucky frontier towns such as Baker City were built on Oregon's gold rush and today, they brim with brewers, chocolatiers, and artisans preserving traditional Western crafts, from boot making to millinery. In the state's far southeast, you will reach the most surprising of all Oregon's natural wonders: the stark Alvord Desert, which swoops out in the shadow of Steens Mountain.

Happily, even Eastern Oregon's remotest pockets can be accessed via a network of dazzling scenic byways – there is Journey Through Time, which uncovers the region's fossil-jeweled west; High Desert Discovery, plunging south into some of the state's best birding territory; and Blue Mountain and Hells Canyon, which both twist into their namesakes.

The land – from the wild Walla Walla River to the thrusting Blue Mountains – has long been a home for Native Americans, though many have been forcibly moved into two reservations in the

region: they belong to the Confederated Tribes of the Umatilla Indian Reservation and the Burns Paiute Tribe.

PAINTED HILLS

Push east from Central Oregon on US-26 and the state's vast eastern plains begin to unfold – the skies grow larger, the air drier. Muscular cattle graze in the shadow of thrusting peaks and sagebrush scatters the roadside. You will route through the **Ochoco National Forest**, with its vast tracts of ponderosa pine and Douglas firs, and

Main attractions
Painted Hills
Thomas Condon
  Paleontology Center
Baker City
Tamástslikt
  Cultural Institute
Blue Mountains
  Scenic Highway
Malheur National
  Wildlife Refuge
Alvord Desert

Maps on pages
180, 188

John Day Fossil Beds National Monument.

you will find the turning for **Painted Hills ①** (37375 Bear Creek Road; tel: 541-987 2333; www.nps.gov/joda) – one of three units in the **John Day Fossil Beds National Monument** – around 5 minutes before you reach **Mitchell**.

You will know you are on the right track: as you push along Cougar Mountain Road, color-splashed hills begin to reveal themselves and the rocks, formed some 30 million years ago, are contoured into dramatic ridges by erosion. Eons of volcanic activity caused soil to build in distinct stratas: then weathered and oxidized minerals gave the hills their striking hues, which appear in reddish brown, ocher, butter yellow, and salmon pink.

Various hikes reveal the wonders of this rainbow-colored region, and a very easy taste of the monument can be found along the **Painted Cove Nature Trail ②**. A gently rising boardwalk brings you through a patch of squat, rust-colored hills – you can see the cracked earth up close and read interpretative signs about the geological wonder. There is even a wooden bench

Wildflowers add even more color to the Painted Hills.

along the way for walkers to sit down and drink in the view. There are slightly more strenuous hikes to be tackled – the 1.6 mile/2.6km (round-trip) **Carroll Rim Trail** is short but steep, and offers some of finest views around.

Here, the boardwalk is swapped for a more rugged gravel and clay path, and you will climb about 400ft (122 meters) in elevation.

JOURNEY THROUGH TIME SCENIC BYWAY

Continue along US-26 and the road soon morphs into the otherworldly **Journey Through Time Scenic Byway**. Multimillion-year-old rock shoots up in weathered bluffs at the roadside as you venture eastward. Your next stop should be the excellent **Thomas Condon Paleontology Center ③** (32651 OR-19; tel: 541-987 2333; daily 9am–5pm; www.nps.gov/joda) at the John Day Fossil Beds' **Sheep Rock Unit** – here, fascinating and diverse displays put the fossil-rich region into context. You will see detailed exhibits revealing the way Oregon's landscapes have

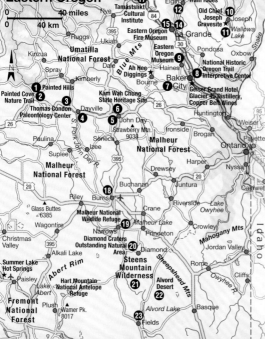

evolved over some 44 million years, from soupy swamps like the modern-day American South to lush forests and savannahs. More than 500 fossil specimens, plucked from the John Day Fossil Beds, are on display. Visitors can pore over the jaws of ancient camels, bones of giant cats, and the skulls of formidable "beardogs," which walked the region some 20 million years ago. There are seven hikes on offer in this unit. The **Blue Basin Overlook Trail** is a 3.5-mile (5.6km) loop offering spectacular vistas of the unit's plunging, ridged ravines and across the John Day River Valley.

Around 9 miles (14km) to the southeast, drivers will pull into the pocket-sized town of **Dayville** ④, which has a real Old West feel. There is little here but a mercantile and the **Dayville Cafe** (212 Franklin Street; tel: 541-987 2122; www.thedayvillecafe.weebly.com; Tue–Sun 7am–3pm), and that is precisely what makes it so charming. Stop in the café for a spot of lunch: it serves a solid menu of sandwiches, salads, burgers, and fried fish dishes, plus

home-made pies (don't miss a slice of the marionberry).

Another 30-minute drive east will land travelers in history-steeped **John Day** ❺. Here, the highlight is the **Kam Wah Chung State Heritage Site** ❻ (tel: 541-575 2800; www.stateparks.oregon.gov; tours May–Oct 9am–4pm). John Day was home to some of the first Chinese immigrants in the state, and this former Chinese general store, medical clinic, and private residence is thought to have been built in the 1870s. It is now preserved as a museum, with a separate interpretive center.

The byway follows the path of the John Day River as it twists eastward toward **Prairie City**, which is backed by the Strawberry Mountain Wilderness. The main drag, Front Street, is a string of charming Western false-front buildings filled with cafés and stores. Stop in for refreshment at the down-to-earth **Roan Coffee Company** (154 Front Street; tel: 541-820 4455; Mon–Fri 8am–5pm, Sat 8am–4pm, Sun 9am–2pm), which serves espresso, cakes, and light lunches.

Displays at the fascinating Thomas Condon Paleontology Center.

⊙ Tip

Take a tour of Baker City with Go Wild: American Adventures (tel: 541-403 1692; www.gowildusa.com). Knowledgeable guides will lead you around the compact Downtown core, revealing the town's layered history and stopping for tastings at the local gourmet hotspots. Go Wild also offers hiking and paddling trips that beat into Eastern Oregon's rugged backcountry.

The Journey Through Time Scenic Byway wends through rural, mountainous scenes.

Once fueled up, push on to **Whitney**, an atmospheric ghost town whose cracked buildings sit in sun-baked grasslands. Whitney was originally founded in 1900, along the Sumpter Valley Railway. It became an important logging town, with a sawmill built by the Oregon Lumber Company, but when the industry declined and the railroad was abandoned residents leaked out of the town. Now, the barns and houses remain eerily deserted.

BAKER CITY

Convivial **Baker City ❼** – flanked by the Elkhorn Mountains to the west and the Wallowa Mountains to the east – is the final stop along the Journey Through Time Scenic Byway. First incorporated in 1874, the city became known as the "Queen City of the Inland Empire" or the "Queen City of the Mines" – at the end of the 1800s, the region's "gold belt," which occupied a swathe of Baker and Grant Counties, turned up approximately 60 percent of all the gold and silver mined in the state. And at the turn of the century, the city was one of the largest in Oregon. A small population of Chinese people lived in Baker City in the 1800s and early 1900s – many were miners and some also opened laundries downtown. Local tour guides will point out the city block that served as the original Chinatown.

Book a night at the **Geiser Grand Hotel** (1996 Main Street; tel: 541-523 1889; www.geisergrand.com), an Italianate Victorian dame that has stood proud on the city's main street since 1889. A bold feature of the exterior is the four-storey clock tower that locals say has been shot out by cowboys on multiple occasions. The interiors are richly clad in dark mahogany, with ornate railings, chandeliers, and a striking stained-glass skylight, and rooms are sumptuous, some with fireplaces and slouchy leather couches. It is said to be haunted by more than a few ghosts.

Back out in town, the walkable Main Street is well worth a wander. Stop in for a tasting at **Glacier 45 Distillery** (901 Main Street; tel: 541-519 0081; www.glacier45.com; Mon–Fri 11am–6pm,

Sat until 2pm), which specializes in imaginative flavors of vodka such as huckleberry and cucumber, plus bourbon and gin. Another top spot is **Copper Belt Wines** (1937 Main Street; tel: 541-519 0949; www.copperbeltwinery.com), whose wines are produced in the eastern Snake River Valley AVA. Come by to try bold reds such as Cabernet Sauvignon, Syrah, and Tempranillo – the Cheese Fairy Cheese Shop is also located within the tasting room.

Another of Baker City's nicknames is "the base camp for Eastern Oregon," and the town is a springboard for many outdoor adventures in the surrounding areas. Just 15 minutes east of the city center, you will find the **National Historic Oregon Trail Interpretive Center** ❽ (22267 OR-86; tel: 541-523 1843; www.blm.gov/learn/interpretive-centers/national-historic-oregon-trail-interpretive-center; temporarily closed for renovations). The historical site brings the Oregon Trail to life through various re-enactments, while at the Ruts Access site you can see grooves carved out by original wagons on portions of the historic trail. West of the city is the access point for the challenging **Elkhorn Crest Trail** – the highest in the soaring Blue Mountains. Hardy hikers are rewarded with sweeping panoramas of the Baker Valley as they travel the roughly 23-mile (37km) route.

Another detour west of the city is the **Ah Hee Diggings Interpretive Site**. The drive is spectacular, traveling on the bucolic **Elkhorn Drive Scenic Byway**, which strikes into the jagged Elkhorn Mountains, skirting Phillips Lake and routing through tiny historic mining towns such as **Sumpter** and **Granite**. The site features stacked rock tailings left behind by Chinese miners.

A short drive north of Baker City, the **Eastern Oregon Museum** ❾ (610 3rd Street; tel: 541-856 3233; www.easternoregonmuseum.com; Memorial Day–Labor Day Thu–Sat 10am–1pm) has a vast collection of historic items that tell the story of the local area, including farming equipment, relics from Oregon Trail travelers, and military and rodeo artifacts.

Geiser Grand Hotel in Baker City.

HELLS CANYON SCENIC BYWAY

A trip on the **Hells Canyon Scenic Byway** is a great way to see a broad sweep of Eastern Oregon's dramatic scenery, defined by the sharply ridged Wallowa Mountains and its namesake – the deepest river canyon in the USA. Spread across 650,000 acres (260,000 hectares), **Hells Canyon National Recreation Area** is managed by the Wallowa-Whitman National Forest, and can be explored on foot, by bike, on horseback, or via a white-water raft.

Edge eastward out of Baker City towards **Richland** and the Scenic Byway twists and curves, inching out between dramatic mounds and dancing with the Snake River and the Idaho border as it pushes north. Your first stop should be the **Hells Canyon National Visitor Center** (tel: 541-785 3395; spring through late summer 8am–4pm), two hours northeast of the city. The center is perched beside the Wild and Scenic Snake River and offers exhibits on natural history and wildlife, plus guidance on trails and recreational activities. There is also a boat launch here.

Striking wildflowers like the Aquilegia formosa grow in the Elkhorn Mountains.

Back on the road, and returning across the border in Oregon, set your sights on the **Hells Canyon Overlook** (NF-490), which offers a spectacular view across the rugged gorge. Interpretative panels put the vistas into context, with highlights including the Seven Devils Mountains, marching across the border in Idaho. There is also a picnic area.

A roughly 90-minute drive northwest will bring you to **Joseph ⑩**. Swaddled by the Wallowa Mountains, the small town is a jumping-off point for adventures on **Wallowa Lake ⑪** and in the **Eagle Cap Wilderness**. It is worth lingering in the town itself, too. It has become something of an artists' hub, with a downtown core filled with charming cafés, studios, and galleries. The area is particularly well known for its bronze sculptures, and you will see these fine works of art dotted across the streets. Pay a visit to **Valley Bronze of Oregon** (307 W Alder Street; tel: 541-432 7551; www.valleybronze.com; gallery Thu–Sat 10am–5pm), a bronze foundry that has been operating since the 1980s. Stop by the downtown gallery to see a range of works, from bronze animal effigies to busts, plus paintings. You can also organize a tour of the foundry.

A mile south of Joseph is the **Old Chief Joseph Gravesite** (Oregon Hwy 82; www.nps.gov), the burial site of a Nez Perce leader who refused to sell his Wallowa homeland to white settlers in the 1800s. Having declined to sign the 1863 Treaty, he died on his ancestral lands in 1870 and his remains were reburied here in 1926.

Continue on to **Wallowa Lake State Park** (tel: 800-551 6949; www.stateparks.oregon.gov), whose namesake is a shimmering glacial water body hemmed in by soaring peaks. You can strike out on the water with kayak or boat rentals from Wallowa Lake Marina, and there is access to the Wallowa Lake Trailhead, which leads to a plethora of trails beating into the **Eagle Cap Wilderness**. You will find year-round camping here, with full hook-up RV and tent sites, plus a pair of yurts.

The **Wallowa Lake Tramway** (59919 Wallowa Lake Highway; tel: 541-432 5331; www.wallowalaketramway.com; May, June, Sept 10am–4pm, last tram 4.45pm; July 9am–4.30pm; Aug 10am–4.30pm) is another local highlight. The dizzying lift pushes 3,700ft (1,128 meters) skyward toward the summit of Mt Howard – at the top, the reward is sweeping views of Wallowa Lake.

EAGLE CAP WILDERNESS

The seemingly boundless Eagle Cap Wilderness is the largest wilderness area in Oregon, parceled up in the raw Wallowa Mountains and rippling out for almost 360,000 acres (145,000 hectares). This is the ancestral homeland and hunting ground of the Nez Perce, who are thought to have occupied the land since at least 1400 AD, alongside the Shoshone, Cayuse, and Bannock peoples. Euro-American settlers first arrived around 1860.

Today, it is a trekker's paradise, offering a raft of backpacking adventures, plus some day hiking opportunities.

In the southern portion, the roughly 10-mile (16km) out-and-back North Fork Catherine Creek Trailhead is a popular and moderately difficult route, whisking hikers along a waterway hemmed in by spruce and fir trees (the closest town is La Grande).

In the Wallowa Lake area, the challenging (given the steep and rugged terrain) West Fork Wallowa River Trail beats through open meadows and woodland, hugging its namesake waterway, and leading to Frazier Lake and Little Frazier Lake, where you will be granted views of dramatic cliffs and a waterfall. The closest town is Joseph.

The Eagle Cap backcountry is wild and unfettered, and you should only strike out alone if you are experienced. Otherwise, hire a guide – Go Wild: American Adventures (tel: 541-403 1692; www.gowildusa.com) offers a range of experiences in Eagle Cap, from rugged backpacking trips to more deluxe catered adventures with gourmet eats and cocktails around the campfire.

Around 30 minutes north of Joseph, drivers will reach the **Nez Perce**

Hells Canyon National Recreation Area.

BLUE MOUNTAINS

The Blue Mountains, spreading out in Oregon's wild northeastern corner, conceal layers of history and cultural heritage in their ancient folds.

The Blue Mountains are the oldest in the state. Rocks here date back over 300 million years, before the region now known as Oregon had been formed. Then, the land was a series of fragments and islands that was eventually banded together by tectonic movement – rocks formed off the coast of what is now Idaho and, as these rocks collided with the shoreline, Oregon's first crust (and the beginnings of the Blue Mountains) was created. Over millennia, uplift occurred as bedrock was eroded – and the range took shape.

Now the Blues – as they are affectionately known – ripple out over some 15,000 square miles (40,000 sq km), though their exact delineations are indefinite. Their boundaries can be roughly drawn out from Snake River in Hells Canyon to the east, and encompassing the Ochoco and Maury mountains to the west. Also folded

Happy Canyon Chiefs of the Confederated Tribes of the Umatilla Indian Reservation.

within the range's great expanse are the Elkhorn Mountains. In this swathe, the range's tallest peak, Rock Creek Butte, soars to around 9,100ft (2,780 meters). The range is thickly forested, with subalpine firs and mountain hemlock carpeting the upper reaches and western junipers dominating the lowest elevations.

There is a whole lot of history crammed in this jungle of peaks. They have long formed part of the homeland for Native Americans, including the Northern Paiute, Cayuse, Umatilla, and Nez Perce peoples. The region, with its thrusting peaks, sweeping river valleys, and forests, proved to be fertile hunting and gathering grounds for these Indigenous groups. It later became mining country. The industry boomed here in the early 20th century, with natural deposits of everything from gold to chromite (a chromium and iron compound) supporting a thriving trade.

Today, the Blue Mountain Scenic Byway cuts a fine figure through the region, stretching 145 miles (233km) from near the Willow Creek Wildlife Area down toward the North Fork John Day Campground. You will route through the Old West towns of Ione and Lexington, with frontier architecture dating back to the 19th century, and on to Heppner, nicknamed the "Gateway to the Blues." The town, which was established by Irish immigrants in the 1880s, provides access to the Blue Mountain Century Scenic Bikeway, a challenging route that snakes out for 108 miles (174km). You will wend through rugged valleys, into the dense Umatilla National Forest, and past great swathes of cattle-dotted rangeland. There are various hikes, including the strenuous Bald Mountain Trail and the Willow Creek Trail, known for its wildflowers. Heppner is also home to the Morrow County Museum (444 N Main Street; tel: 541-676 5524; www.morrowcountymuseum.com; Mar–Oct Tue–Fri 1–5pm, Sat 11am–3pm), which is focused on the region's rural history and has a large store of antique farming equipment.

Around 40 miles (64km) south, a highlight of the byway is Potamus Point – a lookout spot that grants fabulous river canyon views. Another worthy stop is the teensy town of Ukiah, arranged around Camas Creek. It is particularly well known for its abundance of pretty purple-blue camas plants, whose roots have long been considered an important food source by Native American peoples.

Wallowa Homeland Visitor Center and Tamkaliks Celebration Grounds (209 E 2nd Street; tel: 541-886 3101; www.wallowanezperce.org), which holds displays on Native American culture and lifeways. Artifacts include items such as a handcrafted elderberry flute, beaded moccasins, and a buffalo headdress. The visitor center runs an array of workshops themed around traditional skills such as weaving and basketry and plant identification.

Follow the wiggling Wallowa River due northwest and pull into the **Minam State Recreation Area** (tel: 541-432 8855; www.stateparks.oregon.gov). This is your gateway to the Wallowa River, with activities including rafting and boating on offer, plus plenty of picnic spots and campgrounds. Look out for elusive Rocky Mountain bighorn sheep.

Another short 15-minute jaunt west and you will reach **Elgin** ⑫, departure point for **Eagle Cap Train Rides** ⑬ (300 Depot Street; tel: 541-437 3652; www.eaglecaptrainrides.com). The train skirts along the edge of the Wallowa and Grande Ronde rivers and twists between tree-carpeted bluffs as it travels the historic Joseph Branch rail line.

LA GRANDE

The final stop on Hells Canyon Scenic Byway is **La Grande** ⑭, home of Eastern Oregon University and a smattering of interesting museums and cultural attractions. The setting is a boon: the tiny city is sandwiched between the looming Blue and Wallowa mountain ranges, meaning it is a springboard for even more epic backcountry adventures.

The **Grande Ronde Symphony Orchestra** (www.granderondesymphony. org) is the oldest community orchestra in Oregon and there are regular public concerts. Another cultural hotspot is the **Art Center East** (1006 Penn Avenue; tel: 541-624 2800; www. artcentereast.org; Wed–Fri noon–5pm, Sat 10am–2pm), whose Main Gallery showcases a range of fine art and holds talks and artist events.

Do not miss a visit to the **Eastern Oregon Fire Museum** ⑮ (102 Elm Street; tel: 541-605 0163; open by

⊙ **Tip**

La Grande hosts the Eastern Oregon Film Festival in October, offering a platform for up-and-coming directors, and including screenings and live music.

The elusive Rocky Mountain bighorn sheep are a top spot.

⊙ Tip

Every year, the Pendleton Whisky Music Fest lures bighitters like Flo Rida and Macklemore to the stage at this one-day music extravaganza (www.pendletonwhisky musicfest.com).

Pendleton has a rich Western heritage.

appointment), where you will find a series of vintage fire trucks and exhibitions about firefighting. The display shares space in Oregon's historic firehouse with **Side A Brewing** (1219 Washington Avenue; tel: 541-605 0163; www.sideabeer.com; Tue, Wed 4–9pm, Thu–Mon 11.30am–9pm), which produces hoppy IPAs and serves American comfort food such as burgers and mac and cheese.

In nearby Union, the **Union County Museum** (331 S Main Street; tel: 541-562 6003; www.ucmuseumoregon.com; Mother's Day to Sept Thu–Sat 11am–3pm) houses exhibits focused on cowboy culture, railroad history, and vital Eastern Oregon industries such as logging and agriculture.

Meanwhile, roughly an hour southwest, you will find **Anthony Lakes Mountain Resort** (47500 Anthony Lakes Highway; tel: 541-856 3277; www.anthonylakes.com), a winter-sports hub that has the highest base elevation in Oregon at 7,100ft (2,164 meters), with runs ranging from green to single black diamond. Other activities include cross-country skiing, and there is also a saloon hosting live-music sets.

PENDLETON

From La Grande, an hour's journey northwest on I-84 will bring you to **Pendleton ⑯**, a city that mushroomed in the second half of the 19th century, and is known for its Western heritage. The downtown core is wonderfully walkable, sprinkled with cafés, down-to-earth restaurants, and artisan shops, some of which preserve traditional Western crafts. They include the **Pendleton Hat Company ⓐ** (141 S Main Street; tel: 360-739 7289; www.pendleton hatco.com; Wed–Sat 10am–4.30pm), which specializes in handmade fur fedoras. Another master maker is **Staplemans Boots and Leather ⓑ** (7 SE Court Avenue; tel: 509-531 4703; www. staplemans.com; Mon–Sat 8am–6pm), which makes artful cowboy boots with custom patterns by hand.

Just across the river, you will find the **Pendleton Center for the Arts ⓒ** (214 N Main Street; tel: 541-278 9201; www. pendletonarts.org; Tue–Fri 10am–4pm,

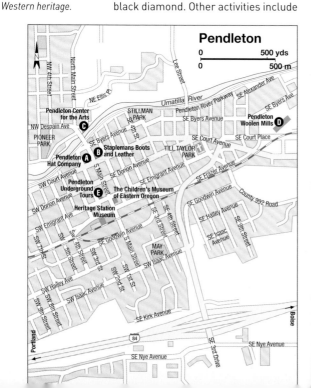

Pendleton

Sat noon–4pm), which hosts cutting-edge contemporary art exhibits and live-music performances from piano shows to folk-band sets.

Make time for a tour of the **Pendleton Woolen Mills ⓓ** (1307 SE Court Place; www.pendleton-usa.com; Mon–Fri 11am–3pm). The city has been a wool-shipping center since the 1800s and the mills opened back in 1893 – today, they craft fine woolen blankets, clothing, and accessories.

A great way to get to grips with Pendleton history is with a guided tour. **Pendleton Underground Tours ⓔ** (31 SW Emigrant Avenue; tel: 541-276 0730; www.pendletonundergroundtours. org) whisk visitors beneath ground to a network of tunnels and subterranean sights, including a Chinese laundry and living quarters and a Prohibition card room, while experienced guides narrate stories from Pendleton's past. Back above ground, you can also visit a bordello once owned by the notorious Stella Darby.

Spreading out for some 172,000 acres (70,000 hectares) to the south and southeast of Pendleton, the Confederated Tribes of the Umatilla Indian Reservation is the home of the Cayuse, Umatilla, and Walla Walla peoples. Traditionally, the Walla Walla and Umatilla tribes made their home along the Yakama, Umatilla, and Walla Walla rivers and confluences with the mighty Columbia. The Cayuse also lived around the upper tributaries of these waterways and in the rugged Blue Mountains. The Oregon Trail, which saw settlers from the eastern US travel westward across the country, routed through these ancestral homelands. The travelers on the Lewis and Clark Expedition would have encountered these Native Americans.

Set aside ample time to explore the excellent **Tamástslikt Cultural Institute ⓱** (47106 Wildhorse Boulevard; tel: 541-429 7700; www.tamastslikt.org; Tue–Sat 10am–5pm). Detailed exhibits explore the relationship of the Cayuse, Umatilla, and Walla Walla peoples with the natural world, ancient trading practices, and the Native Americans' changed lifeways and challenges after

The cracked plains of the Alvord Desert.

⊘ ALVORD DESERT

Perhaps no part of the state feels wilder or more remote than the starkly beautiful Alvord Desert. It is a striking sight: a cracked, pancake-flat expanse watched over by the hulking and jagged Steens Mountain. The barren landscape stretches out for approximately 8 miles (13km) in width and 70 miles (113km) in length, and would have been covered by an ancient lake until around 15,000 years ago. Today, geothermal springs such as Alvord Hot Springs burst through the dry surface, and you can take a relaxing soak in the therapeutic mineral waters at Alvord Hot Springs Bath House and Campground (36095 E Steens Road; tel: 541-589 2282; www.alvordhotsprings. com). There are both tent sites and simple bunkhouses here for those who want to plan an overnight stay.

the arrival of Euro-American settlers. You will see life-size dioramas and recreations of traditional dwellings, plus interesting displays of intricate basketry and beadwork.

Very close to the Institute is the popular **Wildhorse Resort and Casino** (46510 Wildhorse Boulevard; tel: 800-654 9453; www.wildhorseresort.com), which is also owned and operated by the Confederated Tribes of the Umatilla Indian Reservation.

THE HIGH DESERT DISCOVERY SCENIC BYWAY

For those truly wanting to get off the beaten track, the wild expanse of Southeastern Oregon feels like the end of the Earth. This is the place for real off-grid adventures, characterized by raw, rippling desert; formidable mountains; wild horses; and abundant birdlife.

The High Desert Discovery Scenic Byway is an epic route into this remote wonderland, spreading out 127 miles (204km) – you could travel for miles and not see a soul. The region is also home to the Burns Paiute Tribe, who

Burrowing owl in Malheur National Wildlife Refuge.

have been living in this High Desert area for eons and whose traditional lifeways are intricately bound up with the land, from the fish-filled lakes to the abundant forests.

You will find some life in **Burns** ⑱, a blink-and-you'll-miss-it town that acts as a solid base for exploring the rest of the region. Stay at the **Historic Central Hotel** (171 N Broadway Avenue; tel: 541-413 0046; www.historiccentralhotel. com), which offers ultra-stylish digs on the town's restaurant-dotted main street. Grab dinner at **El Toreo** (239 N Broadway Avenue; tel: 541-573 1829; Mon–Thu 11am–8.30pm), a well-loved Mexican spot next to the hotel that dishes up classic tacos, enchiladas, and chimichanga.

Make time to visit **Oard's Museum & Gallery** (42456 US-20; tel: 541-493 2535; www.oardsgallery.com; Mon–Sun 8am–6pm), which focuses on showcasing the jewelry and artwork created by nine Native American tribes, including the local Paiutes. Expect to see a range of intricate pottery, rugs, beaded art, and paintings.

⊙ PENDLETON ROUND-UP

The Pendleton Round-Up (www.pendleton roundup.com) is one of the largest rodeos in the country. The long-running and storied event has been running since 1910, and still draws crowds in their thousands to Pendleton during the first week of September. The event celebrates Native American heritage, with the Confederated Tribes of the Umatilla Indian Reservation hosting a large village filled with teepees, plus traditional dance performances, competitions, and pageants. Indigenous artisans also gather at Roy Raley Park to sell their handmade wares. Traditional rodeo events include bronc riding, steer roping, and bull riding. Rodeos are a longstanding part of Western heritage, though they are often criticized by modern-day animal-rights activists.

Burns is a jumping-off point for the **Malheur National Wildlife Refuge ⑲** (36391 Sodhouse Lane; tel: 541-493 2612; www.fws.gov), which spreads out 187,000 acres (750,000 hectares) at the northern edge of the Great Basin and is hailed as one of the finest places for birdwatching in the state. It has a long history, having been established by 26th President Theodore Roosevelt in 1908, and is now a critical habitat for species including ibises and great blue herons. The refuge sits beneath the Pacific Flyway, a major route for migratory birds that reaches from Patagonia in South America, all the way to Alaska.

If you fancy, you can take a detour and strike onto the **Diamond Loop Tour Route**, a 69-mile (111km) drive that takes in a region of dramatic volcanic basalt formations. There is **Diamond Swamp**, 25,000-year-old lava fields that ripple out in an inky sea. Then, after driving ten minutes east, you will come to **Diamond Craters Outstanding Natural Area ⑳** (Lava Beds Road; tel: 541-573 4400; www.blm.gov), with its striking volcanic phenomena, from rumpled lava tubes to cinder cones.

Otherwise, continue due south and you will push toward the **Steens Mountain Wilderness ㉑**, one of the state's most remote, rugged, and rewarding hiking and backpacking destinations. You can branch off on the 59-mile (95km) **Steens Loop Tour Route**, which ripples out from **Frenchglen** and travels on the highest road in the entire state as it strikes into the Steen Mountains (you will reach dizzying elevations nudging 10,000ft (3,048 meters) in height). Do not miss the **East Rim Viewpoint** (Steens Mountain Rd), which offers sweeping panoramas of the starkly beautiful **Alvord Desert ㉒**.

The High Desert Discovery Scenic Byway itself routes all the way south down to **Fields ㉓**, a tiny ranching town home to **The Fields Station** (22276 Fields Drive; tel: 541-495 2275; www. thefieldsstation.com; store Mon–Sat 8am–6pm, Sun 9am–5pm; café Mon–Sat 8am–4.15pm, Sun 9am–3.15pm), a quaint hotel, general store, and café known for its burgers and milkshakes.

Malheur Maar in the Diamond Craters Outstanding Natural Area.

The mighty Columbia River Gorge.

MOUNT HOOD AND THE COLUMBIA RIVER GORGE

Two epic natural wonders are synonymous with this stirring region: the mighty, snow-crowned bulk of Mount Hood – Oregon's highest peak – plus the gushing Columbia River and its snaking basalt ravine.

You can feel the full force of nature in this bucolic slice of Oregon, where waterfalls hang like lace curtains and the snowy crown of the Cascades' Mount Hood inches toward the sky. This is a place ultimately shaped by water. Beginning high in the Canadian Rockies, the mighty Columbia River is the region's showpiece: it rushes through millennia-old basalt, marking out the border with Washington state, and its spectacular gorge twists out for 80 miles (129km) and plunges down 4,000ft (1,219 meters) – a true geological wonder. In fact, the Columbia River Gorge National Scenic Area (which spills into southern Washington) is the largest in the country. It is easily explored via the Historic Columbia River Highway Scenic Byway, which throws up the best of the region's small cities, viewpoints, and trails.

You will find some of the best powder in the state here: runs at various ski resorts crisscross snow-blanketed Mount Hood, which is dubbed the second-most climbed mountain in the world (only behind Japan's Mount Fuji).

Meanwhile, volcanic soils and a temperate climate mean that the Hood River Valley is one of the finest fruit-growing regions in the country – a popular driving route, the Hood River Fruit Loop, joins together farms and orchards that showcase the region's bounty.

Vista House perched on Crown Point.

WEST COLUMBIA GORGE

Quaint towns and the sheer cinematic drama of the gorge characterize this subregion, roughly delineated by the Sandy River. If you are driving east from Portland on the I-84, then the dinky city of **Fairview ❶** will serve as your introduction to the region. The historic downtown is a pleasant place to stroll and is anchored by the **Heslin House Museum** (60 Main Street; tel: 503-618 0946; tours Sept–June, third Saturday of each month noon–4pm; July, Aug Sat noon–4pm), an 1890s

⊙ Main attractions

Multnomah Falls
Hood River Fruit Loop
Mosier Twin Tunnels Trail
Columbia Gorge Discovery Center & Museum
Timberline Lodge
Mount Hood

Map on page 194

Tip

For a weird and
wonderful diversion,
swerve south of Fairview
and hotfoot it to the town
of Boring, where the
North American Bigfoot
Center is anything but.
This curious museum
(31297 SE Hwy 26; tel:
503-912 3054; www.north
americanbigfootcenter.
com; daily 10am–5pm),
run by a local researcher,
pays homage to
sasquatch through
displays of artifacts such
as footprint casts.

building that serves as a fine example of a 19th-century Western farmhouse. Free tours are available of the house, which is filled with period artifacts.

But the town's real drawcard is **Blue Lake Regional Park** (21224 NE Blue Lake Road; tel: 503-665 4995; www.oregonmetro.gov/parks), which spreads over 101 acres (41 hectares) and centers on an attractive spring-fed lake. It is a hotspot for fishing, picnicking, and disc golf (there is a well-regarded course on site). A series of sculptures honors the Chinook people who are the traditional owners of this land. It's estimated that some 30,000 to 40,000 Chinooks once inhabited the lower Columbia region. This is thought to have been the site of a seasonal fishing village named Nichaqwli; look out for a net sinker carved from basalt and benches sculpted into the shape of canoes. Just a few minutes east of Fairview, **Wood Village** (affectionately known as "the Village") also makes an easy base with no-frills budget hotels.

The community of **Troutdale** ② is slightly larger than its neighbors but does not let up on the small-town charm. Tipped as the "Gateway to the Gorge," the city marks the beginnings of the Historic Columbia River Highway Scenic Byway. It also has more than a few treasures of its own. Make time to dip into the **Barn Exhibit Hall** (32 E Historic Columbia River Highway; tel: 503-661 2164; www.troutdalehistory.org/barn-exhibit-hall; Wed–Sat 10am–3pm, Sun 1–3pm), housed in one of the region's charming cherry-red barns. Exhibitions here usually last several years – since 2016 displays have focused on the Historic Columbia River Highway (nicknamed the "King of Roads"), covering its construction and preservation. Meanwhile, the **Depot Rail Museum** (473 E Historic Columbia River Highway; tel: 503-661 2164; www.troutdalehistory.org; Mon–Thu 9am–3pm, Fri–Sun until 5pm) looks at the area's defining railroad history and is housed in an early 20th-century depot building. This is also the location for the **Gateway to the Gorge Visitor Center** (475 E Historic Columbia River Highway; tel: 503-491 4000).

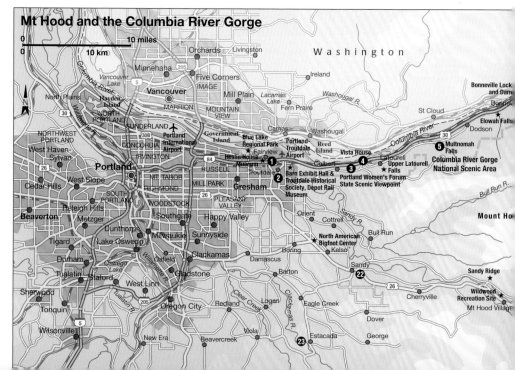

Mt Hood and the Columbia River Gorge

HISTORIC COLUMBIA RIVER HIGHWAY SCENIC BYWAY

Troutdale is within kissing distance of some of the region's finest viewpoints. Heading east on the Historic Columbia River Highway Scenic Byway (which runs south of, but roughly parallel, to the I-84 – though it is much curvier), the first of note is the **Portland Women's Forum State Scenic Viewpoint** ❸ (39210 Historic Columbia River Highway; tel: 800-551 6949; daily 6am–9pm). The land here was donated by its namesake, an organization dedicated to preserving the region's natural beauty. The majesty of the gorge area – with its sheer forested slopes and glistening water – is on full display. From here, you can also spot **Vista House** ❹ (40700 Historic Columbia River Highway; tel: 503-695 2240; www.vistahouse.com; Fri–Mon 9am–5pm), an elaborate Art Nouveau observatory perched on a dramatic gorge bluff called **Crown Point**. The observatory was built in 1918 by renowned Portland architect Edgar M. Lazarus and it commands its own pinch-yourself views of the gorge.

It also houses a gift shop, a café, and displays on the construction of the Historic Columbia River Highway.

WATERFALL ALLEY

This stretch of the Historic Columbia River Highway Scenic Byway packs a punch when it comes to natural wonders. There are eight named waterfalls within a 30-minute driving stretch, from the **Lower and Upper Latourell Falls** in the west to **Elowah Falls** in the east. Bookended by these cascades are: Shepperd's Deli Falls, Bridal Veil Falls, Wahkeena Falls, Multnomah Falls, Oneonta Falls, and Horsetail Falls. Hikes for differing abilities lead to the cascades, including the storied **Multnomah Falls** ❺ (www.fs.usda.gov).

Leaving from the **Multnomah Falls Lodge** (53000 Historic Columbia River Highway; tel: 503-695 2376; www.multnomahfallslodge.com), you can take a relatively easy paved trail to the scenic Benson Bridge, which shoots across the Multnomah Creek – the dramatically situated bridge offers a fabulous vantage point from which to take in the

> ⊙ **Tip**
>
> During the high season (late May to early September daily 9am–5pm), you will need a permit to drive along the busy waterfall corridor of the Historic Columbia River Highway Scenic Byway. Timed use permits for the popular Multnomah Falls are also required during this time. See www.oregon.gov/odot/waterfall-corridor-permits for info.

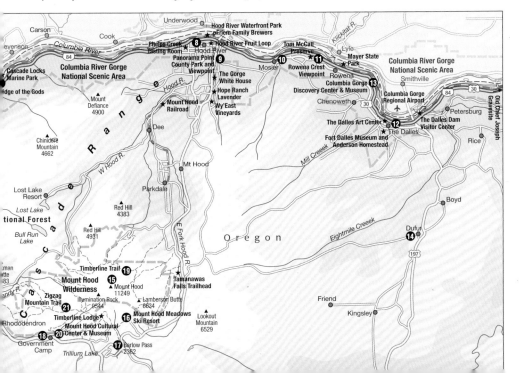

thundering cascade (though, be aware that it may be busy in high season).

You could stop here or continue for a five-mile (8km) round-trip hike that also takes in **Wahkeena Falls** – the onward portions are significantly more strenuous with steep sections and switchbacks, but you will likely shake off some of the crowds that collect around the bridge. If you want a short hike, try the route to **Bridal Veil Falls** (46701 Historic Columbia River Highway; tel: 503-695 2261; www.stateparks.oregon.gov). Though it is steep, it is only around 0.3 miles (0.5km) to the cascade, which is an impressive curtain of water rushing over moss-licked basalt. You could then continue onto the clifftop lookout, which offers sweeping views across the gorge. There are picnic tables and grassy spots near the parking lot if you need to rest up and refuel.

BONNEVILLE DAM AND CASCADE LOCKS

If you are keen to learn more about the mighty force that is the Columbia River, the Bradford Island Visitor

Wahkeena Falls.

Center (Star Route; tel: 541-374 8820; www.nwp.usace.army.mil/bonneville; daily 9am–5pm) at the **Bonneville Lock and Dam ❻** is a great place to set your sights on. The lock and dam were the first to be installed along the wild river, in 1938, and are operated by the US Army Corps of Engineers. Further powerhouses were built later in the 20th century. Today, exhibits at the visitor center cover everything from river wildlife such as salmon to the dam's construction, and how water is managed as a resource for the community.

Push east along the snaking Columbia and you will reach the community of Cascade Locks, which is sold as the "Heart of the Gorge." For years, the Columbia Gorge Sternwheeler glided through the waters here though, sadly, 2022 was the last season for the historic vessel. Get your camera ready for the mammoth **Bridge of the Gods ❼**, whose dramatic appearance befit its lofty moniker. The giant cantilevered structure thrusts across the Columbia – it was first built in 1926 and was later raised in the 1930s as water

⊘ KING OF ROADS

It took more than a decade to build the Columbia River Highway (the "Historic" was added later) with construction running from 1913 up until 1922. Upon its completion, it ran from Troutdale in the west out to The Dalles in the east and totaled some 75 miles (121km). Car assembly and ownership was growing significantly in the 1910s, but ultimately most of the state's roads were unwieldy dirt tracks at this time. The State Highway Commission was established in 1913 to make improvements to Oregon's roadways and the "King of Roads" – as the Columbia River Highway came to be known – was one of the most ambitious projects. It was conceived of, and led by, entrepreneur Sam Hill, who called on his engineer friend Sam Lancaster to lead the endeavor. In their plans, the pair considered both the efficiency of the route and the best way to flaunt the region's jaw-dropping natural beauty. However, their original route became quickly choked with ever-increasing traffic and they built a new, waterside roadway that could better deal with demand, abandoning portions of their scenic project in the process (I-84 was also begun in the 1950s). Today, various tracts of the picturesque original highway are preserved and open to motorists, while others have been restored for use by pedestrians and cyclists.

levels increased. A Native American story involving an ancient stone bridge and a pair of brawling mountain brothers swirls around the structure. As the legend goes, this wasn't the first bridge to stand here. The original Bridge of the Gods was apparently built from stone by the Great Spirit named Manito. It was guarded by an old woman named Loo-Wit, while Manito's three sons – Klickitat (Mount Adams), the totem-maker; Multnomah, the warrior; and Wyeast (Mount Hood), the singer – lived in the valley. Eventually, beautiful Squaw Mountain also moved into the valley, causing strife between brothers Wyeast and Klickitat, who both loved her. The siblings fought in explosive brawls involving fire and rocks – until, one day, the Bridge of the Gods got caught in the crossfire and fell into the river.

The **Cascade Locks Marine Park** (355 Wa Na Pa Street; tel: 541-374 8619; www.portofcascadelocks.org/marine-park) is another popular spot, with its beach, boat ramp, and picnic tables. Also within the park, Thunder Island offers fine views of the Bridge of Gods.

HOOD RIVER VALLEY

The Hood River Valley is an epicurean enclave. Around 350 commercial farms grow everything from apples and pears (a Hood River specialty) to lavender and berries. In fact, the first fruit trees were planted way back in 1855, and Native Americans including the Wasco people have been farming these lands long before that. After heading east from Cascade Locks, the I-84 will eventually lead you towards **Hood River ❽**. This hip small city is at once a gateway to some of the region's natural marvels (including Mount Hood itself) and a gem in its own right. Downtown, independent stores and family-owned restaurants jostle for space with brewpubs and wine-tasting rooms.

The centrally located **Hood River Hotel** (102 Oak Street; tel: 541-386 1900; www.hoodriverhotel.com) makes a great basecamp, with a cozy, fire-warmed common area, and an excellent breakfast at **Broder Øst** (102 Oak Street #100; tel: 541-436 3444; www.brodereast.com; daily 8am–3pm), the adjoining Scandinavian-style

Bonneville Lock and Dam, the first to be installed on the Columbia River.

⊘ EAGLE CREEK FIRE

Started in 2017 when a teenage boy threw a firework into an area of dry tinder during a burn ban, the Eagle Creek Fire rampaged for almost three months in the Columbia River Gorge region. It had a devastating effect on the area, resulting in millions of dollars' worth of damages, destroying property, killing wildlife and ravaging their natural habitat, and impacting local businesses. Some hiking trails, or sections of routes, are still closed because of the scale of the damage caused by the fire. If you are heading to the area, pay attention to signs and ensure you have up-to-date trail maps, or call information lines ahead of time to double-check routes. The scenic Oneonta Gorge is among the areas that remain closed to the public.

☉ Tip

Take a trip through the bucolic Hood River Valley with MountNbarreL (1850 Country Club Road; tel: 541-490 8687), which organizes guided bike, e-bike, or shuttle tours through local wine country, stopping for regular tastings and a catered lunch.

restaurant. Art lovers should make the most of the **Hood River BIG ART Walking Tour** (www.art-of-community.com).

A series of sculptures – some permanent; others on loan from artists – is strung along the streets of the Downtown area. They range from bold abstract pieces to effigies of flora and fauna. You can download a trail map and the Otocast app (featuring voices of the artists) from the website. Beer lovers should beeline for **pFriem Family Brewers** (707 Portway Avenue #101; tel: 541-321 0490; www.pfriembeer.com; daily 11am–9pm). The brewery's Downtown tasting room offers a raft of the brand's classic IPAs, pilsners, and lagers, as well as a selection of creative barrel-aged beers. The food menu has German-inspired plates, including Jägerschnitzel and Bratwurst. It sits right across from **Waterfront Park**, a popular spring/summer hangout spot that spreads out by the Columbia.

One of the region's most spectacular viewpoints unfolds close to Hood River. It is an easy drive up to **Panorama Point County Park and Viewpoint** , a lookout

area with stellar vistas of some of the region's show-stopping peaks, including Mount Hood and Mount Adams, as well as lush orchards and vineyards.

East of Hood River, the little town of **Mosier** ⑩ will put you within easy reach of several trails and viewing hotspots. Among them is the dramatic **Rowena Crest Viewpoint** ⑪ (6500 Historic Columbia River Highway; tel: 800-551 6949; www.stateparks.oregon.gov), which offers breathtaking views of the gorge region, including the lush **Mayer State Park** and a striking horseshoe-shaped stretch of road, known as the Rowena Loops. From here, trails wiggle into the **Tom McCall Nature Preserve** (Historic Columbia River Highway; tel: 503-802 8100; www.nature.org), home to the spring wildflower-scattered Plateau Trail, which covers 2.6 miles (4.1km).

Outside of Hood River, a charming place to stay is the **Old Parkdale Inn Bed and Breakfast** (4932 Baseline Drive; tel: 541-352 5551) in Parkdale. The quaint inn was built over a century ago, and sits in the shadow of Mount Hood, surrounded by orchards and

Lavender farms paint the Hood River Fruit Loop in purple hues.

☉ WATERY ADVENTURES

There are few better ways to experience the power and beauty of the Columbia than to paddle on it. You will find numerous launch points along the 146-river-mile Lower Columbia River Water Trail, which stretches all the way from Bonneville Dam out to the Pacific Ocean. Dalton Point Boat Launch is a popular put-in spot and from here you can paddle out west towards Rooster Rock. Note, however, that high winds can sometimes cause rough water in these parts, so the route is not necessarily recommended for beginners. Local guides operate along various stretches of the river. Hood River SUP and Kayak (The Hook; tel: 541-490 5286; www.hoodriversupandkayak.com) comes highly recommended, offering daytime sunset tours, plus organizes custom itineraries.

vineyards. Rooms are cozy with chintzy throws and floral watercolors.

THE DALLES

The rugged Dalles region is known for its High Desert scenery – a shift from the lush landscapes in the region's west – and its Oregon Trail history. It is thought that the city of **The Dalles** ⑫ is one of the oldest continuously occupied places in the state, estimated to have been home to Native Americans for more than 10,000 years. Its prime position in a bend of the Columbia River made it an important trading point and transport route, while the waterway's bounty of fish sustained the resident populations. The nearby rapids were documented in journals kept by explorers Meriwether and Clark, and later the area became a critical stop along the Oregon Trail.

This history is explored at the **Fort Dalles Museum** (500 W 15th and Garrison Street; tel: 541-296 4547; www. fortdallesmuseum.org), housed in preserved officers' quarters in a mid-19th-century military complex. There is an impressive store of antique vehicles,

including wagons, a stagecoach, and traditional surrey carriages. Meanwhile, the on-site Anderson House preserves a finely crafted 1895 log house built by a Swedish immigrant.

The **Dalles Art Center** (220 E 4th Street #2206; tel: 541-296 4759; www. thedallesartcenter.org; Thu–Sat 11am–5pm) is also worth a visit, showcasing the work of regional artists in a range of mediums, from paintings to sculpture.

The grand dame of the area's museums is the mighty **Columbia Gorge Discovery Center & Museum** ⑬ (5000 Discovery Drive; tel: 541-296 8600; www.gorgediscovery.org; daily 9am–5pm), which houses exhibits on the ravine's geology and wildlife, and the region's human history and local industries.

You can also pay a visit to **The Dalles Dam Visitor Center** (3545 Bret Clodfelter Way; tel: 541-296 9778; www. nwp.usace.army.mil/columbia/The-Dalles; Memorial Day to Sept Fri–Sun 9am–5pm) to learn about one of the largest hydropower dams in the USA.

The little city of **Dufur** ⑭, right at the eastern edge of the gorge, is

The dramatic Rowena Crest Viewpoint.

⊙ MOUNT HOOD RAILROAD

The historic Mount Hood Railroad (110 Railroad Street; tel: 541-399 8939; www. mthoodrr.com) offers a unique way to take in Hood River's bucolic valley. It began operation more than a century ago (with various defunct periods) and is now locally owned. Excursions see the train chug through woodland and alongside orchards and vineyards, with Mount Hood making regular cameos along the way. There are also seasonal, family-friendly events, including an Easter and a Christmas train. If you're feeling adventurous, you could try rail biking. These unique vehicles fit to the railroad track and offer an open-air alternative to the train – excursions stop at the long-running Fruit Company (2900 Van Horn Drive; tel: 541-387 3100; www.thefruit company.com), which includes a shop selling gourmet goods, plus museum exhibits.

FRUIT LOOP

The popular Hood River Fruit Loop knits together 28 of the region's top wineries, orchards, and pick-your-own farms in this fertile river valley.

Organized food trails are now abundant in Oregon – and across the nation as a whole – but the Hood River Fruit Loop was one of the earliest in the state. The driving route wriggles out for 35 miles (56km), promising pastoral views of scarlet barns amid blossoming pear orchards and hillsides criss-crossed with grape-heavy vines.

You will travel south from Hood River on the OR-35, whose early stretches follow the city's watery namesake. Early stops include Pearl's Place (1860 OR-35; tel: 541-86 3888), a quaint farm stand

Hood River is famed for its plump Bartlett Pears, best sampled at the region's pick-your-own farms.

that hawks fruit, including apples, pears, cherries, and nectarines grown by Viewmont Orchards. Just a minute's drive south is The Gorge White House (2265 OR-35l; tel: www.thegorgewhitehouse.com), which offers everything from hard cider and wine to fruit and flowers, and is centered on a gorgeous white-washed, 1908-built house. The food truck here is run by a Le Cordon Bleu chef, and features a menu that draws upon Hood River Valley's natural larder, dishing up everything from burgers made with local beef to pear quesadillas.

Lavender farms are a feature of the trail: follow your nose to Hope Ranch Lavender (2585 Fir Mountain Road; tel: 541-399 4634; www.hoperanch lavender.com) to see rippling fields of lilac, where you can cut your own bouquet. Hood River Lavender Farms (3823 Fletcher Drive; tel: 541-490 5657; www. hoodriverlavender.com) is another top spot.

Beyond the fruit and the flowers, wine also defines the route. The fertile valley is another of Oregon's top-notch grape-growing regions, with its undulating terrain resulting in elevation changes that make for many different microclimates. The abundance of rich volcanic soil is a boon. One of the finest stops along the Fruit Loop is the boutique Phelps Creek Vineyards (301 Country Club Road; tel: 541-386 2607; www.phelpscreekvineyards.com). Five-wine tasting flights are poured in the attractive and airy tasting room, with the primary output being Pinot Noir, Chardonnay, and Pinot Gris.

Mt Hood Winery (2882 Van Horn Drive; tel: 541-386 8333; www.mthoodwinery.com) is another worthy stop for oenophiles, so named for its cinematic views of the region's famous peak. Drink in mountain views through the tasting room's soaring windows as you sip Pinot Noir Rosé, Dry Riesling, Gewürztraminer, and a classic Pinot Noir. There is even pear wine, made from local Comice pears.

Wy'East Vineyards (3189 OR-35; tel: 541-386 1277; www.wyeastvineyards.com), meanwhile, has a wonderfully laid-back vibe with a bocce court and a food truck, plus more epic mountain views to boot.

Note that opening times for tours and tastings vary with the season – check websites and social media pages of individual outlets for the most up-to-date information.

another must-stop for history lovers. The **Dufur Living History Museum** (40 Main Street; tel: 541-467 2205) brings the local past to life through preserved homesteads and old farming tools.

MOUNT HOOD

The mighty hulk of **Mount Hood** ⑮ – Oregon's highest peak – defines this spectacular region and rears its head at every possible occasion. You'll spot the snow-crowned peak from hilltop tasting rooms, from downtown boulevards, and right from the road. The Mount Hood Scenic Byway throws up cinematic vistas of the famous peak along its 100 miles (161km), beginning in Hood River and winding all the way west to Wood Village.

Around a 30-minute drive south of Hood River, you will come to the trailhead for **Tamanawas Falls**. The pleasant hiking route leads along to an attractive 100ft (30-meter) cascade.

Several major ski areas cover snow-plastered Mount Hood, including the largest – **Mount Hood Meadows Ski Resort** ⑯ (14040 OR-35; tel: 503-337 2222; www.skihood.com), which sits on the

peak's southeastern face. Beginners can take lessons at this resort, which also has runs for experts, including the double diamond Heather Canyon and Super Bowl. Other winter activities include snowshoeing and Nordic skiing. There is plenty of life at the resort in the summertime too: visitors can enjoy chair rides offering sweeping mountain views, guided hikes, and live music.

Nudging west, **Barlow Pass** ⑰ is a significant point along the Scenic Byway – it was a critical point along the Oregon Trail, as travelers would have pushed through and over the Cascade Mountains, and it soars to 4,155ft (1,266 meters). **Barlow Pass Sno-Park** is a jumping-off point for winter adventures in the region's backcountry, with plenty of ungroomed ski trails (only attempt alone if you are a pro skier and well versed in navigating Oregon's wild backcountry in the winter).

Continuing along the byway, the next place you will reach is the pretty mountain town of **Government Camp** ⑱, the base camp for the popular **Timberline Trail** ⑲, a key Mount Hood hiking trail. It

☉ Tip
Time your trip for the Vintage Dufur Days festival, which celebrates the region's agricultural heritage (particularly dryland wheat farming) through feasts, farming demos, artisan markets, and a tractor parade.

Bridge of the Gods.

☉ RIVER HIGHWAY TRAIL

Hood River is a good base camp for the Historic Columbia River Highway State Trail, a series of paved hiking and biking trails that follows old Highway 30 (once the only way to journey from Portland to the Dalles). There are three separate portions – the Bonneville Segment, which routes from John B. Yeon to Cascade Locks; the Mitchell Point Segment, which connects Wyeth and Viento; and the Twin Tunnels Segment, which ripples out from Hood River to Mosier. Altogether, they form a 12-mile (19km) route, though the 4.5-mile (7km) Twin Tunnels stretch is the most popular (as its name suggests, the route preserves a pair of historic tunnels). Epic views of the Columbia River unfold beneath you as you hike or cycle the scenic trail.

Tip

The Jonsrud Viewpoint (15652 Bluff Road) is one of the region's finest, granting far-reaching vistas over the Sandy River Valley, as well as out to Mount Hood, the area's enduring celebrity.

routes into the rippling Mount Hood Wilderness and circumnavigates the peak, covering more than 40 miles (64km) and taking in meadows, waterfalls, and high alpine panoramas. You can complete the whole route on a backpacking trip, or tackle a section with a day hike. Government Camp is home to the **Mount Hood Cultural Center & Museum** ⊉ (88900 Government Camp Loop; tel: 503-272 3301; www.mthoodmuseum.org; daily 9am–5pm). Exhibits focus on Mount Hood's natural history, as well as the area's skiing and mountaineering heritage. The kid-friendly museum includes a scavenger hunt. Nearby, **Trillium Lake** in the Mount Hood National Forest is popular for boating and swimming, and the perfect pyramid of Mount Hood is reflected squarely in the water on clear days. There is a campground here.

The **Zigzag Mountain Trail** ㉑ (beginning at Forest Road 1819/East Mountain Drive) is another of the region's glorious hiking trails, routing through the Mount Hood Wilderness Area and climbing 3.5 miles (5.6km) over 4,400ft (1,341 meters) of namesake Zigzag Mountain.

The trail's real drawcard is the excellent views of Mount Hood along the way.

Hikers will love the **Wildwood Recreation Site** (65670 US-26; tel: 503-622 3696; www.blm.gov), which provides access to some impressive old-growth forest (including ancient Douglas firs and Western red cedar), as well as the scenic Salmon River. Gentle paved and boardwalk trails offer a change of pace from some of the region's more strenuous mountain routes (though the 4.7-mile/7.6km Boulder Ridge Trail, which climbs Huckleberry Mountain, tests the mettle of even the most hardened of hikers).

A short jaunt northwest, the town of **Sandy** ㉒ has become a hub for mountain bikers. The **Sandy Ridge Trail System** spreads out in the foothills of the Cascades, and its 17 miles (27km) of trails range from beginner routes to double black diamond runs that demand a high level of technical ability.

Around 20 minutes southwest of Sandy, **Estacada** ㉓ provides access to **Milo McIver State Park**, which is a hub for boating and kayaking on the Clackamas River.

Trillium Lake.

⊘ TIMBERLINE LODGE

Perhaps the most famous of all Oregon's ski resorts is **Timberline Lodge** (27500 E Timberline Road; tel: 503-272 3311; www.timberlinelodge.com), not least because it served as the exterior for the Overlook Hotel in 1980 horror movie *The Shining* (based on the Stephen King novel of the same name). The resort is touted as having the longest ski season in all of North America (mid-Nov through May). The lodge itself is perched at 6,000ft (1,829 meters), and the area offers 4,540 vertical feet (1,384 meters) of ski and snowboard runs. Other activities include snowshoeing, cross-country skiing, and snowcat rides on the Palmer Snowfield. In summer, you can ride the Magic Mile Chair Lift and take to a range of hiking and biking trails. Among them is a section of the Pacific Crest Trail. Rock climbing is also popular in the area.

Multnomah Falls.

The US Route 101 traces the entire Oregon Coast.

OREGON

TRANSPORTATION

GETTING THERE

Oregon is well connected to the rest of the USA by air, and there are also non-stop flights from Mexico, Canada, the UK, and Iceland. Roads route into the state from various northern, southern, and eastern access points, while some cities in the Portland and Willamette Valley area are served by Amtrak, the USA's National Railroad Passenger Corporation.

By air

Portland International Airport (PDX) is 12 miles (19km) northeast of Downtown. It is a 40-minute ride to and from the city on the Red Line of the TriMet MAX light-rail system (www.trimet.org), which typically departs every 15 minutes from the south end of the ticket lobby on the airport's main level. An Uber ride will likely cost you around $35 and should take 20 minutes depending on traffic.

Portland International Airport.

Airlines

Major airlines that fly into PDX include (but are not limited to):
British Airways
American Airlines
Southwest
Alaska
Frontier
United
Delta
Air Canada

By rail

Train services into Portland are limited, though several Amtrak (tel: 800-872 7245; www.amtrak.com) services offer a pleasant way to explore a swathe of the West Coast. The Cascades route runs all the way from Vancouver in Canada's British Columbia to Oregon's Eugene, stopping at Seattle and Tacoma in Washington, and Portland and Salem in Oregon on the way. In its entirety, the route takes just over 10 hours. Portland also features on Amtrak's Coast Starlight route, which travels

⊙ On foot

Many of Oregon's cities have compact and walkable downtown cores. They include Bend (Central Oregon), Eugene (Willamette Valley), and Hood River (Columbia River Gorge and Mount Hood region). Portland's Downtown core is walkable too, and so are neighborhoods such as Montavilla, Mississippi, and the Pearl District.

from Seattle to Portland and on to California's Sacramento and Los Angeles. The Empire Builder runs begins in Chicago and travels west to Portland via St Paul Minneapolis and Spokane (from Spokane there is also the alternative option to route toward Seattle).

Mount Hood makes a spectacular appearance as you travel down through the Columbia River Gorge towards Portland. Amtrak trains are generally modern and comfortable, with charging ports, reclining seats, and food for purchase.

By bus

The national bus line, Greyhound Lines (tel: 800-231 2222; www.greyhound.com), operates a number of routes across Oregon. Most leave from Portland – you can reach Bend, Medford, Corvallis Eugene, Seattle (Washington), and Sacramento (California) from the city.

There are also services from Medford to Eugene.

By road

There are myriad ways to approach Oregon by road. Highway 101 bleeds down the coast, from northern Washington, through Oregon, to California (where it eventually branches off into famous Highway 1). Interstate-5 is another major north to south route, running all the way from the Canadian border to the border with Mexico. A key route in from the east is on Interstate-84. The highway gets started in Echo, Utah, and routes north through Idaho, before crossing the border (and the Snake River) near Ontario, Oregon. From here, it travels toward Portland via La Grande, Pendleton, The Dalles, and Hood River.

The TriMet MAX light-rail system and Portland Streetcar in Downtown.

GETTING AROUND

Oregon is the ninth largest state by area, so distances are long. Particularly in the state's rugged and remote east, a car is the only viable mode of transportation (and, happily, road trips here are richly rewarding offering cinematic views).

Otherwise, a smattering of bus routes crisscrosses the state, and a few cities are also served by Amtrak. Portland International Airport (PDX) is the state's major air hub, but cities including Eugene (Eugene Airport) and Medford (Rogue Valley International–Medford Airport) have regional airports.

To and from the airport

It is a 40-minute ride from Portland International Airport (PDX) into the Downtown area on the Red Line of the TriMet MAX light-rail system (www.trimet.org). An Uber ride will likely cost you around $35 and should take 20 minutes depending on traffic.

From PDX, you can reach Eugene by car in around 2.5 hours and be in Bend in just over three hours.

Public transportation in Portland

Portland's public transit is coordinated by MAX (tel: 503-238 7433; www.trimet.org; 2.5 hours at $2.50, all-day pass $5). Buses radiate through the city from a downtown transit mall on 5th and 6th avenues, while five color-coded light-rail lines channel riders around central downtown and Old Town, and out to the suburbs. The Portland Streetcar runs three routes through the city center, covering both sides of the river (tel: 503-222 4200; www.portlandstreetcar.org).

By air

Portland International Airport (PDX) is the state's main airport, offering flights across the state, nationwide, and overseas. The Willamette Valley is also served by Eugene Airport (EUG), which operates carriers including Alaska Airlines, Allegiant, and American Airlines, and reaches destinations including Salt Lake City, Phoenix, and Denver. You can travel from Pendleton to Portland via the Eastern Oregon Regional Airport, or to Portland, Denver, Los Angeles, and Phoenix from the Redmond Municipal Airport (RDM) in Central Oregon.

The Southwest Oregon Regional Airport (OTH) (operating from North Bend) connects the Oregon Coast with Denver and San Francisco,

while Rogue Valley International–Medford Airport (MFR) connects Southern Oregon to Portland and Seattle, as well as to Los Angeles, San Francisco, and Denver.

By rail

You can travel from Portland Union Station to Albany, Eugene, Oregon City, and Salem on the Amtrak Cascades train. A range of scenic tourist trains operate in the state too. Among them is the Eagle Cap Excursion Train (300 Depot Street; tel: 541-437 3652; www.eaglecap trainrides.com), which travels along the Wallowa and Grande Ronde rivers, and the Oregon Coast Scenic Railroad (402 American Avenue; tel: 503-842 7972; www.oregoncoastscenic. org), which covers the Tillamook

⊘ Renting a car

National car-rental companies are located at all airports and large towns. To secure the best rates, it is advisable to book your car rental in advance; if you're flying in with a major airline, check to see whether it offers discounted car rental. You must be at least 21 years old to rent a car (often 25) in the US, and you must have a valid driver's license that you have held for at least a year already, along with a major credit card to guarantee your booking. Foreign travelers should always expect to have to show a license from their home country; an international driver's license will not be enough. Standard rental vehicles have automatic transmissions; expect to pay extra if you require a

manual ("stick shift") car. Be sure to take out collision and liability insurance, which may not always be included in the base price of the rental.

Alamo: tel: 844-354 6962; www.alamo.com
Avis: tel: 800-633 3469; www.avis.com
Budget: tel: 800-218 7992; www.budget.com
Dollar: tel: 800-800 5252; www.dollar.com
Enterprise: tel: 855-266 9565; www.enterprise.com
Hertz: tel: 800-654 3131; www.hertz.com
National: tel: 844-382 6875; www.nationalcar.com
Thrifty: tel: 800-847 4389; www.thrifty.com

☉ Taxis

There is typically a minimum fare for cab rides in Portland (often around $3.80) and usually an additional $3.50 airport charge. Taxi companies include Flat Cab (tel: 503-970 0033) and PDX Yellow Cab (tel: 503-841 6328). Ride-sharing apps such as Uber and Lyft also operate in Portland. The Bend Cab Company and Shuttle Services (tel: 541-389 8090; www.bendcab. com) operates in Central Oregon, while Crater Lake Taxi (tel: 541-333 3333; www.craterlaketaxi.com) covers Southern Oregon areas, including Ashland and Medford.

Bay area, with rides leaving from Rockaway Beach and Garibaldi.

By coach/bus

Nationally recognized chain Greyhound Lines connects Portland with Bend, Medford, Corvallis, and Eugene. Meanwhile, the Sunset Empire Transportation District (tel: 503-861 7433) operates buses in Clatsop County in northwestern Oregon, servicing destinations such as Astoria, Cannon Beach, and Seaside. NW Connector (www.nworegontransit.org) is a useful tool for planning transit in the region without a car. Southern Oregon is served by the Rogue Valley Transportation District (tel: 541-779 2877; www. rvtd.org), which connects destinations such as Medford and Ashland. In Central Oregon, Cascades East

The iconic US 101 route.

Transit (tel: 541-385 8680; www.cascadeseasttransit.com) joins hubs such as Madras, La Pine, and Bend.

By road

Driving in Oregon is a joy, with an extensive network of designated Scenic Byways stitching together the state's most spectacular spots. A small sampling includes the Mount Hood Scenic Byway, which travels through the bucolic region around the famous peak; the Journey Through Time Scenic Byway, in rugged Eastern Oregon; and the fabled Pacific Coast Scenic Byway, which snakes along Oregon's seaboard. Major routes also include the north–south I-5 and the I-84 (which travels in from Idaho).

Ensure you are adequately prepared for driving in Oregon during the winter. Snow can make roads hazardous, particularly in the state's mountainous areas, and it is highly recommended that you rent a 4WD vehicle. If you have a 2WD, it is mandated by law that you carry traction tires or chains with you and use them as instructed along the highway.

Drivers are required to carry a valid license at all times. Visitors from English-speaking countries are typically allowed to use their full domestic licenses. Be sure to also have with you a certificate proving you have liability insurance. It is illegal to drive without these items, and you are required to show them to any law enforcement officers who stop your car.

Laws for safety

Belts and child seats. State laws in Oregon require that every passenger wear a seat belt. If a child is eight years old or younger and is under 4'9" tall, use of a child-restraint system is still mandated.
Cell phones. It is illegal to talk on a cell phone while driving unless you are able to operate it hands-free.
Emergency vehicles. When a fire truck, ambulance, or police vehicle approaches from either direction with flashing lights and/or a siren, you must immediately pull over to the side of the road.
Helmets. All motorcycle riders are required to wear helmets.
Roadside assistance. The Highway Patrol cruises the highways, not just monitoring speed limits but also

looking for drivers in trouble. If you have any emergency that won't allow you to continue the trip, signal your need for help by raising the hood. Motorists are often advised that it is safest to stay in the car with the doors locked until a patrol car stops to help.

Rules of the road

Those roads that are restricted to one-way traffic only are identified by a black-and-white sign with an arrow pointing in the permitted direction of travel. At an intersection with a four-way red stop sign, motorists must completely stop and then proceed across the intersection following the order in which they arrived at the stop. If you arrive at the same time, the person to the right has the right of way, but usually one person just waves on another. It is legal to make a right turn on a red light after making a full stop, unless signs indicate otherwise.

Speed limits for roads and highways are posted on white signs to the right, as are all other road signs. Unless otherwise indicated, the speed limit is 65mph (105kmh) on freeways, 55mph (88kmh) on two-lane highways, and 25mph (40kmh) near schools and in residential or business districts.

Watch for white signs warning that you will be in a different "Speed Zone Ahead." Be prepared to slow to the lower speed you will soon see posted on upcoming white signs.

☉ Cycling

Portland is often held up as one of the USA's premier cities for cycling. There are miles of designated bike lanes in the city, as well as trails routing through large green spaces such as Forest Park. The city operates the Biketown bike-share program (www.biketownpdx.com), which is inclusive of 1,000 bright-orange bicycles. Designated scenic bikeways cover miles of the state, from Central Oregon's Three Sisters Scenic Bikeway to the Willamette Valley Scenic Bikeway or the Wild Rivers Coast Scenic Bikeway. Oregon is also a mountain-biking hub. Top destinations include Oakridge in the Willamette Valley and Sandy in the Mount Hood region.

Accessible travel

US legislation requires public buildings and most public transportation to be made accessible to travelers with disabilities. Greyhound buses offer priority seating to disabled passengers, while many are equipped with wheelchair lifts, and the railroad system, Amtrak, offers discounted tickets.

Oregon Adaptive Sports (tel: 541-306 4774; www.oregonadaptivesports. org) is an adaptive sports foundation committed to making outdoor recreation accessible to all. Winter programs include accessible skiing, snowboarding, and snowshoeing at Mt Bachelor or the Hoodoo Ski Area.

There is also a range of accessible hiking routes in Oregon, including boardwalk and paved trails. The Willamette Partnership has produced an accessible travel guide covering the whole state; it can be found online at www.willamettepartnership.org/accessible-travel-guide.

Accommodations

Oregon offers a broad range of accommodations, from historic hotels to rustic lodges in the woods. Most of Oregon's state parks have campgrounds, many with RV sites as well as tent pitches – some also have cabins or yurts. In Oregon's cities, lodgings run the gamut from swish hotels – such as the Sentinel in Portland (614 SW 11th Avenue; tel: 503-224 3400; www.provenancehotels. com/sentinel-hotel) – to basic budget chains such as La Quinta Inn and Days Inn.

Admission charges

Most large museums charge entrance fees, which tend to range from $10 to $25. Smaller art galleries are often free. Special exhibitions usually cost extra, but many museums have free general admission on certain days each month or once a week in the evening.

Age restrictions

The legal age to consume alcohol and marijuana is 21. The legal age for driving is 17.

Budgeting for your trip

If you're looking for a hotel room with an acceptable minimum level of comfort, cleanliness, and facilities, a reasonable starting point for the price of a double room is $85; upping your budget to at least $150 will make a significant difference in quality. For between $150 and $300, a whole range of hotels opens up, from functional spots geared toward business travelers to hip little boutiques or luxurious woodland cabins.

Eating out costs range from $5 to $10 for street food and fast food such as hot dogs to $50 for a two- or three-course meal at a contemporary restaurant. You might pay $100-plus at a fine-dining place. A glass of house wine is usually under $10, and a beer is around $7.

Getting around by public transportation can cost as little as $3–5 a day. Bus or train tickets typically cost around $2.50.

Children

Oregon is well suited to a family vacation. Many spots along the coast are particularly geared toward families with kid-friendly attractions such as aquariums and traditional arcades. Other family-focused attractions include ziplines (such as Crater Lake Zipline in Southern Oregon, www.craterlakezipline.com); museums like the Eugene Science Center (2300 Leo Harris Parkway; tel: 541-682 7888; www.eugenescience center.org; Tue–Thu, Sat, Sun 10am–5pm, Fri until 7pm); and wildlife-watching places such as the Sea Lion Caves (91560 US-101; tel: 541-547 3111; www.sealioncaves.com; daily 9am–5pm).

Climate

A mild, humid climate predominates in the area west of the Cascade Mountains, with moisture-laden clouds moving in from the Pacific and bringing considerable rainfall. Portland and the Willamette Valley generally have daily high temperatures in July reaching 81°F (27°C), dropping to 57°F (14°C) at night, while the equivalent averages for January – the coldest month – are 46°F (8°C) in the day and 37°F (3°C) at night.

Things are considerably cooler in Oregon's mountainous areas, which receive a generous amount of snow during the winter months – snowfall in regions such as Southern and Central Oregon might begin in October and last all the way through to early April. In Bend, average highs are 41°F (5°C) in January and 82°F (28°C) in July

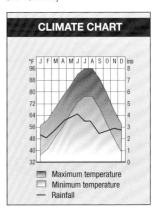

CLIMATE CHART

Maximum temperature
Minimum temperature
Rainfall

Portland's temperatures drop to 46°F (8°C) in the depths of winter.

Your visit to landmarks such as Crater Lake National Park will be significantly different in winter than in summer: for example, at Crater Lake, roads such as Rim Drive are closed from October all the way through to July and snowshoes may be required during this time.

Crime and safety

Much like in any city around the world, you should exercise caution in Oregon. Portland, like many other American cities, has seen an increase in crime in the past year, though it typically occurs outside of the principal tourist areas (and levels of violent crime is generally lower than the national average).

Common sense is typically an effective safeguard. Keep a careful eye on your belongings. Never leave your car unlocked. Never leave children by themselves. When driving, never pick up anyone you don't know and always be wary of who is around you.

Hotels usually warn that they do not guarantee the safety of belongings left in the rooms. If you have any valuables, you should lock them in the hotel safe.

Customs regulations

There is no limit to the amount of money you can bring into Oregon with you – but if the amount exceeds $10,000, you must fill out a report. All agricultural products must be declared (and some, such as meat and raw veg are prohibited). For details, contact the US consulate nearest you or the US Department of Agriculture.

Adults are allowed to bring in one quart (1 liter) of alcohol for personal use, tax free. Dogs, cats, and other animals may be brought into the country with certain restrictions. Automobiles may be driven into the US if they are for the personal use of the visitor, family, and guests.

For a full list of prohibited or restricted items, see www.cbp.gov/travel/us-citizens/know-before-you-go/prohibited-and-restricted-items.

Eating out

Oregon is a food-lover's delight. There is an abundance of cuisines to try, from classic American and contemporary "New American" food, to all manner of global cuisines. From Europe, you will find Italian trattorias, French bistros, German beer halls, and Mediterranean eateries. As for Asian foods, cities such as Portland, Bend, and Hood River offer the opportunity to sample Indian curries, Vietnamese pho, Korean barbecue, sushi, and dim sum, plus Americanized fusion fare. The state has also wholeheartedly adopted Mexican favorites such as burritos, quesadillas, and tacos *al pastor*. And don't forget the extraordinary array of ultra-fresh seafood that's available across the Pacific Northwest.

Regions such as the Willamette Valley and Hood River Valley are particularly well known for their bounty of fresh produce (especially pears, berries, and hazelnuts), and imaginative restaurants make the most of this cornucopia. These regions – along with the up-and-coming Rogue Valley – also produce some of the finest wines in the nation. Craft beer has long been a specialty of the state, and now artisanal cideries, and gin, whiskey, and vodka distilleries are popping up across Oregon, too.

Electricity

The standard electric current in the United States is 120 volts, and outlets are generally for flat-blade, two-prong plugs. Foreign appliances usually require a converter and an adaptor plug. Many hotel bathrooms have plugs for electric shavers that work on either current.

Embassies and consulates

The nearest embassies and consulates are as follows:
Australia 575 Market Street, San Francisco. Tel: 415-644 3620; www.usa.embassy.gov.au.
Canada 1501 4th Avenue, Seattle. Tel: 415-834 3180; www.international.gc.ca.
Great Britain 1 Sansome Street, Suite 850, San Francisco. Tel: 415-617 1300; www.gov.uk.

Emergencies

In the case of an emergency, dial 911 from any telephone for the police, fire department, or ambulance service.

Etiquette

People usually address each other in friendly, rather than formal, terms. "Mr" and "Ms" are used in business and formal settings if the person is a superior. "Mrs" is rarely heard or used. When meeting someone, a handshake is typical. If you are invited to someone's home, a bottle of wine, a box of candy, or a small personal token is thoughtful. Political discussions can be divisive.

Festivals and events

Here are just a few of the most popular festivals and cultural events across Portland:
January
Portland Folk Festival, Portland www.portlandsfolkfestival.com
Local and regional artists gather in a celebration of roots, Americana, and folk music.
February
Oregon Winter Fest, Redmond www.oregonwinterfest.com
Come to Central Oregon for a winter extravaganza including live music, ice carvings, and light displays.
Northwest Black Comedy Festival, Portland www.nwblackcomedyfest.com
Black comics from across the nation

are brought together for showcases and live podcasts.

March
SheBrew, Portland
www.shebrew.beer
Female-identifying brewers from across the Pacific Northwest are showcased at this festival, with tastings, competitions, and food carts.

April
Oregon Country Fair, Veneta
www.oregoncountryfair.org
This wholesome, family-friendly event combines an artisan market and street food with stages hosting everything from hip-hop performances to puppet shows.

May
Florence Rhododendron Festival, Florence
www.florencechamber.com/annual-events/rhody-festival-2
See this cute coastal town in full bloom, with colorful parades, classic car shows, and local food vendors.

June
Lincoln City Kite Festival, Lincoln City
www.oregoncoast.org/events/annual/summer-kite-festival
A world of colorful creations fills the skies during this Oregon Coast event, which also hosts kite-making workshops and carnival games.
Portland Rose Festival, Portland
www.rosefestival.org
One of the state's most popular festivals celebrates the humble rose and includes parades with flamboyant floats, music concerts, and fireworks. (The organization now also hosts the Oregon Brewers Festival.)

July
Waterfront Blues Festival, Portland
www.waterfrontbluesfest.com
A summer celebration of the soulful genre, this festival includes concerts, dance shows, and family-focused activities, and draws big names such as The Mavericks.

August
Pickathon Experiential Music Festival, Happy Valley
www.pickathon.com
Genres run the gamut from hip-hop to bluegrass at this historic summer music festival taking place at Pendarvis Farm.

September
Pendleton Round-Up, Pendleton
www.pendletonroundup.com
This classic and long-running rodeo in Eastern Oregon also has a focus on Native American heritage.

October
Oregon Shakespeare Festival

www.osfashland.org
One of the nation's most highly regarded theater companies runs its season from April through to October, showcasing the Bard's classic tragedies, comedies, and histories.

November
Portland Book Festival, Portland
www.literary-arts.org/about/programs/portland-book-festival
This literary showcase features readings and workshops, a large book fair, and food carts.

December
Umpqua Valley Festival of Lights, Roseburg
www.uvfestivaloflights.com
Beginning late November, this festive Southern Oregon jamboree dazzles with drive-through lights display.
Oregon Whale Watch Week, various coastal locations
Volunteer interpreters are stationed at different spots along the Oregon Coast to help visitors glimpse these majestic mammals during their winter migration.

Health and medical care

There is nothing cheap about being sick in the United States. It is essential to have adequate insurance and to carry an identification card or policy number at all times.
Walgreens and CVS drugstores (pharmacies) typically have 24-hour locations in major cities.
Providence Portland Medical Center 4805 Glisan Street Northeast; tel: 503-215 6079; www.providence.org.
OHSU and Doernbecher Emergency Room 3181 SW Sam Jackson Park Road; tel: 503-494 7551; www.ohsu.edu/health/emergency-care.

Portland has a thriving nightlife scene.

CVS 640 SW Broadway; tel: 503-535 6032; www.cvs.com; daily 8am–10pm.

Internet

Pretty much every coffeehouse in the US gives customers free wi-fi access. Many local and state visitor centers also have free wi-fi, and it would be very rare to find a hotel that didn't offer wi-fi access in its guestrooms and common areas. Most public libraries have free terminals too.

Left luggage

File claims for damaged or missing luggage with the relevant airline before leaving the airport. For queries and complaints, contact the Office of Aviation Consumer Protection (tel: 202-366 2220; www.transportation.gov/airconsumer).

LGBTQ+

Portland, alongside other hubs such as Eugene and Bend, are known to be exceptionally welcoming to LGBTQ+ travelers. In fact, Portland has one of the largest LGBTQ+ populations in the country. The city has a large Pride celebration in July, while Dayton, in the Willamette Valley, is the home of the world's first queer wine festival. Travelers can find and support LGBTQ+ businesses and find particularly welcoming establishments by searching Portland's Gay Directory: www.gaypdx.com.

Maps

State and local visitor centers throughout Oregon are invaluable

sources of free maps, while commercial maps are also widely available. You can download a range of transit and tourist maps via the Travel Portland website at www.travelportland.com/meetings/maps-transit. Meanwhile, www.traveloregon.com has information on the state's seven distinct regions.

Media

Television and radio

Television and radio are sources of up-to-the-minute information about weather, road conditions, and current events. Television and radio listings are published in local newspapers. Sunday editions usually carry a detailed weekly guide to events and activities.

Newspapers, magazines, and websites

First published in 1850, Portland's *Oregonian* (www.oregonlive.com) has the largest circulation of any Oregon newspaper. Some of the free local weekly newspapers, available in cafés and newspaper boxes on the street, are also excellent sources of current information about what's going on in a particular town. The *Portland Business Journal* is another highly regarded publication, as is alternative newspaper *Willamette Week*.

Money

Cash. Most banks are connected to a network of ATMs, which dispense cash 24 hours a day.
Credit cards. Not all credit cards are accepted everywhere, but most places accept either Visa, American Express, or MasterCard. Major credit cards can also be used to withdraw cash from ATMs; look for those that use one of the banking networks indicated on the back of your credit card, such as Plus, Cirrus, or Interlink. Most likely, there will be a charge.
Travelers' checks. With the popularity of ATMs, credit cards, and debit cards, travelers' checks are becoming increasingly rare. Still, banks, stores, restaurants, and hotels generally accept US dollar-denominated travelers' checks. If yours are in foreign denominations, they must be changed to dollars. Banks readily cash large travelers' checks, although be sure to take along your passport. When lost or stolen, most travelers' checks can be replaced; record the checks' serial numbers in

a separate place to facilitate refunds of lost or stolen checks.

Opening hours

Standard opening hours are 9am to 5/6pm weekdays (though these, of course, can vary). Most department stores open at 10am; many stores, especially those in shopping malls, stay open until 9pm; and major cities tend to hold a handful of 24-hour restaurants. A few supermarkets and convenience stores are also open around the clock.

Bank hours usually run from 9am to 5pm, although some stay open until 6pm. Many branch offices also keep Saturday morning hours. However, most banks are equipped with 24-hour ATM on the outside of their buildings, which you can use for simple transactions at your convenience. Be careful when withdrawing money at night.

During public holidays, post offices, banks, government offices, and many private businesses are closed.

Postal services

Post offices typically open during regular working hours, from Monday to Friday. Many also open for a few hours on Saturday morning but are typically closed all day Sunday. If you don't know where you will be staying in any town, you can receive mail by having it addressed to General Delivery at the main post office in that town. You must pick up General Delivery mail in person and show proper identification.

You can buy stamps in most convenience stores, although you may have to buy a book of stamps. You can also buy them at a post office.

Public holidays

National US holidays are:
New Year's Day January 1
Martin Luther King Jr. Day 3rd Monday in January
President's Day 3rd Monday in February
Memorial Day Last Monday in May
Independence Day July 4
Labor Day 1st Monday in September
Columbus Day 2nd Monday in October
Veteran's Day November 11
Thanksgiving 4th Thursday in November
Christmas Day December 25

Religion

There is no official religion in the US, though the largest majority of Americans identify themselves as having a Christian faith, including Protestant or Catholic. Non-Christian religions (including Judaism, Islam, Buddhism, and Hinduism) collectively make up about six percent of the adult population, according to the Pew Research Center.

Shopping

Shopping is tax-free in Oregon, so many travelers come from out of state to get their retail fix. The state's shopping locations run the gamut from outlet malls (such as Columbia Gorge Outlets in Troutdale; 450 NW 257th Way; tel: 503-669 8060; www.shopcolumbiagorgeoutlets.com) to upscale destinations such as Portland's Pioneer Place (700 SW 5th Avenue; tel: 503-228 5800; www.pioneerplace.com). Portland is also known for its high concentration of quirky indie clothing and curio stores and vintage shops, while you will find fun gift and souvenir stores along the coast.

Smoking

Smoking is banned in almost all indoor public places and workplaces, including bars, clubs, and restaurants, and outdoors within 10ft (3 meters) of entrances and exits to public buildings and places of employment. You may find it difficult to reserve a smoking room in a hotel; check when you book.

Student travelers

With a current school ID, a student traveler can take advantage of discounts at some museums, in movie theaters, and on public transportation.

Tax

There is no sales tax in Oregon.

Telephones

US phone numbers are 10-digit numbers (including a 3-digit area code). The country code for the US is "+1." Make use of toll-free numbers when possible (indicated by 1-800, 855, 866, 877, or 888).

Foreign travelers hoping to use their cellphones in the US should check with their service providers; it's very likely that your phone will work, but calls may well incur substantial roaming charges. Ideally, if possible, try to use online services such as FaceTime or Zoom. Alternatively, it's possible to buy pay-as-you-go phones from major electrical stores in the US, or prepaid SIM cards from the likes of AT&T.

Coin-operated telephones are becoming rare but might be found in gas stations or lighted booths on street corners.

Time zone

Oregon is on Pacific Standard Time (PST), which is two hours earlier than Chicago, three hours earlier than New York and eight hours earlier than Greenwich Mean Time. During Daylight Savings time, which occurs from the second Sunday of March to the first Sunday of November, the clocks are rolled forward one hour, and PST becomes only seven hours earlier than GMT.

Tipping

Just as in other parts of the country, service personnel in Oregon rely on tips for a large part of their income. In most cases, 18–20 percent is the going rate for waiters and bartenders, and 15 percent for taxi drivers. The accepted rate for baggage handlers at airports and hotels is around $1 per bag. The rule of thumb is to leave a minimum tip of one or two dollars per night stayed in for house-keeping staff. A doorman expects to be tipped at least $1 for unloading your car or for other services. You should also aim to tip your tour guide around 10–20 percent of the trip cost.

Tourist information

Travel Oregon
Tel: 800-547 7842; www.traveloregon.com
Portland
Tel: 503-427 137; www.travelportland.com

Tour operators and travel agents

Cycle Portland Bike Tours
Tel: 844-739 2453;
www.portlandbicycletours.com
Cycling tours of downtown Portland and the Willamette River; longer trips include stops at two city breweries.
Lost Plate Food Tours
www.lostplate.com

Gourmet trips tapping into Portland's food scene, including food carts and pods, breweries, and coffee and donut spots.
Hellgate Jetboat Excursions
Tel: 541-479 7204; www.hellgate.com
Jet-boat tours of Hellgate Canyon on Oregon's Rogue River, departing from Grants Pass. Choose between a gentle one-hour ride or a five-hour wild water extravaganza.
Best Oregon Tours
Tel: 503-572 5323;
www.bestoregontours.com
This Willamette Valley-based tour company offers excursions exploring the region's covered bridges and wine country, plus jaunts out to the coast.
South Coast Tours
Tel: 541-373 0487;
www.southcoasttours.net
Head out on expert-led paddling tours in the South Slough National Estuarine Research Reserve and on the Coquille River.
Main Street Adventure and Wine Tours
Tel: 541-625 9845;
www.ashland-tours.com
Main Street tours strike out into Crater Lake National Park and explore Southern Oregon's backcountry with hiking and snowshoe trips. It also offers tours in wine country and historic Jacksonville.
Wanderlust Tours
Tel: 541-389 8359;
www.wanderlusttours.com
Operating from Bend, this adventure tour company promises Central Oregon adventures from scrambles through volcanic caves to snowshoeing in the Cascade Mountains.

Pioneer Place in Portland.

Go Wild: American Adventures
Tel: 541-403 1692; www.gowildusa.com
Multiday hiking and paddling trips in Eastern Oregon's backcountry are the drawcard of this operator, which also offers history tours of Baker City.
Pendleton Underground Tours
Tel: 541-276 0730;
www.pendletonundergroundtours.org
Check out subterranean sights in historic Pendleton with this company, whose tours include a visit to a Chinese laundry, a Prohibition-era card room, and a historic bordello.
MountNbarreL
Tel: 541-490 8687;
www.mountnbarrel.com
Guided bike, e-bike, and shuttle tours exploring wineries and fruit farms in the charming Hood River Valley.

Visas and passports

Citizens of 40 countries – including the UK, Ireland, Australia, New Zealand, and most Western European countries – are allowed to vacation in the US for up to 90 days without visas. Instead, under the Visa Waiver Program, you must apply for ESTA (Electronic System for Travel Authorization) approval before you leave home.

This is easily done, via the ESTA website (www.esta.cbp.dhs.gov), but you may have to wait for as long as 72 hours before you receive your authorization number. The ESTA authorization certificate costs $21 and is valid for up to two years, unless your passport expires first. If you come from a country that's not covered by the Visa Waiver Program – check www.travel.state.gov – contact your local US embassy or consulate to obtain a visa.

Websites

Bureau of Land Management
www.blm.gov/oregon-washington
Oregonian newspaper
www.oregonlive.com
Oregon State Parks
www.stateparks.oregon.gov
Travel Oregon www.traveloregon.com
US Fish and Wildlife Service
www.fws.gov

Weights and measures

The US generally uses the imperial system for measurement, with Fahrenheit for temperature and miles for distance.

FURTHER READING

Sometimes A Great Nation by Ken Kesey. Set on the Oregon Coast, this novel centers on the Stamper family, a logging group whose decision to work during a union strike causes community outrage.
The Jump-Off Creek by Molly Gloss. The trials of a widowed homesteader, settling into Oregon's rugged mountains in the 1890s, are explored in this title.

GENERAL

Wild: From Lost to Found on the Pacific Crest Trail by Cheryl Strayed. Memoir documenting a woman's epic solo journey on the fabled hiking trail – from the Mojave Desert through California and Oregon all the way to Washington.
Fugitives and Refugees: A Walk in Portland, Oregon by Chuck Palahniuk. A string of vignettes and offbeat travel tips from the lauded author of *Fight Club*.
Oregon Wine: A Deep-Rooted History by Scott Stursa. An in-depth look at the history of winemaking in Oregon, from Prohibition to the origins of Pinot Noir.
The Oregon Trail: A New American Journey by Rinker Buck. Follow Buck as he travels some 2,000 miles on the historic route in a covered wagon, sharing entertaining and moving anecdotes from his journey.
Northern Paiutes of the Malheur: High Desert Reckoning in Oregon Country by David H. Wilson Jr. A poignant account of Paiute history, focused on misinformation around the Bannock War.
Jumptown: The Golden Years of Portland Jazz, 1942–1957 by Robert Dietsche. Dietsche uses jazz music as a lens through which to uncover layered and overlooked Portland histories and cultures.
Original Journals of the Lewis and Clark Expedition, 1804–1806 by Meriwether Lewis and William Clark. The explorers filled eight volumes with notes on the Pacific Northwest's flora and fauna, and their encounters with Native Americans; abridged versions are available.
Fire at Eden's Gate: Tom McCall and the Oregon Story by Brent Walth. This work shines a spotlight on the well-known Oregon politician and journalist, celebrated for his environmental policies.

FICTION

Mink River by Brian Doyle. This novel homes in on a fictional town on the Oregon Coast, knitting together the lives of various community members, from a logger to a doctor.
The Lathe of Heaven by Ursula K. Le Guin. Portland is the setting for this gripping science fiction novel, where the dreams of protagonist George Orr can influence reality.
Night Dogs by Kent Anderson. A police novel following a veteran-turned-cop working in the North Precinct of Portland.

☉ Send us your thoughts

We do our best to ensure the information in our books is as accurate and up-to-date as possible. The books are updated on a regular basis using destination experts, who painstakingly add, amend and correct as required. However, some details (such as opening times or travel pass costs) are particularly liable to change, and we are ultimately reliant on our readers to put us in the picture.

We welcome your feedback, especially your experience of using the book "on the road", and if you came across a great new attraction we missed.

We will acknowledge all contributions and offer an Insight Guide to the best messages received.

Please write to us at:
Insight Guides
PO Box 7910
London SE1 1WE

Or email us at:
hello@insightguides.com

GEOGRAPHY AND NATURAL HISTORY

Ancient Places: People and Landscape in the Emerging Northwest by Jack Nisbet. A fascinating overview of the geological and human history of Washington, Oregon, and Idaho, by an eminent historian whose *Sources of the River* traced the journeys of fur trader David Thompson.
Birds of the Pacific Northwest by John Shewey and Tim Blount. Hundreds of beautiful photographs of the distinctive birds of the Northwest make this compendium a delight.
The Other Oregon: People, Environment, and History East of the Cascades by Thomas R. Cox. Enjoy a deep dive into the communities, environmental history, geography, and culture of Eastern Oregon.

GUIDES AND MANUALS

Exploring the Oregon Coast Trail: 40 Consecutive Day Hikes from the Columbia River to the California Border by Connie Soper. A breakdown of the top hiking routes along Oregon's spectacular coast trail, including history, wildlife and practical information.
Oregon Fossils by William N. Orr and Elizabeth L. Orr. A field guide to Oregon's incredible fossils, featuring detailed records of finds that date back some 400 million years.
Foraging Oregon: Finding, Identifying, and Preparing Edible Wild Foods in Oregon by Christopher Nyerges. Learn how to uncover Oregon's wild bounty with this fascinating foraging field guide.
Oregon Wine + Food: The Cookbook by Danielle Centoni and Kerry Newberry. Some 80 recipes sit alongside commentary from Oregon wine professionals in this culinary tome dedicated to the state's fine gourmet credentials.

CREDITS

INSIGHT GUIDE CREDITS

Distribution
UK, Ireland and Europe
Apa Publications (UK) Ltd;
sales@insightguides.com
United States and Canada
Ingram Publisher Services;
ips@ingramcontent.com
Australia and New Zealand
Booktopia;
retailer@booktopia.com.au
Worldwide
Apa Publications (UK) Ltd;
sales@insightguides.com

Special Sales, Content Licensing and CoPublishing
Insight Guides can be purchased in bulk quantities at discounted prices. We can create special editions, personalised jackets and corporate imprints tailored to your needs. sales@insightguides.com
www.insightguides.biz

Printed in China

This book was produced using **Typefi** automated publishing software.

All Rights Reserved
© 2023 Apa Digital AG
License edition © Apa Publications Ltd UK

First Edition 2023

www.insightguides.com

Editor: Joanna Reeves
Author: Jacqui Agate
Picture Editor: Piotr Kala
Cartography: original cartography Carte
Layout: Greg Madejak
Head of DTP and Pre-Press: Rebeka Davies
Head of Publishing: Sarah Clark

CONTRIBUTORS

Insight Guide: Oregon was commissioned by Joanna Reeves and written by Jacqui Agate, a freelance travel journalist who specializes in the USA. Jacqui spends vast portions of each year traveling and researching stories in the States, and she also writes regularly for titles including *The Times*, *The Telegraph*, *National Geographic Traveller* and *Wanderlust*.

ABOUT INSIGHT GUIDES

Insight Guides have more than 45 years' experience of publishing high-quality, visual travel guides. We produce 400 full-colour titles, in both print and digital form, covering more than 200 destinations across the globe, in a variety of formats to meet your different needs.

  Insight Guides are written by local authors, whose expertise is evident in the extensive historical and cultural background features. Each destination is carefully researched by regional experts to ensure our guides provide the very latest information. All the reviews in **Insight Guides** are independent; we strive to maintain an impartial view. Our reviews are carefully selected to guide you to the best places to eat, go out and shop, so you can be confident that when we say a place is special, we really mean it.

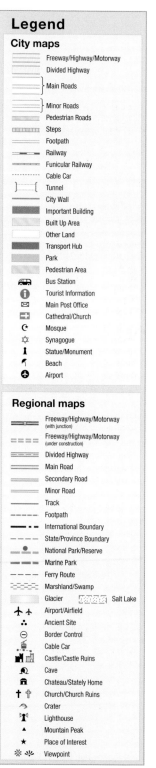

Legend

City maps

	Freeway/Highway/Motorway
	Divided Highway
	Main Roads
	Minor Roads
	Pedestrian Roads
	Steps
	Footpath
	Railway
	Funicular Railway
	Cable Car
	Tunnel
	City Wall
	Important Building
	Built Up Area
	Other Land
	Transport Hub
	Park
	Pedestrian Area
	Bus Station
	Tourist Information
	Main Post Office
	Cathedral/Church
	Mosque
	Synagogue
	Statue/Monument
	Beach
	Airport

Regional maps

	Freeway/Highway/Motorway (with junction)
	Freeway/Highway/Motorway (under construction)
	Divided Highway
	Main Road
	Secondary Road
	Minor Road
	Track
	Footpath
	International Boundary
	State/Province Boundary
	National Park/Reserve
	Marine Park
	Ferry Route
	Marshland/Swamp
	Glacier / Salt Lake
	Airport/Airfield
	Ancient Site
	Border Control
	Cable Car
	Castle/Castle Ruins
	Cave
	Chateau/Stately Home
	Church/Church Ruins
	Crater
	Lighthouse
	Mountain Peak
	Place of Interest
	Viewpoint

INDEX

MAIN REFERENCES ARE IN BOLD TYPE

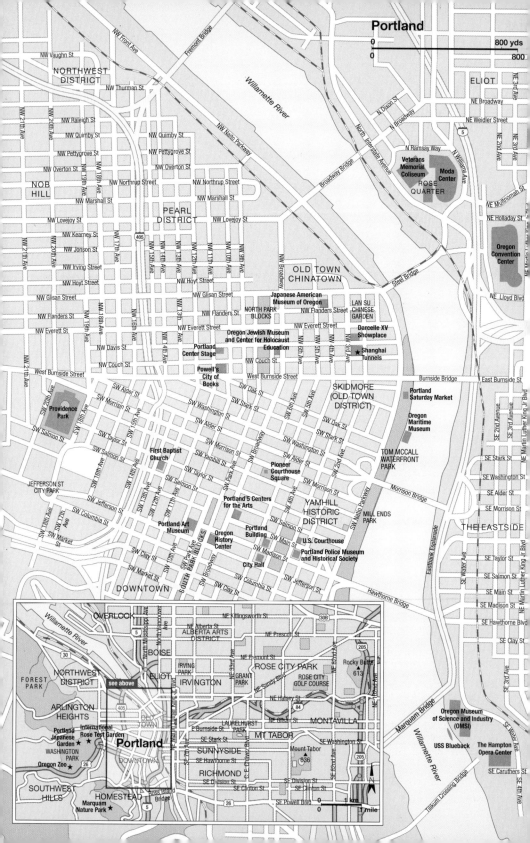

Portland

0   800 yds

0   800

Willamette River

NORTHWEST DISTRICT
NW Vaughn St
NW Thurman St

ELIOT
NE Broadway
NE Weidler Street

NOB HILL
NW Raleigh St
NW Quimby St
NW Pettygrove St
NW Overton St

NW Quimby St
NW Pettygrove St
NW Overton St
NW Northrup Street
NW Marshall St

NW Naito Parkway

N Ramsay Way

ROSE QUARTER
Veterans Memorial Coliseum
Moda Center

Oregon Convention Center

PEARL DISTRICT
NW Lovejoy St
NW Kearney St
NW Jonson St
NW Irving Street
NW Hoyt Street
NW Glisan Street
NW Flanders St
NW Everett St
NW Davis St
NW Couch St

OLD TOWN CHINATOWN
Japanese American Museum of Oregon
NORTH PARK BLOCKS
NW Flanders St
NW Everett Street
Oregon Jewish Museum and Center for Holocaust Education
NW Couch St

LAN SU CHINESE GARDEN
Darcelle XV Showplace
★ Shanghai Tunnels

Portland Center Stage

Powell's City of Books

West Burnside Street

Providence Park

SKIDMORE (OLD TOWN DISTRICT)
Portland Saturday Market
Oregon Maritime Museum

TOM MCCALL WATERFRONT PARK

JEFFERSON ST CITY PARK

First Baptist Church

Pioneer Courthouse Square

Portland's Centers for the Arts

Portland Art Museum

Oregon History Center

Portland Building

City Hall

YAMHILL HISTORIC DISTRICT
U.S. Courthouse
Portland Police Museum and Historical Society
MILL ENDS PARK

DOWNTOWN

Morrison Bridge
Hawthorne Bridge

THE EASTSIDE
Eastbank Esplanade

Burnside Bridge
East Burnside St

Inset map

OVERLOOK
Willamette River

BOISE
NE Killingsworth St
NE Alberta St
ALBERTA ARTS DISTRICT
NE Prescott St

NORTHWEST DISTRICT
FOREST PARK

ELIOT
IRVINGTON
IRVING PARK
GRANT PARK

ROSE CITY PARK
ROSE CITY GOLF COURSE
Rocky Butte 613 ▲

see above

ARLINGTON HEIGHTS
Portland Japanese Garden ★
International Rose Test Garden
WASHINGTON PARK
Oregon Zoo ★

Portland

OLD TOWN
DOWNTOWN

E Burnside St
LAURELHURST PARK
SE Stark St
MT TABOR
MONTAVILLA

SUNNYSIDE
SE Hawthorne St
RICHMOND
SE Division St
SE Clinton St
Mount Tabor 636

SOUTHWEST HILLS
HOMESTEAD
Marquam Nature Park ★
Ross Island Bridge

Marquam Bridge
Willamette River

Oregon Museum of Science and Industry (OMSI)
USS Blueback
The Hampton Opera Center

Tilikum Crossing Bridge

0   1 km
0   1 mile